The Awakening Of An American: How My Country Broke My Heart

MERIA HELLER

WWW.MERIA.NET

Edited by
Deborah M. Alexander

A Dandelion Books Publication

www.dandelionbooks.net

Tempe, Arizona

A Dandelion Books Publication
Dandelion Books, LLC
www.dandelionbooks.net
Tempe, Arizona

Library of Congress Cataloging-in-Publication Data

Heller, Meria.
The awakening of an American: how my country broke my heart

Library of Congress Catalog Card Number 2003100592
ISBN 1-893302-39-3

Cover and book design by Amnet-Systems, Limited
www.amnet-systems.com

Cover photograph of Meria Heller at age 7 by Harold Levy

Disclaimer and Reader Agreement

Reader Agreement for Accessing This Book

Dandelion Books, LLC
www.dandelionbooks.net

This book is dedicated to my granddaughters, Jenna and Jessica, and to children all over the world, for the next seven generations

ACKNOWLEDGMENTS

I want to thank my father and mother, John and Leah Rubino, for teaching me some of the most important lessons in life. Among those lessons were, "Question everything," and "Never, *ever* be afraid to say what you think."

Many kind friends and relatives patiently transcribed my interviews: Debbie Alexander, Towana McDonald, Dotti Flanagan, Gina R. Gee, Scott McCleary, Bema Neal, "Jackson Thoreau," Diane Warth, and my sister, Joyce Rubino-Grimm. Not an easy job when trying to keep up with a fast-talking New Yorker!

For the cover of the book, my friend, Scott McCleary, "enhanced" a picture of me taken 45 years ago.

Sincere thanks to countless numbers of wonderful, loving people I have known in my life and have had the pleasure of working with, as well as the wonderful, intelligent beings I have had the true blessing to be able to interview on my shows for over two years now.

I am everlastingly grateful for Jordan Dorf of NetRadioLive who made my show possible, and for my listeners, fans, supporters, friends, clients, students, teachers, sisters, children, grandchildren, and people worldwide who support the basis for humanitarianism, which is freedom for all living things. Without any one of these people, I just wouldn't—or couldn't—be Meria.

FOREWORD

Catherine Austin Fitts is the Chairman of Solari, Inc., which specializes in equity investment in neighborhood databanks and investment advisors. She is a former managing director and member of the board of Dillon, Read & Co., Inc., a former Assistant Secretary of Housing-Federal Housing Commissioner in the first Bush Administration, and President of The Hamilton Securities Group, Inc. Ms. Fitts is a member of the advisory board of Sanders Research Associates in London and publishes "The Real Deal" column in *Scoop Media* in New Zealand.

If you are reading this, you are already smart. You are learning about our world by investing your time and money in Meria Heller. As someone who has worked at the highest levels of government and on Wall Street, I assure you there is *nothing* more important to ensure your family's physical and financial security than getting "the real deal" from leaders like Meria and the people she brings to her global Internet webcast audience.

News media divides into two groups. One is corporate media. Corporate media manipulates the news to encourage you to act in a manner that serves the interests of large corporations, banks, and investors. The owners of corporate media make money by using media to promote their profits not just on their media investments, but on *all* their investments, including warfare, organized crime and money laundering, and government corruption.

Real media is the media that tells you the truth about what you need to know to act on behalf of your *own* enlightened self-interest in your everyday life, whether voting at the polls or voting in the marketplace with your time, your attention, and your purchases, deposits or investments. *Real* media helps us build better maps of how the money and power really work around us in a way that enhances our safety and well-being.

If you want the rich to stop getting richer through fraud, organized crime and warfare, the first thing you must do is make sure that you and your friends and family stop watching, listening or buying corporate media and switch your vote in the marketplace to *real* media leaders like Meria.

As Assistant Secretary of Housing in the *first* Bush Administration, I once advised Jack Kemp, then Secretary of the Department of Housing and Urban Development (HUD), that we could not do something he had ordered because it was illegal. He said he did not care, to go ahead and do it anyway. His general counsel was Frank Keating, now Governor of Oklahoma, who had come to HUD from the Department of Justice. Frank regularly advised Jack that he could make sure Jack was free to break the law when it was politically expedient. "Ahh, f___ 'em, Jack, by the time they win in court, we will be gone anyway," was one of my favorite Frank Keating quotes. Frank seemed expert at abrogating constitutional rights, property rights, and contract law to help Jack cover up Iran-Contra fraud, keep slush fund operations growing, and make life nice for major Republican donors. He had been trained at the Department of Justice. In Frank's book, a good conservative was someone who did not need to *bother* with the law. The law was simply a tool to get your way—and that "way" was often criminal.

So, I changed tactics and said, "But, Jack, we will get caught. The career civil service will leak what we are doing to the press. We will take a bad headline. The headline will be very bad for us." At that point, Jack *always* relented as he saw the merits to his quest for the Presidency of not getting a *bad* headline. It turned out that freedom was *entirely* a function of having a free press.

What I also learned working in both the Bush Administration and with the Clinton Administration as an investment banker helping to clean up billions of S&L, BCCI and HUD financial fraud was this. The way politicians and their corporate, banking, and investment backers increasingly avoid taking a bad headline is through monopoly control of our media. I watched both administrations and both political parties manipulate the top newspaper and TV news outlets in ways that were shocking, if not criminal. And I watched the top media corporate chieftains get paid back with lots of regulatory and government "treats" in exchange for their suppression of the news about how money and power really worked in Washington.

I have a friend who introduced my conference speech about the influence of organized crime in our lives by saying, "Who here saw the movie, *Enemy of the State*? The woman who is about to speak played Will Smith in real life." Starting in 1996, I was targeted by an "Enemy of the State" process involving 18 audits and investigations, a smear campaign, and several years of physical harassment and surveillance. Numerous members of the corporate media supported this effort. I endured years of printed lies, refusals to use or check facts, and cheap dishonest smear campaigns. Sure enough, all of it was proved false after *many* years in court and the expenditure of millions of dollars.

I watched this not only in my own situation, but I saw it happen to many other honest people, including honest reporters who were moved out because they would not "play ball." Short and sweet, throughout the 1990s, corporate media helped move honest people and businesses out of all sectors of our economy while senior management stole significant money from government, corporations, pension funds, communities, and citizens. The story of Enron is just the tip of the iceberg of the fraud that corporate media helped make possible. The cost to our jobs, our pension funds, our social security and our healthcare support is far greater than most people yet realize. Corporate media did not warn us that the fox was in the chicken coop and that we needed to do something about it. That is because corporate media *is* the fox.

I was lucky. After I realized that corporate media could not be trusted, I sought out the truth-tellers in the media, particularly those who have started and built important radio talk shows. As a result, I was able to speak and publish and create the knowledge and networks I needed to in order to transform beyond any dependency on corporate media and their false maps. I am alive and I am a winner today because of *real* media.

In the process, one of the leaders I found was Meria Heller. Now, you have found her, too. Meria and the people she brings into our lives are "the real deal." Enjoy Meria's book. Enjoy being a subscriber to her Internet webcast show. Once you discover Meria and her talent for engaging the real leaders among us, as the Temptations used to croon, you will "never, never let her go."

Catherine Austin Fitts
November 2, 2002

CONTENTS

INTRODUCTION

Within the following pages, you will read what other people in over 60 countries have been able to "hear" on my Internet webcast for over two years now. *The Meria Heller Show* has been breaking Internet records—and for good reason. Many intelligent, caring human beings in the world need to have a voice. I have taken it upon myself to become that voice, and so I have been dubbed "the Mouth that Roars."

You may choose to argue, agree, discount or verify any of the interviews. All I ask is that you keep an open mind as you read the stories that have made me rethink my own life after living over a half century in a country that has been billed as being "free."

To know that my work/love is appreciated to the point of being nominated for The Peabody Award for Excellence in Broadcasting is amazing to me. In my earlier years, I never had one single conscious desire to be a radio personality, but I have always desired to be a voice. I think I have found my "home."

I was born in the last week of 1949, in Brooklyn, New York. I am a second-generation American-Italian (American FIRST). Both sets of grandparents arrived in America through Ellis Island, like so many other immigrants in the early 1900s. Both my mother and father were born in New York City. I was lucky enough to grow up in America just after World War II, during the "Happy Days" period in our history. We lived in a three-story brownstone in a section called "Cobble Hill," near Brooklyn Heights. I had four sisters to play with and my mother's parents lived on the floor above us. My father was a humble man, a barber, yet one of the wisest philosophers who ever walked the planet. I had a "stay-at-home" mother who taught us the joys of laughing and singing—and cooking.

I attended the public school system in Brooklyn and obtained a wonderful education. From the time I was a small child, whenever I saw the American flag or heard the national anthem, all the hairs on my body would stand at attention. I loved my country more than anything in the world. The words to the song, "God Bless America" were natural to me. I truly felt that America was the greatest country in the world, the chosen country to lead the world in peace and prosperity.

When I graduated from high school, I began my work-life. I learned the business of business in what I think of as the greatest city in the world: New York City (Manhattan). Of course, I was not unaware of the social problems facing our society as a young person. Like a lot of my peers (the baby-boomers), we occasionally made our voices heard, but for the most part we were busy getting on with our lives.

As I started raising a family of my own, I began to become more socially aware. I could no longer just think about a future for myself, but now had the futures of two children to worry about. The world was indeed changing. Our environment was spiraling out of control. Politics had become a dirty word and the world situation was heating up. Then, I became a grandmother and the thought of the future of the next seven generations become *very* real. I look at my granddaughters and wonder what type of world—IF ANY—will they inherit?

I became an involved environmentalist in 1988 and started doing my homework. In 1991, I moved to Arizona. One day in 1998, I tripped across an opportunity to do a local Phoenix radio show. I thought it sounded like fun, and the next thing I knew I was on the air, staying with the station for nearly two years.

When I thought I had done all I could with that program, Jordan Dorf of NetRadioLive approached me with the idea of doing an Internet radio show. As a self-admitted computer geek, I couldn't resist. When we met, neither Jordan nor I had any idea what we would accomplish in a short period of time.

My net show started off as part entertainment and part news. Then the campaign for the 2000 election began. My show took another turn as I started realizing how dire the consequences could be if the wrong man took office at a time when the environment was at its most critical juncture. We are now seeing the results of that "election."

When the Supreme Court's "Felonious Five" selected the President of the United States in 2000 prior to and regardless of the votes (either Republican or Democratic) having been completely counted or reported by the Electoral College, I felt I had lost my country. Where was *my* America? Where was democracy? What happened to "by the people and for the people"? I sat down and cried over the loss of our democracy and the subversion of the tenets of the U.S. Constitution.

Then, I snapped out of it (as Cher told Nicholas Cage to do in *Moonstruck*). Now, I had the fire of every true patriot and founding father/mother of our country. I knew what needed to be said and began saying it my first day back on the air.

As a result of many of the books I have read and guests I have had on my show, I have learned many ugly things about my country. I have learned terrible things about U.S. foreign policy, racism, domination, greed, corporate/government media manipulation, the military-industrial complex and what other countries truly think about America and Americans. I have learned about the role we have played in the global madness of today: globalization as a system of genocide worse than any Hitler could have imagined, the attempts to destroy our Constitution, the lies our government has been handing us for DECADES, and worldwide suffering visited upon our fellow human beings in the name of "GOD" (Gold, Oil, and Drugs). My *own* country has broken my heart.

We currently have an administration that was NOT elected BY the people; a government that does NOT cooperate in global projects for peace or the environment; a government that has made us the enemy of the world; a government of lies and secrets; a government that has stolen ALL our votes. We have, as Americans, become a laughingstock to the rest of the world for not standing up against those who stole the election from us. We have been attacked by terrorists for our business policies as well as international atrocities committed under the guise of "democracy" and "freedom." We preach democracy abroad and have seen our own democracy and rights diminished by the power of the money machine. Our "war on terrorism" has set a bad example for the rest of the world to duplicate; feeding into the hands of the corporate International Monetary Fund (IMF), the World Trade Organization (WTO), and One World Order capitalistic take-down of society.

This book is not meant to tear down America, but to help Americans realize that tears need to be shed for the atrocities committed against the innocent in many lands, in OUR names. We must not let this continue. It is time to "snap out of it" and get busy. We need to do our homework and speak out. We no longer have the luxury of letting the country be run by the government while we go about living our individual lives. Too much is at stake here—quite literally, the future of this country and the whole world.

Don't just take my word for it. Listen with your heart as you read the words of many of the best thinkers in America today in the pages that follow. America, it's NOT too late.

Meria Heller
November 2, 2002

ONE

THE BETRAYAL OF AMERICA
Meria with Vincent Bugliosi

"Get over it" isn't flying with top prosecutor Vincent Bugliosi.[1] Well known for being the prosecutor who sent Charles Manson to prison, Bugliosi is the author of *The Betrayal of America: How the Supreme Court ndermined the Constitution and Chose Our President.* For too long, Bugliosi has been the only public figure stating the simple fact that the "Supremes" are criminals and should be impeached. An exciting, educated, informed citizen of the USA discloses how and why all America's votes were disenfranchised to deliver the presidency to George W. Bush. (Interview taped/broadcast on July 31, 2001.)

MH: For those of you who don't know, besides this book, Vincent is the criminal prosecutor who prosecuted Charles Manson and wrote the book, *Helter Skelter.* He also wrote the book *Outrage,* basically on how O.J. Simpson got away with double murder. The topic of my show is the stolen election. What a lot of people don't know, Vincent, is that you truly are the only public figure presently out there saying these Supreme Court Justices are criminals and they should be impeached. Why is that?

VB: I hate to use those words, "public figure," but for lack of a better term, I'm the only recognizable name that is saying these people are criminals; that in a fair and just world, they deserve to be behind bars; and that they should be impeached. Now, there are many people saying that they should be impeached, but they are not public figures and I would hope that, eventually, other recognizable names would join me, but as of the present moment, unfortunately, I'm the only one with a recognizable name who is saying these people are criminals who belong behind bars and should be impeached.

MH: Maybe through your efforts and your work, more people will jump on the bandwagon. Sometimes it's just the fact that people don't know. We have media in this country that certainly do *not* work to educate the people.

VB: One person I'm trying to get on my side is Alan Dershowitz. Alan has written a good book, *Supreme Injustice,* and I recommend it. He and I were on the *Good Morning America* show about two weeks ago. I said they should be impeached and he flat out said they should *not* be impeached. He would be a good candidate to join my side because he is, like me, attacking the Supreme Court ruling. So far, Alan doesn't feel there should be any consequences to that, that they should *not* be punished and, of course, I feel there's no more serious crime than stealing a presidential election. How can you deter subsequent justices in the future from doing things like this if there are no consequences for what happened this time?

MH: Exactly. And people will say what I hear all the time: what's the point in voting? And, then, they really *have* achieved what they wanted.

VB: If the United States Supreme Court had done for Al Gore what it did for George Bush, I can give your audience out there a 100% guarantee that I would have written the same identical book, *The Betrayal of*

America, which, incidentally, this week is up to No. 5 on the *New York Times* trade paperback bestseller list, so it's doing fairly well. To summarize my views, Meria, on December 12th, five Supreme Court Justices committed one of the biggest and most serious crimes in American history when they stopped the recount in Florida, took the election away from the American people and handed it to George Bush. Yet, at the moment I'm talking to you right now, they have completely gotten away with it. Despite the monumental crime, they're still, obviously, seated on the highest court in the land; they're still treated with the utmost respect by the established institutions of America, including the mainstream media.

The mainstream media, by the way, don't even want to talk about what the Court did any more. Their position is the election is over with; we've gone on to covering other matters. Now, not to defend President Clinton, but this is the same identical group that pursued Clinton, not just day after day, not just week after week, not just month after month, but year after year, for lying about a private, consensual sexual affair. But here, we're talking about the theft of the presidency and they're saying, "The election is over with; we've gone on to covering other matters." That would be like the Nazi war criminals at Nuremberg saying, "The war is over with; let's get on with our lives."

Obviously, the election being over with is not a defense to what these Justices did and, with respect to what they did, I will stake my prosecutorial reputation on the fact that within the pages of my book, I prove beyond all reasonable doubt that these five Justices deliberately set out to make sure that George Bush became President. The evidence against them is overwhelming. They left their incriminating fingerprints everywhere.

Two people wrote forewords to my book. Molly Ivins said the book is "the modern equivalent of 'J'Accuse'" (the famous indictment against the French government in the Dreyfus affair). Gerry Spence also wrote a great foreword and Spence is considered by many to be the leading criminal defense attorney in this country. How could even a Gerry Spence have defended these five Justices when they, themselves, in so many words, in effect confessed to the crime?

Now, if you just give me 30 seconds or so, I'll try to explain to you how they confessed to the crime. They confessed by necessary implication when they said their ruling that different standards to count votes in Florida violated the equal protection clause only applied to *Bush v. Gore*, not to other cases. If their ruling set forth a valid legal principle that was good enough for *Bush v. Gore*, why wasn't it good enough for other cases? This is the first time (constitutional scholars will tell you this) in the 210-year history of the Court that the Court limited its ruling to the case before it, saying it did not constitute legal precedent for other cases. This fact alone (and all by itself) shows that these five Justices were up to no good, that they themselves knew their ruling was bogus and fraudulent, and only a means to hand the election to George Bush—because if their ruling was based on the law, there is no reason under the moon why they would have said it did not apply to other cases.

All lawyers know Supreme Court decisions enunciate legal principles that the Court itself, as well as other courts and litigants, cite in the future to support a position they are taking. Most of the people who are hearing me or reading what I'm saying, obviously, are not lawyers. And for those who are not lawyers, let me read to you from an opinion of Justice [Antonin]

Scalia in a 1996 case, *United States v. Virginia* (the citation is 518 U.S. 515 at page 596) and here's what he says: "The Supreme Court of the United States does not sit to announce unique dispositions. Its principal function is to establish legal precedent; that is, to set forth principles of law that every court in America must follow." But not in Bush v. Gore, the only exception in the 210-year history of the Court.

Now, the reason for this here—why they didn't apply the ruling to other cases, obviously—is that they knew if they did, it would invalidate elections throughout the entire country, because different standards to count votes exist throughout the 50 states. In fact, 44 out of 50 states don't even have uniform voting methods, much less uniform methods to count votes. They showed that they were up to no good three days earlier. The previous day, December 8th, the Florida Supreme Court, pursuant to Section 102.168 of the Florida Election Code, ordered a manual recount of all the undervotes in the State of Florida. There were about 60,000 and the recount was going to take place in all 67 counties of Florida. So, that started the recount at 8:00 the following morning, on Saturday, December 9th.

At 2:00 in the afternoon, Scalia steps in with an emergency order supported by the four other conservative Justices, and this is what he truly said—you can't make up stuff like this; it's just too far out—he said we've got to stop the recount because if it continues, it could (these are his exact words) "threaten irreparable harm" to George Bush. So, even though the election had not yet been decided, the incredible Scalia (and there's no other adjective I can use to describe this fellow) was presupposing that Bush had won the election; indeed, had a right to win it; and any recount that showed that Gore had won would "threaten irreparable harm" to George Bush.

Now, if that doesn't show these five Justices were trying to steal the election for Bush, I don't know what would. I would ask your audience to hypothesize a reversal of roles. Let's assume Gore was ahead as Bush was. When the recount started, Bush's lead over Gore had shrunk to 154 votes. Let's assume now that Gore was ahead of Bush by 154 votes on December 9th at 8:00. Would Scalia have done the same thing for Gore that he did for Bush?

Who is Scalia? Well, he's not a typical conservative or a typical Republican. What he is, he's a right-wing ideologue of the Rush Limbaugh school. He's the judicial darling of the far right. To him, someone like Gore is probably anathema, an execration. It is absolutely inconceivable that Scalia would have stepped in and said we've got to stop this recount because if it continues it could "threaten irreparable harm" to Al Gore. That would not have happened. That could not have happened. Anyone who can tell me, with a straight look on their face, that that would have happened, I will personally nominate for an Academy Award. Anyone who can imagine that happening, I suppose could also imagine seeing someone jump away from their own shadow, or Frenchmen no longer drinking wine.

It would not have happened. Now, what does it mean when it's obvious that Scalia would not have done for Gore what he did for Bush? Well, what it means, obviously, is that Scalia's order was not based on the law, because if it was based on the law, obviously, it would apply equally to both parties. And many legal conservatives have severely denounced the Court's ruling; they don't go on to say these people are criminals and deserve to be impeached, but they say the Court's stopping of the recount was just absolutely wrong.

I'll just give you one example. Terrance Sandalow (a former dean of the University of Michigan Law School; a judicial conservative who opposed *Roe v. Wade* and supported the nomination to the Court of the right-wing icon Robert Bork), said Scalia's order was "incomprehensible" and "an unmistakably partisan decision" that had no foundation in law.

MH: How clear does it have to be? Your book spells out that this was a stolen election.

VB: And now there's the equal protection argument. Let's explore it a little further. We already know the Court itself did not believe in it because if it did, it would have said that it applied to other cases. Because they based their ruling on the equal protection clause, let's examine it a little further. What evidence could there possibly be — empirical, anecdotal or otherwise — that different standards to count votes in various of the Florida counties would hurt George Bush more than Al Gore? How could there *possibly* be any evidence to support that proposition? Indeed, the Bush legal team, in all arguments before the Court and in legal briefs, never even made that allegation. Now, if the Court was not concerned about George Bush, but about the voters themselves, as they so fervently claimed to be, then under what conceivable theory would they, in effect, tell these voters, "We're *so* concerned about the fact that some of you undervoters may lose your vote because of the different standards to count votes in Florida, that we're going to solve the problem by making sure *none* of you undervoters have your votes counted"? They threw out all 60,000 undervotes.

How preposterous can the Court get? Sixty thousand Floridians did not have their votes counted. So, in effect, the Supreme Court told 60,000 Americans, "We're going to protect your right to vote by not counting any of your votes." I just mention this to show you the equal protection argument was nothing but a legal gimmick the Court itself did not believe in, to hand the election to George Bush, and that an election for an American president can be stolen by the highest court in the land under the deliberate pretext of an inapplicable constitutional provision, has got to be one of the most frightening and danger- ous events ever to have occurred in this country. If anyone in your audience is not frightened by what happened, then I would say to them, they should be; they certainly should be.

MH: I totally agree, and my audience is pretty much on our side, trust me. Even though everyone seems to be focused on the fact that the Supreme Court disenfranchised the voters in Florida, that the Supreme Court picked a president even before the Electoral College did, doesn't that mean they pretty much disenfranchised voters throughout the whole United States with that move?

VB: There's no question about it. When they ruled on December 12th, effectively handing the election to George Bush, at that particular point in time, not all of the votes had been counted. Sixty thousand undervotes in Florida had not been counted. So, then when Bush is inaugurated on January 20th, he's inaugurated solely and exclusively because of what the Court did on December 12th, not because on January 20th, it had been determined that he got the majority of votes. And, of course, by their ruling, they disenfranchised the 50 million voters who voted for Al Gore. These Justices had no respect, no regard, for 50 million Americans whose votes for Vice President Gore they knew they were erasing as if never cast. No concern, apparently, at *all* about a betrayal of trust—that's why I call the book *The Betrayal of America*—a betrayal of trust that may be unparalleled in the annals of American history.

MH: You have a couple of quotes in there I want to "steal" because they are too good. A little piece on the bottom of page 37 says, "So not only did a century-old technicality enable Bush to win the national election even though he lost by over a half million votes, but he won Florida by mistake. Yet there were human mutants who loudly protested outside the Vice-President's home in Washington, D.C., before the election was over, demanding that he 'get out of Cheney's home.'"

VB: I view myself primarily as a trial lawyer who happens to be writing, as opposed to a writer who happens to be a trial lawyer, but now and then, I do come up with a decent line. I think one of my better lines in the book was when I referred to the many members of the media who are very liberal, but who cater to the far right and try to convince the far right they are "good liberals," while in the process they aid and abet the far right. I pointed out that these liberals are physiological marvels who are somehow able to sit and stand erect in front of a camera without a spine.

MH: Another one was when you were talking about Clarence Thomas, "who doesn't even try to create the impression that he's thinking."

VB: He's a professional mynah bird for Scalia. Whatever Scalia says, Thomas goes along with it. Both Scalia and Thomas are disgraces to the legal profession and the judiciary. They are nothing but rubber stamps for the right wing in this country.

MH: I'm glad your book exposes it. What are the chances of actually getting these people prosecuted or disbarred?

VB: They're not going to be prosecuted because, technically, they didn't violate any law. I mean, people have specifically asked me, "Mr. Bugliosi, you say they're criminals and they committed a crime. What crime have they committed?" With full knowledge, on December 9th, that there certainly was a possibility, a real possibility, that the recount would show that Gore had won (who would disagree with that?), that there was certainly that possibility on the afternoon of December 9th (his lead had shrunk to 154 over Gore), with sole knowledge of that possibility that Gore might be the actual winner, they stopped the recount, took the election away from the American people, and handed it to Bush. Now, if anyone thinks that is not a crime of the most serious magnitude, then I say there's something wrong with that person. But did they commit any technical crime? Answer: No. Why? Because no Congress had ever dreamed of enacting a statute making it a crime to steal a presidential election. It is so far out, and so unbelievable, there was no law then on the books for them to have violated.

All true crimes require two elements: one, morally reprehensible conduct, and two, they are offenses against society. If stealing a presidential election is not morally reprehensible AND an offense against society, what in the world would be? So, in terms of natural law and justice, which is the protoplasm for all eventual laws on the books, these five Justices are criminals in the very truest sense of the word. In a fair and just world, they would belong behind bars as much as any American white-collar criminal who has ever lived. Now, there is one option—it's not a realistic option, but there is one option out there—and that's impeachment. You need a crime in order to prosecute, but you do not have to have a violation of law to impeach. What you have to have is a breach of the public trust, or a violation of law, of course, too, but you don't need it.

From Alexander Hamilton and The Federalist Papers down through Joseph Story's commentaries on the Constitution, there are all types of historical precedent for impeaching public officials without their having violated a specific law. In fact, the only Supreme Court Justice who was ever impeached is Samuel Chase back in 1804, and there were seven Articles of Impeachment against him. Not one of them alleged a violation of law; they were all breaches of the public trust.

A national legal organization contacted me a couple of weeks ago by letter to inform me their executive committee is giving very serious consideration to using *The Betrayal of America* as somewhat of a legal brief, a legal foundation, for asking the House Judiciary Committee to institute impeachment proceedings against these five Justices. Realistically, Congress is not going to impeach these five Justices. They don't have the spine to do that. However, any movement for impeachment, and any consideration at all given by Congress to the impeachment movement, I think, would have enormous sociological significance. Along these lines, last Friday, a woman from the office of Representative [John] Conyers [Jr.], from the Detroit [Michigan] area, called and wanted to know if he could introduce my article "None Dare Call it Treason," which I wrote for *The Nation* back in February [2001], into the Congressional Record. Of course, I said yes, so apparently the whole article's going to be in the Congressional Record.

MH: A lot of people don't know this book actually started out as an article.

VB: It started out as an article in *The Nation* (in the oldest magazine in this country—dates back to 1865, the last year of the Civil War). The editors of *The Nation* said that the biggest response from their readers in the 136-year history of the magazine was to my article. Because of that, they asked me to do a book around the article and I agreed to write *The Betrayal of America*.

MH: I really don't think most Americans get it that *every* single vote in this country was discounted by the Supreme Court, whether it was Democrat or Republican. The Supreme Court picked the President. I know Bush's cabinet was really upset with what Julian Bond had said at the NAACP [National Association for the Advancement of Colored People] convention: "We didn't vote for 'Let's get over it' or for 'It's over and done with.'" You know, everybody tried to say he was being too hard; I thought his speech was great. And I don't think this is something that, as Americans, we *should* get over. I went into a crying jag, and then a depression after this happened. My friends thought I was nuts. I asked them, "Do you have *any* idea of the enormity of what just happened in this country?" I felt like I had lost my country. There are a lot of people, like yourself and a lot of my listeners and a lot of my guests, who aren't letting this go, but they need the exposure. This is part and parcel of why I do my show, because they're all welcome on my show. You wrote in your book that it's remarkable that arguably the most consequential and far-reaching decision the U.S. Supreme Court has handed down since its inception will undoubtedly alter, for good or bad, the course of American history and, therefore, world history. Then, you added that it was also unsigned and anonymously written.

VB: The decision was so bad and the Supreme Court—the five Justices, whom I refer to as the "Felonious Five" in the article and the book—*knew* it was so bad that they issued it in the form of a *per curiam* opinion. Now, *per curiam* opinions, as students of the Supreme Court will tell you, almost invariably are issued for situations where you have unanimous decisions, that is, nine to nothing; where the Court wishes to be brief, that is, a two- or three-page opinion; and when the case is not a controversial one. Here, none of those three situations were present. It was a 5–4 decision, the opinion ran to 62 pages, and it couldn't *possibly* have been a more controversial case. So, why did the Court issue its ruling as a *per curiam*, which is Latin for "by the court," ruling? It just so happens that *per curiam* opinions have two very wonderful features that were particularly appealing to these five Justices, and that's that these opinions are *unsigned* and *anonymously* written.

So, after these five Justices did their dirty work in rendering worthless the votes of 50 million Americans who voted for Vice President Gore, they apparently wanted to stay away from the decision the way the devil stays away from holy water. And it's really remarkable that, like you just read, arguably the most consequential decision in American history by the Court was unsigned and anonymously written. Many legal scholars believe Justice Anthony Kennedy is the one who actually ended up writing the *per curiam* opinion for the five Justices. But it seems that perhaps they felt since their names would not be on this legally sacrilegious opinion maybe, just maybe, the guilt they knew they bore would be mitigated at least somewhat in posterity.

MH: I don't understand how these people can even live with themselves after what they did.

VB: I talk about that in my book. Unless they're judicial sociopaths, in which case they're even more dangerous than I already think they are, this is a very, VERY serious thing. I agree with you that we have to energize America because America follows the cue of the media. In all deference to the media, and there certainly are some exceptions, it's a group that, for the most part, can always be counted on to do a minimum of thinking. Somehow, out of stupidity, or what-have-you, they have gone on to covering other matters.

MH: And, yet, this is the biggest story to ever hit. I was following the stories of the G-8 protests in Genoa [Italy] and then I got to read some of the stuff people were posting online from Europe. *Their* opinion on *our* opinion on their protest was, "You people had your election stolen and you laid down for it. We don't really care what you have to say because you people had no guts to fight against having your rights stripped away with that election."

VB: I said something similar to that last night. I was speaking at a synagogue in East Hampton. I was saying, "We already know about the moral bankruptcy of these five Justices, their deficiency of character," but I said, "If we allow this to happen without a whimper of protest, without demonstrating our absolute outrage, what does that say about *our* character, *our* values, *our* worth as human beings?" And I went on to say, also, what you just said, that if they can commit this terrible, terrible act, and we take it lying down, what does that say about us?

The people at the synagogue said, "Well, what can we do, Mr. Bugliosi, to help?" I told them to promote my book. That may sound self-serving, but it's not. I did not write this book to make money; I wrote this book in a state of rage. For the first time in my 25-year literary career, I'm now having a difficult time getting on national TV. I *always* automatically got on for all of my books. There now seems to be a resistance to having someone like me on national TV, sitting down with someone and saying these people are criminals, they belong behind bars, and they should be impeached.

If you believe in what I'm saying, if you believe in my message, the way to help is call any columnist you know at your local newspaper or national newspaper and try to get the book reviewed or a column written on it. If you know any producer or host of a local or national radio or TV show, contact them and try to get them to interview me, because then when I get on and give my message, I can reach millions and millions of people. I would ask your audience, if they know anyone who can help me get on the air, on radio or TV, or in the newspapers, with my message—and of course you don't want to do that if you don't believe in what I'm saying—but if you do believe in what I'm saying, and in the message of *The Betrayal of America*, that's the way to help; to get me on shows where I can get this message out to all of America. Right now, most Americans are not on the same wavelength; they don't even know the book is out there, even though it's No. 5 now on the *New York Times* bestseller list.

MH: This is a book people should be buying. Get a dozen copies each and just give them out to people you know. This is a book that should be in every history class, teachers going over it with their students in class. One of my listeners has asked, "The damage is too much. How can we rid ourselves legally of the usurper?" The "usurper," I'm assuming, is Mr. Bush. "Is there anything we can do to impeach *him*?"

VB: My book is not, *per* se, an anti-Bush book. I don't claim, as some people have said, that *Bush* stole the election. What I claim is that the *Supreme Court* stole the election *for* George Bush. I don't think he can be impeached here. I don't see any impeachable offense, but certainly, theoretically, the Supreme Court could be impeached because of the enormous, *colossal* breach of trust. There's another Article of Impeachment that could be brought against them—a very clear one—and that gets into the issue of motive.

MH: What *were* they thinking? What were their private agendas? I've had a lot of people on who have made the connection between the Justices and some Cabinet members and big corporations, etc., and money. What do you think is their deal?

VB: To prosecutors, motive is not an element of the *corpus delicti* of a crime. You never have to prove motive, but the jury wants to know why, because the presence of motive is circumstantial evidence of guilt. The absence of motive is circumstantial evidence of innocence. I never would have written this book if all I had was motive. A prosecutor doesn't want to go into court and have the jury, in effect, say to the prosecutor, "All right, the defendant had a motive, but did he do it?" These are two separate things, and there's an enormous amount of evidence in here that the Court did precisely what I said they did.

The motive could not be more clear here. Obviously, they wanted George Bush to win. No one would have the crazy audacity to say they were voting for Al Gore and they wanted Al Gore to win. Let's talk about some of the examples of motive here. The night of the election, November 7th, Justice Sandra Day O'Connor was at a cocktail party in Washington, D.C., with her lawyer-husband, John. Dan Rather comes on the air at 8:00 and says, "It looks like Florida is going to Al Gore," whereupon she blurts out, "That's just terrible." She was angry; she was upset.

Her husband explained to the guests that the reason his wife was so upset is that they had planned to retire to Arizona and now they weren't going to be able to do so for four years. They were going to have to wait another four years because she did not want a Democrat to appoint her successor. Now, the *Wall Street Journal* found three guests who were at that party to confirm the story and they wrote an article about it. *Newsweek* also wrote it up; they had found two guests. Both the *Wall Street Journal* and *Newsweek* went to Sandra Day O'Connor for a comment and she declined comment.

Clarence Thomas' wife works for the Heritage Foundation, a very conservative think tank, which assisted Governor Bush in his transition to power. Scalia, everyone knows (it's not a big secret) wants to become the Chief Justice of the U.S. Supreme Court, and certainly there's no way he could become the Chief Justice if Al Gore became President. Also, he has two sons who were working for law firms that were heavily involved in the Bush campaign, so the motive here is very clear. Title 28 of the United States Code, Section 455, says this: "Any justice, judge or magistrate of the United States *shall*" (it's mandatory) "disqualify himself in any proceeding in which his impartiality might reasonably be questioned. He shall also disqualify himself in the following circumstances: he or his spouse, or a person within the third degree of relationship to either of them, is known by the judge to have an interest that could be substantially affected by the outcome of the proceeding."

These three Justices had a duty, *under the law*, to recuse themselves (disqualify themselves) and they did not do that. That, again, would be a separate Article of Impeachment that could be brought against them, but I'm being realistic when I tell you that Congress does not have the spine to impeach these people.

MH: I really think the economy and the stock market not recovering has everything to do with people having lost their faith in the country since this election. We have a President who's made us the enemy of foreign countries, the laughingstock of the world, and who is referred to in Europe as the global village idiot.

VB: I heard the *Los Angeles Times* reported when Bush was in Germany, he "forgave" Germany for Pearl Harbor. That's kind of embarrassing.

MH: I'm a baby-boomer and I grew up at a time when I was so proud to be an American. Patriotism runs through me. I hear "The Star Spangled Banner" and I cry. When this election got stolen, everything about America that I believed in was robbed from me, and I went into the pits of hell over this.

VB: I don't have any anger with Republicans *per se*, but I do have an enormous animus towards the right wing of the Republican Party. My animus for them is without limits. This is the group that lionizes Rush Limbaugh. They wear their patriotism on their sleeves with very, very little left inside; and I've challenged these people on radio and television. They're starting to read the book—you don't get up to No. 5 if they're not reading the book—and I've challenged them. I've said, "Listen, this is a good $10.00 litmus test for you"—the trade paperback is $9.95—"because if you're honest with yourself, and you read this book, you're going to find out very quickly how much you really love America or whether your primary allegiance is to the Republican party."

It's my belief that any true conservative who loves this country—and I'm talking about the John McCains of the world, not the right-wing fanatics that Barry Goldwater had no use for—has to be deeply, *deeply* disturbed over what the Court did, even though it happened to inure to their individual benefit. I'm still waiting for the first conservative who read the book to say to me, "You did prove your point and because of it, these five Justices should be hung in the town square at noontime."

Liberals reading the book are getting even more angry than they already were and they *do* want to hang the Justices of the Supreme Court at noontime, but conservatives—even when they feel I've made my point in the book—not *one* of them I've personally met is angry about it. What this means is that *their* guy got in, and they don't care how he got there. And I don't know what that says about *their* morality, that they don't *care* how he got in. Whether it was wrong or not, a Republican got in. I'm sure there's some conservative out there who is going to say these people are criminals and they belong behind bars.

MH: Is what they did treason?

VB: It's not technically treason. Treason is the only crime that's defined in the United States Constitution, and there are two types of treason. One is an insurrection against the government—certainly we don't have that here. The second type is the most common type, and that's aiding and abetting an enemy during wartime. The essence of treason, obviously, is that an American citizen—which these five Justices are—is doing something extremely harmful to the country. It's kind of a distinction without substance. I mean, how much difference is there between helping someone *else* hurt our country, as opposed to hurting our country yourself? It's not technically treason, but certainly there are implications of treason here.

MH: You want some of these Republican conservatives to come out publicly on your side, but they don't.

VB: I'm talking about the ones that come up to me and compliment me on the book, but they have no anger over what happened, no anger at all.

MH: Don't you think people need to stop defining themselves as a member of any party and just define themselves as a citizen of the United States and realize this is what has happened to *all* of us?

VB: These are the people, of course, who are the flag-wavers, the ones that are always speaking about the virtues of democracy. And my position is that the right-wing are the most un-American people out there. Many of them, of course, have always felt that I was conservative because of my background in law enforcement. Actually, I'm a moderate, but they thought I was conservative, and several have called in on shows, saying, "I'll never read another book that you write, Mr. Bugliosi," even though they haven't read this book; just the fact that what I'm saying goes against their interests, they're not going to buy another book.

MH: But what *you're* saying, the whole *world* is saying about our current administration. One of my listeners said, "I'm ashamed that Europeans are doing *our* protesting." Why did Greg Palast of the BBC have to be the first person to write about how the election was stolen in Florida, *from London*, when our own media won't touch it? And yet the media wastes time every night on what congressman is banging this girl instead of how about the fact we *all* got banged by the Supreme Court? The perspective of corporate media is way out of whack.

VB: When the conservatives come up to me, there are two things they say, "Even if what you say is true, Mr. Bugliosi, what difference does it make? The newspaper recount showed Bush won anyway." And they emphasize the word *"anyway."* Well, that's the first argument they use, and there's a second one that I will get to shortly. It's not clear at *all* that Bush is going to win the newspaper recount. The most recent *USA Today/Miami Herald* survey of May 11th said that using two standards to count votes, Bush wins; using two other standards, Gore wins. "The Consortium"—that's the *Los Angeles Times*, the *Chicago Tribune*, the *New York Times*, the *Wall Street Journal*, the *Washington Post*, and several other major dailies—hasn't come out with its findings yet.

But, let's assume, for the sake of argument, that Bush ends up winning anyway. It's totally, completely, utterly irrelevant. When you commit a crime, the bell is rung the moment you engage in your conduct; nothing that happens thereafter can unring that bell, and, therefore, it's completely irrelevant. To judge these Justices by the final result, as opposed to their state of mind or their intentions at the time they engaged in their conduct, would be like exonerating someone who shoots to kill if the bullet happens to miss the victim. Or "A" murders "B," and then some doctor says, "Well, you know, 'B' was going to die anyway in a couple of days, so I guess we should forgive what 'A' did to 'B.'" It's silliness, and it's nonsense. Now, the second argument the conservatives are making is that even if what I say is true, the Court had to do what it did to "avoid or avert a Constitutional crisis."

MH: And what bigger Constitutional crisis is there than stealing the election?

VB: The translation to what they're saying when they say the Court had to do what it did to avert a Constitutional crisis is that if an election of an American president is not close, then the Court doesn't have to intervene, but if it is *bitterly* close—as all close elections are—then, it's better for the Supreme Court to pick the President, whether or not he won the election, than to have the dispute resolved in the manner described by law.

Now, what is the manner described by law? The Twelfth Amendment of the United States Constitution clearly, expressly says all electoral disputes are to be resolved by Congress—*Congress, not* the United States Supreme Court. The United States Supreme Court usurped the power of Congress here, and these are the so-called strict constructionists. They weren't very strict in their construction here, because if they were, there's no ambiguity to the Twelfth Amendment, ratified in 1804. It should have been resolved by Congress. In a close election, as this one was, this Court had no more business intervening to resolve it than the Des Moines Rotary Club or the Boston Symphony.

And if any fine-feathered conservative friend of yours says, "Well, the Court had the authority to do that," you just ask them, "What case gave them that authority? What case, what statute, what rule, what regulation, what historical precedent?" There is none. It's nonsense.

MH:	It's like you said, if they had to extend that deadline for a few days for the counting of votes to determine who the rightful winner of a presidential election is, if that doesn't constitute a sufficient cause for a short extension of time, then what in the world does?

VB:	We're getting into the separate issue here of Title 3, Section 5 of the U.S. Code supposedly setting a deadline for the counting of votes of December 12th. If you look at Title 3, Section 5, there's no indication in that statute that it's a deadline for the counting of votes. It's a "safe harbor" statute, meaning if presidential electors are selected by December 12th, they cannot be challenged in Congress, but it has nothing to do with a deadline for the counting of votes. In fact, the Bush team, in their legal briefs (in the last brief to the Court on December 10th) talking about that issue, never said December 12th was a deadline for the counting of votes. What they did say is that the Florida Supreme Court was enacting new law in violation of Title 3, Section 5. Title 3, Section 5 *does* deal with that issue.

Very briefly, the Florida Supreme Court did not enact any new law. What they did, they interpreted old law. Assuming, for the sake of argument, that December 12th was a deadline for the counting of votes (which it is not, but let's make that assumption), any lawyer who practices law and goes to court in this country will tell you there's always an elliptical clause to mandatory deadlines—like to file a brief, to file a motion, etc.—and that elliptical clause is "except where there's good cause."

Mandatory dates are constantly waived by judges around the country. I'll give you a hypothetical. The lawyer says, "Judge, my secretary was out sick last week and we didn't get the thing in on time." "Fine, counsel, how much time do you need?" And it's a mandatory statutory deadline. And if extending the deadline for counting votes by a couple days is not good cause — where you're trying to find out who's the rightful winner of a presidential election — what in the world *would* constitute good cause?

Here's a third and, perhaps, the most important point. The recount started on December 9th. It was scheduled to conclude at noon on December 10th. The Court aborts that on December 9th, unlawfully — without any legal basis — stops the recount, and then has the audacity, the barefaced audacity, at 10:00 p.m. on December 12th (two hours before the deadline expires) to say that Gore ran out of time. Well, why did he run out of time? He ran out of time because the Court improperly stopped the recount at 2:00 p.m. on December 9th. Now, this is the type of sophistry that could tee off a saint. How *dare* they? Who were they to use an argument like that? Yeah, he ran out of time because of what the Supreme Court did.

MH: Well, the whole thing is insulting to anyone with any kind of intelligence, to believe what happened here was a normal, typical thing, or "a day in the life."

VB: What happened here is not the sunlight of democracy, but the very dark and ominous shadows of totalitarianism, despotism, fascism; there's no question about it. That message has not got out there, and if anyone can help me get that message out there, I would deeply appreciate it.

MH: I'm going to keep helping you because I refer to your book a lot. I always talk about the real side of what's going on in the news and I'm sure all my listeners will be happy to support you. Where do we go from here, because we're just about at the hour line?

VB: I'm taking my message around the country because this is just unbelievable what's happened here, and as of the moment, they have completely gotten away with it.

MH: We've just got to let people know what really happened because most people are in a trance over it. If we can wake them up, we can certainly make a difference. Just keep spreading the word, one person telling another person, and that's the way it works.

TWO

WHAT REALLY HAPPENED IN FLORIDA?

Meria with Greg Palast

Britain's *London Observer* is being sued by Barrick [Gold Corporation] of Canada for the investigations by journalist, Greg Palast.[2] Why? A witch hunt perhaps? Could it be because Palast was one of the first reporters to expose the illegal voting mess in Florida 2000? Are there connections to these two stories? Palast's article (now a book) is *The Best Democracy Money Can Buy: An Investigative Reporter Exposes the Truth about Globalization, Corporate Cons, and High Finance Fraudsters.* Freedom is *never* free. (Interview taped/broadcast on April 25, 2002.)

MH: There are troubled times in the 70-year friendship between the U.S. and the oil-rich desert kingdom [Saudi Arabia]—bin Laden and 15 of the 19 alleged hijackers on September 11th have Saudi roots and that's something nobody seems to be investigating any harder than Greg Palast.

GP: I'm calling you from deep in the bowels of BBC Television in London.

ME: Okay, how *are* the bowels today?

GP: Oh, they're moving slowly. I apologize to everyone listening in for being late, but I've been making several panicked calls into Venezuela to get set up to get the real story there.

MH: God knows we haven't been told the real story here. The whole Internet was buzzing with the fact that you're going to be on the show today. I'm glad to see that your book is doing so well, so let me plug the name of your book, *The Best Democracy Money Can Buy: An Investigative Reporter Exposes the Truth about globalization, Corporate Cons, and High Finance Fraudsters.*

GP: That's right. Amazingly, gratefully, I even made the *New York Times* bestseller list. It shocked the heck out of the entire publishing industry because they don't follow the Net. My book is put out by a teeny-weeny British publisher called Pluto Press and they were shocked too, because they didn't print anywhere near enough books. They are printing another 30,000 books very quickly, so if you're not seeing them in the stores—even Amazon was saying they couldn't get them—you will start getting quick delivery on these books.

The alternative networks, like Pacifica Radio Network, have been heavily promoting the book and I have to say thanks to Michael Moore, as well. If you've read *Stupid White Men,* you know from the opening of his book that several of the key stories are based on my reporting. He's been very gracious in crediting my work and promoting my book, as well, on his tour, so that's also helped. They've exiled me; they're trying to keep my stories off the main media, but they're having a tougher time because of you, Meria, and the Net world, and Michael Moore.

I finally broke into American television by being on *Politically Incorrect.* If I make a joke of the demolition of our democracy, I can get on the air. The question is, will I be allowed to report the *real* stuff? I'm here at BBC Television telling the rest of the planet what's up with the information I'm uncovering, but it's a hard-sell into the United States still.

MH: The good thing is, I've been talking about your book and I get letters and e-mails from a lot of my listeners asking where they can find your book. I think the tide is turning because people are ready to hear what you have to say. Just the fact that these books, like yours and Michael's, are flying off the shelf, means that people are pretty much disgusted with the lies we've been told.

GP: I don't sell my book on my website, but you might want to go to my website to get some of my latest stories and you can sign up and get them. You can even watch the BBC Television broadcasts, which you're not allowed to see on American networks, if you go to my website, which is www.GregPalast.com. You'll see a list of booksellers who have the book and can get them for you.

MH: I tell my listeners all the time, go into your bookstores and *demand* the book. If people ask for it, they're going to find a way to get it.

GP: My publisher decided to print 7,000 books for the USA and 8,000 bookstores ordered the book, so less than one book per bookstore. It's been a little tight, but we're correcting that as quickly as we can. People should know what's up and not only what's in the book, but what I'm working on now and why I was delayed in getting on the line with you, what's happening here with my investigations for BBC Television and the *Guardian* newspapers of Britain.

MH: You're one of the last of a dying breed of journalists who actually do their investigative homework.

GP: Every time I see the word "muckraker" or "the last of the investigative reporters," I know my agent cringes because that means I'll never get work in the USA. Literally, I've been told this, that being identified as a muckraker, and especially as a good one, is absolute career death in America. They are looking for actors. They think people who are muckrakers are out to get someone. I'm out to get the story and, yeah, there are bad guys out there and I probably *am* out to get them, or at least out to tell the truth on them. I thought that was a *good* idea. Apparently, it doesn't work very well for American television.

    You see the gutlessness of American television. It's horrendous. I've been screaming about Enron for eight years. You'll see in the book, which was written before the collapse of Enron, that I have 10 pages on it. You can see off my website, the BBC broadcast about Enron, where I stand in front of their old baseball stadium and say, "This is Enron. You've never heard of them, but they control America's energy policy." You couldn't get a story on Enron on American television, unless it was how wonderful they were.

MH: We *still* don't hear anything about it.

GP: I have to say that *60 Minutes* finally ran out and talked about Enron's vile, vicious operations in India. Now, you have to understand, that story has been reported worldwide for *six* years. *60 Minutes* finally runs out and does a six-year-old story on a company that is now bankrupt and basically disappeared so they can't punch back. They were "courageous" enough to wait six years until they didn't have to worry about the corporate power and I thought that was an absolute indication of how American television works. But, God forbid, they should do Enron *before* the fact.

I have to say, *60 Minutes* called me about doing one story. This was about George Bush's gold mining company, Barrick, and they talked to me about doing a story about George Bush and how he makes his money—George "Poppy" Bush—and how the family became suspiciously wealthy. I said, "You're not going to run the story," and *60 Minutes* said, "Oh, we don't know whether it'll be one segment or one of Ed Bradley's one-hour specials." I said, "You're not going to run the story." *60 Minutes* will *not* run the story about George W. Bush and George "Poppy" Bush and where they got their money. It took about three days before they got back to me and they said, "Oh, we changed our mind. We're not running this story."

MH: What a surprise.

GP: It's much more important to run stories about how wonderful General Electric's CEO, Jack Welch, was. That's *their* kind of investigative reporting, which is to ask General Electric's CEO, "And why is it that you're so wonderful?" That's how they go after corporate America.

MH: Bill Moyers had a special last night on the Hudson River and he didn't make Jack Welch look all too good.

GP: Moyers is a rare oasis of intelligent information and God bless him for being there. I should note that [Hudson River] story was originally done by *NBC Dateline*. You never saw it, though, because NBC is owned by General Electric. A young woman who was the producer did a story showing how GE covered up its continuing pollution of the Hudson River—Jack Welch almost certainly knew about it—and how he conned the public. Her story was not run.

Now, did it happen because it was about the ill-doings of her boss, General Electric, and her boss, Jack

Welch, that she couldn't report on him? I don't know, but it obviously came out somewhere else. That's your American television for you. Of course, PBS has been a nightmare as well. They did a program called "Commanding Heights," six hours of a version of globalization—just complete garbage; complete crap. We're getting a bunch of reports about the wonders of globalization and, by the way, that program was paid for first by Enron Corporation and then when Enron ran a little short of cash, it was taken over by British Petroleum, so basically what you had is an infomercial on how wonderful multinational corporations are, paid for by British Petroleum.

I can tell you, British Petroleum does not give any money to the BBC, the British Broadcasting Corporation. I would lose my job if I took money from a corporation.

MH: I don't think people really understand what you're up against. One of the good examples, besides the threats and lies people threw at you, is that you made the cover of a magazine called *The Moron*, where it says, "Is this the world's most evil man?"

GP: That was a send-up. One of the British newspapers, the *Mirror*, ran a full-page picture of me under a four-inch headline, a big screaming headline, that said, "The Liar"—that was the front page of the *Mirror*, which is the second largest newspaper in Britain. That's because I had uncovered the fact that Tony Blair's cabinet was open for purchase, was for sale. I pretended, in fact, that I was an Enron lobbyist, and saying I was from Enron was like abracadabra; it just opened all the doors. Of course, there was a price to be paid—an entry fee.

There was a consulting firm that said for 5,000 pounds (that's about $8,000.00) a month, they would connect me with their old partner, who was a guy very, very close to Blair inside Downing Street, and one of the key people in Blair's cabinet. I met this man and he said, "You hire that consulting firm. Tell me what you want and who you want to meet and I'll take care of it for you."

MH: That's the chapter you call "Lobbygate."

GP: It was famous. It was the story of the year in Britain. That was interesting because one of the things I discovered in that investigation was that, in fact, Enron Corporation had basically rented the British cabinet. All the tricks Enron used ultimately in affecting the policies—purchasing the policies of the U.S.—were first tested elsewhere, in Britain and Argentina; in Brazil and India. In fact, I just filmed here, Senator Rudolfo Terrano of Argentina who told me that George W. Bush called him in 1988 and basically said, "My daddy was just elected President of the United States" (or was about to be; it was November of 1988) "and he would really appreciate it if you would give a pipeline" (privatize and sell off a state pipeline) "to a company called Enron." This is 1988. If you remember, George W. Bush said he didn't get to know Ken Lay, the CEO of Enron, until 1994, when he ran for governor.

MH: He's a liar. How many times does he have to be proven to be one?

GP: I challenged Senator Terrano, who is very conservative. He actually knows the Bush family (knows Neil Bush pretty well) and he's the equivalent of a Republican. And I said, "Well, why would you say that, because you are implying that my President is concealing the truth?" Remember, Bush did not say he didn't *work* for Enron; he said he didn't get to *know* the CEO. It does tend to leave out a material fact if he was lobbying for Enron. So, I asked, "Why would my President say this? How could he have possibly forgotten about lobbying for Enron?" And he said, "Because the proposal had a corrupt edge to it." Not from George W., but Enron's lobbyist had basically implied that the deal, which would give up Argentina's resources for one-fifth of their value, was such a sweetheart proposal that some of the money could end up in the minister's Swiss bank account. So, he said that maybe George W. Bush "forgot" about this plan because it was corrupt and maybe it was uncomfortable to remember it.

MH: How convenient. One of the other things that's interesting is that you've never done what I think a lot of people do. Let's face it, this Bush Administration is one nightmare from hell and, because of that, I think people tend to make Bill Clinton look like he was a saint. But you also make very clear that Bill Clinton was in the middle of that Lobbygate, too.

GP: I also have to be very careful. I don't give anyone a pass. The Clinton Administration helped Enron, as well. It was clear that policies were changed in Britain at the behest of Enron and we do know that specific approaches were made to the Blair government to bend Britain's rules and laws by Bill Daly, Bill Clinton's Secretary of Commerce, and, of course, Clinton's spokesman during the Battle of Florida. Now, it was pretty creepy that Clinton would do that.

On the other hand, from my investigations, it was clear that while you can kind of rent the Democratic party, you could *purchase* the Republican party. There was influence on Clinton's cabinet. There was influence on people like Bill Daly. In the case of Enron and the Bush Administration, they *are* the government. You have to understand, for example, Bob Zilich, who is our chief trade negotiator, the guy who deals with the World Trade Organization, he was an Enron lobbyist. I mean, the guys are coming straight out of corporate America. As Jim Hightower puts it, "They no longer lobby the government. They *are* the government," so they don't have to. Paul O'Neill, our Secretary of Treasury, was CEO of Alcoa. It goes on and on. Don Edwards, our Energy Secretary, was CEO of an oil company. Obviously, Dick Cheney was CEO of Halliburton Corporation, so it looks more like a board of directors than a cabinet. You couldn't get this story out in America.

Until Enron collapsed, you couldn't talk about the influence of Enron in shaping our energy policies. You'll see it in the book, for example, exactly how Enron fixed the energy market in California. That story has still not been told. The story of Enron is all about how they cheated stockholders. Well, I don't care about the stockholders, to be very honest. They didn't cry when the stock was doubling and doubling again on the backs of the people they were ripping off in California and India and Argentina. This company seized the water system of Buenos Aires and literally broke the pipes and contaminated the system just to save money. So, the stockholders didn't complain then. They complained when they found out that Enron not only cheated the public, but they cheated their own owners. The executives cheated their own owners, so they're just in a long line of people ripped off.

MH: One of the things that you've become Internet-famous for, of course, was exposing the disenfranchisement of voters in Florida. Here we are, two years later, what do you think has changed? What can we look forward to in 2004?

GP: It will be worse. I'm very interested in getting back to Florida to find out exactly what they're up to there because no one's watching this. In fact, the U.S. media's view is that somehow Katherine Harris and Jeb Bush are so ashamed of what happened two years ago, they wouldn't dare pull a stunt like that again. Not so. They aren't ashamed, they're emboldened. Most of your listeners know this, but let me just give this to you in a sentence.

In the couple of years, and mainly in the last months leading up to the presidential election of 2000, Katherine Harris' office ordered the removal of 57,700 registered voters from the voter rolls on the grounds that they were felons. We know at least 90.2% of the people on that list were innocent of being felons. They had the right to vote, but they *were* guilty of being black. Fifty-four percent of the people on that list were black, *are* black, and we know the vote of the black folks. So, if you do the arithmetic, 57,700 voters targeted for removal, over half of them black (we figure the white voters are more or less evenly split in their vote); the black vote is 90% Gore. Well, there's your election. It was only decided by 537 votes, officially. I have to say, not all 57,700 voters were removed. They were ordered removed. Not all of them *were* removed, but it was enough to absolutely and unquestionably fix the election. They did it deliberately. One thing that has not come out in any U.S. newspaper is that it was deliberate.

The *Washington Post* did allow me to report this story, but *six months* after I wrote it. Don't forget that, it was *six months* after I wrote it. I first broke the story three weeks after the election. Gore was still in the race. A weak and limited version of the story was run by the

Washington Post in June [2001], after the U.S. Civil Rights Commission said our story is basically correct. What is still missing from the U.S. discussion is that it was a *deliberate* purge of black voters. They knew what they were doing. If you go down that list, for example, you'll see conviction dates, dates these people were *supposedly* convicted.

One, in particular, that comes to mind is a Thomas Cooper of Ohio. It says he was convicted on January 30, 2007. You tell me. Obviously, the guy *wasn't* convicted. Now, was that a mistake? Was that what you could call an *honest* mistake? Even if it changed the presidency of the United States, it might have just been a mistake? The ugly news is, if you go back into the e-mails, the e-mail traffic, you will see clerks who said, "My God, we've got people convicted into the future. What shall we do?" Now, what *should* we do? Someone is put on a list that he is supposedly a felon, but he is convicted in the year 2007. I don't know. I went to public school in Los Angeles; I think that person should be allowed to vote. Instead, the Republican functionaries wrote back to the clerks saying, "Well, just blank out the conviction dates and then no one will know." There were 4,000 blank conviction dates on one of the disks that I saw. There were 400-some names of people still listed as convicted in the future.

MH: I'm sure you've seen the book, *Jews for Buchanan*, by John Nichols. He's got ballots in there that are very clearly marked "Al Gore." "Al Gore" is written all over them. You know, just like some of the stuff you have, your documents, throughout your book. If people think you are making this stuff up, let me tell my listeners right here and now, you'd better get this book and get educated because we've been lied to forever. I had Will Pitt on the show and he said very succinctly: "Without the stolen election, 9/11 would not have happened."

GP: There are brilliant writers who like to put things together and make brilliant connections, but I'm not a connector. I'm a dot-maker. I'll give you the dots and you draw the lines.

MH: Pitt saw it as a business deal that went bad.

GP: One thing you will find in my book is a horrendous story about September 11th, which I reported, again, on the BBC and, believe me, you didn't and you won't see it on your television screen in America unless you watch BBC-America. Prior to September 11th, George W. Bush's Administration put a complete quash upon all investigations of Saudi financing of terror, *including* known financing of the al-Qaida network. This also included putting the kibosh on investigations of the bin Laden family, except for Osama, because remember that George W. Bush and "Poppy" Bush are close to the bin Laden family; they're partners in the Carlyle Corporation, so they were given a pass.

Now, I'm not saying—and this is important; I want to make a distinction—I don't have any information that our President *knew* we were going to be attacked or that he had some type of involvement on it. I have no information on that. I'm an investigative reporter; if I haven't investigated it and found it, I don't report it. But, what I *do* know is that he blind-sided our intelligence agencies. I did get high-level intelligence agents who confirmed that the kibosh was put on investigations of Saudi financing of terrorism and you have to understand, it's the old rule, if you can't follow the money, you can't do the investigation. Following the money is the heart of the investigation.

So, while he didn't say you can't investigate the al-Qaida network, he said you can't look at *where* they're getting their money, or you can't look at the Saudi connection.

Remember, almost all the hijackers were Saudi. Now, we bombed Afghanistan into oblivion, or we stirred up the rubble that was already there, I should say (it was *already* in oblivion). While we stirred up the rubble, on the other hand, we're dancing slow and close with the Saudis and no one is telling me why.

MH: Bush has a meeting with the Saudis today.

GP: One thing we did report on BBC Television; I reported for the *Guardian*; in fact, there is a very specific investigation, a very crucial investigation, that was hampered by George W. Bush. When we look at September 11th, it is profound and horrid. Believe me, I had an office at one time in the World Trade Center. These are my friends; these are my colleagues, the people I worked with. In fact, I've got to tell you, a lot of my files were still kept there. The corporate bad guys should take no comfort in that because I have copies of almost everything, but my files went down with the building and certainly much more than that, needless to say.

If this world blows up, it won't be because of Israel-Palestine and it won't be because of bin Laden. It's going to be because there will be a nuclear war between India and Pakistan. How did that happen? How did Pakistan create the so-called "Islamic bomb"? The information appears to be, according to intelligence agents, that the information and equipment was purchased for them by Saudis. The investigation of the Saudi financing of the Islamic atomic bomb was killed off by George W. Bush and his administration.

Now, are the reasons that he wanted America to be attacked or he wants the world to blow up and a nuclear war between Pakistan and India? I don't think so. I think what it's all about is that he had made a political and personal decision that the Saudis who sit on our oil and have joint investments with him and his family must be very good people because who else would be financial partners with the Bush family except very wonderful people? And very wonderful people who co-invest with the Bush family and have financial connections with them, it's hard to imagine that they would help the financing of an attack upon the United States or help financing of the Islamic bomb that could bend the world as we know it.

MH: What you're saying is so right on because he's meeting with the foreign minister of Saudi Arabia today and they've been pretty strong.

GP: I'm sitting here in the BBC studios and I just saw Bush giving this guy a big hug. And I thought, "Gee, after you hug him, you might ask him how much money he gave to al-Qaida." And how much money did he give to the guys who hijacked the planes and flew them into the buildings? And why he did that and when he did that? And what's next? I think those might be nice questions to ask after he's done with the hugging.

MH: From what I've read, they're getting ready to slap George Bush on the wrist or bitch-slap him across the face, especially after what he said about [Ariel] Sharon being a man of peace. I mean, this guy knows how to *really* piss people off. That's his specialty, I think.

GP: I don't mind pissing off the Saudis. They have a lot to answer for.

MH: I agree, but if our government's in bed with them and it's all a big money deal, you don't want to piss them off because he said America and Israel are basically the real evil terrorists on the planet.

GP: So this is what we have to listen to from these guys. First, we give them a pass on the investigation and then they call America the real terrorist. I want to note another Saudi connection—and, again, this is what *60 Minutes* would not bother really investigating or looking into and what I have reported. The story of Bush quashing the investigation is in the book, as well as the stories I'm working now on Argentina. My stories in the book about Argentina—how the World Bank basically drove the Argentine economy into the ground— the stories from my book, are page one news in Argentina for the past two weeks. The phone was ringing off the hook with calls from Argentina. They want to know what's going on even if Americans are denied the information.

Getting back to the Saudi connection, one of the things you'll never see in the U.S. papers is that George "Poppy" Bush went to work for a Canadian mining company called Barrick, after he left the White House. That Canadian gold mining company, Barrick, was a start-up operation funded by Adnan Koshogi, who is the arms dealer. Koshogi is the guy who armed "The Axis of Evil." In the Iran-Contra scandal, he was the bagman. He is the guy who traded the guns that were part of the Guns-for-Hostages deal. So, this is the guy who armed "The Axis of Evil" and George W.'s daddy went to work for him right out of the White House. And another little thing, there is absolutely no connection (I'm forced to say that because I'm sitting here in England) between George Bush going to work for Koshogi's company and the fact that George Bush pardoned Adnan Koshogi as one of his last acts of office.

MH: Yeah, right, there's *no* connection.

GP: There's *no* connection. I want to emphasize that point.

MH: And they were all worried about Clinton and his sex life.

GP: I'll give you the dots; you draw the connection.

MH: My listeners know that I tend to draw the connections a lot quicker than most people. There are other things that you uncover in this book that are phenomenal, especially your favorite guy there, Pat Robertson, and even the things you wrote about Wal-Mart and the globalization. This book covers so many different things, it's totally invaluable. Everyone needs to have this book and learn more about our country and really make their own decision as to whether or not they want to continue to support the way we run our foreign policy and this globalization nightmare.

GP: Read the book because what you'll get in the book also is documentation. You'll actually see some photos of documents; you'll get those BBC reports. In fact, you'll even get some great photos of Clayton Roberts, the head of the Florida Department of Elections, who was in on "the fix." When I went down with my BBC camera crew to ask him some questions about documents marked "Secret and Confidential," which, by the way, those documents are in the book and are explained in the book. I thought, "Gee, Clayton, maybe you'd like some of these documents back from your own file cabinet that are marked 'Secret and Confidential.' I'm sure you'd be interested in explaining *these* to us."

Instead, he rips off his microphone and does a 50-yard dash into his office and calls in the cops and they remove me and my BBC camera crew. There's a great picture of me running after Clayton. I'm saying, "Just explain it to me." So, you'll get the documents; you'll get photos.

MH: I really believe America's ready to hear the truth. They're tired of not getting answers.

GP: The fact that a goofy little book like mine made the *New York Times* bestseller list and that Michael Moore's book is at the top indicates that maybe there's an interest here. You have to understand that the American news producers have *always* used the excuse that Americans don't care about information; that it's not commercially viable to give them the truth. I've got to tell you, whenever the information comes out, people are hungry for the real thing, for the *real* news. It's not like Greg Palast is some great, wonderful investigative reporter. You know what it is, it's just that I have a network and a newspaper that's basically willing to let me tell the stories. We just got all this baloney about what happened in Venezuela. I'm sitting here at BBC and they're willing to fly me to Caracas to get the real story.

MH: Go get the story because it surely looks like the CIA's fingerprints are all over this one.

GP: You'll get the Venezuelan story as I have it. There was a *coup d'etat* against an elected president. Hugo Chavez, the president of Venezuela, was elected by 60% of the vote, an overwhelming landslide—an overwhelming majority of the public elected this guy—and *our* President kept calling him "a dictator." And *our* President is a guy who wasn't elected by *any*one and he's calling a guy who got elected by 60% of the voters "a dictator."

When asked about it, someone in the White House — a White House spokesman — said, "Well, winning a majority of the vote doesn't confer legitimacy on your government." We have a guy who obviously believes that winning a minority of votes is what confers legitimacy on your government.

MH: Doesn't that sound like what [Antonin] Scalia had to say about our right to vote?

GP: Yeah, you ain't got it, baby. So, no one was telling the true story about Venezuela and it's an important story because President Hugo Chavez of Venezuela is a guy who has basically refused to accept the dictates of U.S. oil corporations or the World Bank or the IMF and the U.S. government. He's really trying to give the poor people a break. He instituted a land reform program. Land is not tilled in Venezuela and that place is twice the size of France. There's a lot of land that is simply not used. It's empty. He said that empty land owned by rich landlords has to go to the landless. This got the rich up in arms against him and you know what sealed his fate? Everyone keeps saying he's a friend of Castro and that sealed his fate.

No one cares about Castro. What sealed his fate is that he doubled the royalties on foreign oil companies extracting oil from Venezuela. Venezuela sold more oil to the United States than Saudi Arabia. It *had* been our number one supplier. The U.S. oil companies ran a virtual boycott on Venezuela after they doubled the royalties. Now, when I say doubled them, he doubled them from about 16% to 30%; still the foreign oil companies got to keep like 70% of the value of the oil going out. But that wasn't enough. The idea that anyone would have the temerity to raise royalties on U.S. oil companies basically, as Bush would say, meant they no longer had a legitimate government.

So, Bush is right. In his world view, under a New World Order, we now know it's not whether you have a majority of the vote that makes a government legitimate, but whether you have a majority of the *oil* companies on your side. And I thought this was a story worth telling. It was just complete nonsense. One of the things that happened is, the U.S. press announced that Hugo Chavez, the president, had resigned and, therefore, these guys who directed this *coup* against Chavez had a legitimate government. In fact, it was a completely bogus story. I was able to reach Venezuelan leaders who said, "Chavez has not resigned. He's still president," and within 48 hours, he was back.

MH: And who did they try to slip on in right after that happened, but another big businessman.

GP: You know where that story came from? Ari Fleischer. So, basically our news is what Ari Fleischer, the spokesman for George W. Bush, *says* it is. His complete factoid was complete nonsense, with no backing whatsoever, no basis, *none*, and yet the *New York Times*, the *Los Angeles Times*, *Chicago Tribune*, you name them, every U.S. outlet printed it as truth. And I have to say that my own outlet in Britain, the *Guardian*, unfortunately, picked up that story and ran it as truth, but at least they let me correct it very, very swiftly.

MH: Ari Fleischer's *admitted* to being a liar for everything from the supposed Clintons' destruction of the White House on their way out to everything else.

GP: This was a fake. After Venezuela, I have to get information about Argentina. We'll save Argentina for another day, though if you want to get some information on what's *really* going on down there, go to my website. If you don't want to buy the book, tell your library to get it, *The Best Democracy Money Can Buy.* I've heard that some authors don't like libraries getting books because they can't sell you a bunch. Not me. I love it. I believe in libraries. Tell your library to order it and share it.

THREE

CAN WE HAVE A LEGITIMATE GOVERNMENT?

Meria with Michael Rectenwald

Michael Rectenwald,[3] as the founder of Citizens for Legitimate Government (*www.legitgov.org*), has strong opinions about how our thrown 2000 election figures into the events of today and why we are being lied to constantly. He questions whether bombing Afghanistan is the answer and ponders what price Americans will pay for this policy. He explores why true patriots are being labeled un-American and the part media "whores" play in creating our "history." Rectenwald discusses why real freedom is being repressed on our college campuses, what oil in the Caspian Sea has to do with the current "war," and makes suggestions as to how we can work together to inform America and stop the "war." Anthrax, weapons, tax breaks for the rich, and more are discussed with Rectenwald. This is an interview with information all true patriots need to know. (Interview taped/broadcast on October 24, 2001.)

MH: Citizens for Legitimate Government is a national Internet-based activist group that arose in response to the breach of democratic principles in the 2000 presidential election contest and which continues in the [President George W.] Bush Administration. I went to their website yesterday and I can tell you that almost every news story I've covered on the show the past few weeks is right there. Could you give the audience a little of your biographical background?

MR: I would say that my political lineage dates back to the '60s vis-à-vis my connections with the New Left movement. Most specifically, Allen Ginsberg, who I studied with when I was 19 years old at Naropa Institute [University] in Boulder, Colorado. Basically, I became interested in art and activism at that time and have been involved ever since. My career is academia. I work as an English professor and a writer, and I use the classroom as a vehicle for activism, as well as a way of getting progressive political ideology on the table. We can't proffer it as a belief they have to acquire in order to pass the course, but we get aired. My position at Citizens for Legitimate Government came about simply in response to the travail and cover-up of the election scandal in the 2000 presidential elections, specifically with reference to Florida.

MH: I was re-reading the article about you in the *Democracy Chronicle* [www.Kiosk2000.com], where you tell the story that you and your 14-year-old son were out putting up Gore-Lieberman posters and you got some physical threats while you were doing that, from Republicans. Is that true?

MR: Yes. That's absolutely true, and right in my own neighborhood. We were basically threatened and charged off of the site by a Republican who was brandishing a hammer. So, I knew the extent to which they were going to go to get this election, come terrorism or whatever.

MH: I've been covering that from day one, too. I guess it wasn't exactly Maxwell's silver hammer this guy had in his hand, but it probably had *your* name on it.

MR: It had *my* name on it. And after he ripped down all of
        our signs, he proceeded to put up his own. It was
        basically a battle. This was a very hard-fought state,
        Pennsylvania, and we did win it in the final hour, with
        the kind of struggles we had.

MH: I can only imagine, but I don't think anything
        compares to Florida, that's for sure. It's nice to know
        the Tampa Three are actually suing the City of
        Tampa now, for being arrested at that protest.

MR: The charges were dropped and it's going the other
        way now.

MH: Yesterday, there was a story in the news about how a
        lot of [college] teachers are getting fired for speaking
        to their students about peace protests and anything
        anti-Bush. What do you think about that?

MR: I think it's abysmal, and it shows that academic free-
        dom may be merely a pie-in-the-sky ideal that doesn't
        exist. I have had similar, I would say, warnings, from
        the administration, but nothing overt or outright,
        such as specifically, don't say this or that. Basically, it
        happens with baiting you in forums, public forums,
        for discussions, and that's where you have to be most
        careful, because after inviting you to come and
        express your opinion, it's a way of shaking down and
        getting out all of the oppositional viewpoints, and to
        identify those who have them. It's very strange. I've
        seen that in two cases so far.

MH: I think abysmal *is* the right word for it. As you reme-
        mber, in the '60s, a lot of the peace movement really
        came from the college campuses.

MR: I can say that I've taught in different types of institu-
        tions, from very elite sort of universities that are quite
        expensive, to community colleges and, in any case,

the right-wing ideology has quite a grip on a lot of these young people. It's not pervasive. It's not entirely ubiquitous, but it's there. And they're not very slow to complain to the parents, or whomever, if they think you're trying to foist a political position down their throats.

MH: Then, we have the flip-side of that where the media aren't covering any of the peace protests or anything that's said against the rah-rah-sis-boom-bah-let's-go-to-war Bush Administration.

MR: Very little coverage of anything.

MH: What do you think the chances are of the NORC (National Opinion Research Center) Report ever being given to us about the results of the Florida recount?

MR: I think the report is going to come out, but the question is, who's going to interpret it, and how is it going to be skewed, in terms of interpretation? I do think that eventually we'll get the results, but I think by the time we get them, as in most cases in the U.S., unfortunately, it will be far too late. I think the media, again, are going to have the complete control as to how it gets presented. I do think it's going to come out, but we're going to have to get our own interpreters on this. This is one of the things I was talking about with Bob Fertik [*see* Chapter 4] at Democrats.com and Aaron of *Democracy Chronicle*, is to get our own access, so we can interpret the data ourselves.

MH: Think about it. Just from a commonsense point of view, don't you think if that report showed, at this particular juncture in history, that Bush won, that it would be smeared all over the front page of everything?

MR: Oh, absolutely! So, I think it's very damaging and that's why it's being kept under wraps.

MH: They don't want it to cast an illegitimacy pall on the President, that's what I've been reading.

MR: Especially at this time. I think it's obviously been the case since the beginning, but now, in particular, it seems to be their option to keep this thing under wraps. Ironically, two days before September 11th, *Newsweek* had finally broken something major; the whole issue was basically devoted to the fact that we have an illegitimate President.

MH: I read that *Newsweek* article out loud on the show, and then all of a sudden, this happened.

MR: Yeah, all of a sudden, this happened. Politically, it couldn't have been more auspicious for the current administration to have this happen.

MH: A lot of people are saying that Bush is really not showing good leadership, especially with leaving the country in the midst of all the anthrax going around D.C. What's your feeling about it?

MR: First of all, I think a lot of the problems have arisen from an unwillingness to pay attention to other sources of information and other studies. For example, the airport studies, the terrorist studies that have been done prior to his [Bush's] Administration taking office. The presentation of those studies was utterly dismissed because they were presented by Democrats, for the most part.

MH: Are you talking about the study that Gary Hart presented and the Gore Commission?

MR: Right. That had recommendations, particularly about airport security, and basically the line back then was, "We'll have [Vice President Richard] Cheney study that." It was part and parcel of a consistent dismissal of other people's work, of expert testimony and part and parcel of a whole series of dismissals, from the science on global warming, with respect to the Kyoto protocol; from the science on cigarette smoking for teenagers, and the problem of international advertising; from the cyanide in the water. Everything was dismissed that didn't suit their ideology, that didn't come from the "right" place. So, this was part and parcel of that. As far as the handling ever since, I was hopeful there would be some restraint shown with reference to Afghanistan, and I think it's terrible what's happening; this bombing of Afghanistan is just awful. It just confirms what many of us have always suspected.

MH: That this was what we were going to find ourselves with, because of the results of the stolen election.

MR: That we would find ourselves with the trigger-happy cowboy shooting up the planet, and much in line with the legacy of the Bush family tree, which has deep roots in violence and international conspiracy and terror beyond simply the connections between Bush and the bin Laden family.

MH: They really couldn't be any closer if they were Siamese twins.

MR: It's just incredible, the likenesses, and one way to look at the whole scenario is to say, we have two criminal cartels shooting each up and the citizens of their respective countries are the collateral damage.

MH: Let's look at collateral damage. One of the top opinion stories is postal workers legitimately going "postal" now, over their second-class treatment with this anthrax.

MR: It just so happens they were mostly African-American postal workers in Washington, D.C. and it just confirms the kind of second-class citizenry that this party, this Administration, considers African-Americans. They have no problem with an election that came on the heels of throwing out at least 20,000 of their votes before they even voted, etc. So, they're angry because they were not treated with the same kind of urgency that pertained with reference to the Congress and the White House. They're just not as "equal" as those people.

MH: Right, and there it is. How much clearer does it have to be that the small person, the average Joe Citizen, is really expendable, to say the least? I think we really saw that, with what happened at the World Trade Center and how many lives were lost. But you know, when it comes down to bottom-lining everything, lives are expendable, just like the people in Afghanistan are expendable. I always like to say, the rich get richer and the poor get screwed.

MR: A stray bomb goes off and hits an elderly folks home . . .

MH: And a hospital.

MR: . . . and it's barely an apology.

MH: How do you have a "stray" bomb, in this world of technology, high-tech war? And not even an apology. With [Secretary of Defense Donald] Rumsfeld, of course, everything that comes across his desk is, "Oh, that's ridiculous." When the UN [United Nations] confirmed that we bombed the hospital, then we *still* had no statement. What do you think about the media blackout on this wag-the-dog war?

MR: It's worse than a blackout, I would say. I would consider it a full-scale propaganda campaign and it just goes to show you that the state and the media are so inseparable. The official governmental policy is absolutely 100% kow-towed to by the media. We're supposed to have a critical, at least a distanced, position with reference to what goes on. That's the whole virtue of an independent and free media. We talk about the propaganda in other countries, but the propaganda here is just unbelievable.

MH: This morning, I woke up to the best story yet. I've been comparing this thing to wag-the-dog since day one, but today, our government actually hired Madison Avenue. We have the same woman who put together the Uncle Ben's Rice commercials, who's going to be working to do advertisements for us on that Al-Jazeera station, to show the rest of the world our stand and how wonderful we are, I suppose, in this war on Afghanistan.

MR: Similarly, in the Gulf War, a PR firm was hired.

MH: Don't you find that offensive?

MR: I find it very offensive. Especially that public funds are used to sell an agenda to the public. Basically, we're paying to have ourselves brainwashed, if you look at it that way, and to brainwash the rest of the world. So, our tax dollars are being used to influence us by a public relations firm—one in D.C., that's covering the war. I don't know if this exact firm was used in the Gulf War, but the same thing happened there, and we know about all the lies that took place there. You know, the babies-in-incubators lie. All that made the slippage from support-the-troops to support-the-war so imperceptible to the public, and suddenly they found themselves waving those yellow flags in support of a pogrom of Iraqis. Here, we have the same thing and I refuse to wave a flag at this juncture in history because of what it means. It simply means blood. I will not wave for blood or call for blood.

MH: I went through the same cycle, wrestling day-by-day with this, as everyone else did, especially being an ex-New Yorker. I freaked out when this first happened and you know, I covered everything in flags. And then, after a couple of days, when my senses came back, I took them down. And I said, "I can't support this. This is bullshit." This is not the America I grew up in. What do you think about the fact that anyone like us that's out there talking or saying anything sideways about what's going on is immediately called communists, Nazis or unpatriotic?

MR: Well, I've been threatened. This is not the first time, but it's a little more frightening now because I actually believe these threats could be taken out with much more impunity if they were to be enacted against me. I'm talking about physical threats. And, obviously, as the firemen in Florida who would not fly the flag on the back of their fire trucks said, "This stands in direct opposition to everything the flag represents." To squelch opinion, to squelch free speech, to enforce conformity, all these things are un-American, and true patriots are standing up and speaking their minds.

MH: I remind people that everyone who signed the Declaration of Independence ended up getting murdered or ruined for life.

MR: They were radicals. And the conservatives only like a reform or a revolution that happened in the past. They never like it when it happens now or in the future. They don't like any reform unless it's past-tense. That obviously underscores the contradiction in their political ideology. They don't like to see the face of progress or radicalism, or reform or opposition, that very thing that got them where they are, that got them their rights, that got them all the things they now have. They don't like to see it in the present tense.

MH: They just want to sit on the laurels of the people who died for them, but they don't want to be active in anything. I had a guest on the show recently and he said what really insults him is when you hear the President talk about Americans. He'll say how brave we are, and how strong we are, but you never hear anybody in government refer to how intelligent we are.

MR: And I think it's a very intelligent population. One of the greatest signs in recent history of the resilience and intelligence of the American public came with the Clinton scandal, and the attempt on the far-right to destroy the Clinton presidency and the way the public held firm against the most outrageous onslaught of public relations and smear is a tremendous testimony to the integrity, the mental integrity, of the United States citizen.

MH: It really is an insult to our intelligence, what they're doing with the media and all these PR firms, etc., and blocking us out on what's really going on in the war. When is the rest of America going to wake up and get it? Talk about getting the wool pulled over your eyes. This is better than a movie, watching this.

MR: It's *absolutely* a movie and they're bringing out the old myths, the old simplified dichotomies of good versus evil. It plays right into all of these religious mythologies, so that people are able to consolidate their opinions in the most simplified, inane terms possible. At least, the hope is that you can suggest we're on the side of good and George Bush is going to rid the world of evil.

MH: My thought as soon as he said that was, "Well, how about starting right at home, right in the White House?"

MR: I don't see how he would put an end to evil without looking in the mirror.

MH: Remember when the bombings first happened here, they said the White House was a target and then the Administration, Ari Fleischer, came out and said they lied about that; that it was just a story. So, how could it be that all Americans are not up in arms over that, just being outright lied to?

MR: I wonder about this little jaunt that Bush took right after the attacks and the reason why he was puddle-jumping across the country. I'd like to know what that was all about.

MH: My feeling was that he was probably scared shitless. Let's face it, he didn't make too many friends in the world in the short time he's been the President-select. He could have just poked his fingers in people's eyes like Curly of the Three Stooges. I think that's the only thing he *didn't* do.

MR: One of the other consequences of this particular episode is the fallout. We had a real good pro-democracy movement really picking up steam. We had many groups coalescing and working together and we were starting to pull in a wider coalition with environmental and feminist groups and, basically, all parts of the left that had been fragmented. Then, when this attack happened, we've had some fragmentation again. It's unfortunate.

MH: We had a lot of people threatened, physically threatened, and I don't know if your threatener is just a regular Joe-Schmoe in the street. I know that some of my guests have been visited by different organizations, governmental organizations, and basically told to shut up.

MR: You were supposed to tell me that *before* the show.

MH: Well, nobody's come to see *me* yet.

MR: They want to keep you on the air so they can have their magnet. They need their political magnet, right?

MH: Maybe people are still trying to figure out who the hell she is. What is this woman's deal? There's a cute cartoon in *Newsweek* this week where a wife is looking at her husband sitting in front of the TV and she says, "Ha, if you're *so* important, how come nobody sent *you* any anthrax?" So, that might be the new way to tell whether you're really worth your salt or not. Not that I'm inviting any of that into my reality.

MR: Your importance will be known by that, when you get anthrax.

MH: You'll know you've arrived then. You mentioned Bob Fertik [*see* Chapter 4] a little earlier. He's a pretty ballsy guy. He wrote a little article on 10 differences between what's going on now [and what would be happening if Al Gore were President. The number one thing is, he wouldn't be passing yet another tax break for large corporations right now, while our economy is crashing. The same corporations that are laying people off like crazy, that are getting government bailouts, are going to get even larger tax breaks going back to 1986 for refunds, and the little guy is choking. We're just choking in our own spit, trying to keep our health insurance up, keep paying and making up our unemployment. Oh, they extended unemployment for 13 weeks. Big deal. Al Gore would have been very present. He would have been very out there. I mean, how long did it take for Bush to show up after the World Trade Center got knocked down? That was pretty scary.

MR: He was pretty much dodging things and he wasn't out front.

MH: And then we had that goat-boy story about how when Bush was told, he continued reading to the kids in Florida.

MR: For a half-hour, I think.

MH: That's pretty scary stuff. What was this guy thinking? Or can we even use the word "thinking" in connection with that?

MR: He wasn't surprised. I'm not sure what that means.

MH: No, he wasn't. I'm sure you're familiar with Bob Kunst of the Oral Majority? His feeling is that Jeb Bush has made Florida a target state, but this is definite retribution against the Bush family. I wondered, what if Afghanistan or the Taliban said, "Why don't you guys hand over Bush and we'll trade you bin Laden?" What would the United States do?

MR: That would be an interesting question.

MH: Maybe that's part and parcel of why Bush is spending so much time traveling. He's kind of like, "Where's Waldo?"

MR: It's just too much. Did you read the comparison between bin Laden and Bush? If you ask, "How do you tell a terrorist?" it pretty much runs down their backgrounds and the similarities between the two — Bush and Osama bin Laden. They are *not* that different; there are more similarities than differences.

MH: And then he was going out looking for terrorists and ends up in Italy with [Italy's President Silvio] Berlusconi. And I said, "Is he going to put the handcuffs on him?" because he's another one who rates right up there with terrorists. It's just the pot calling the kettle black.

MR: I guess the question then becomes how can we stop this crazy killing and this crazy bombing campaign, and how do we prevent it from extending to Iraq. This is one of the major reasons why the Middle East, regardless of how they express it, is so angry. Now, we've probably killed 300,000 when we bombed them, and then another million when we starved them with the sanctions, and now we want to attack them again.

MH: They basically know that. They're not stupid people. They said, "Don't go using this as an excuse to come in here and finish old unfinished business."

MR: But it could very well happen. The anthrax could be linked, or supposedly linked, to them, and then we're going to have another country that's mad.

MH: But the key word is "supposedly." How convenient would that be as an excuse for us to go in there and wipe out yet another population? I really try to stay out of conspiracy thinking, but if you have a half a brain and you really look at the way this thing is developing, you see what the intention of our government is from the get-go. Those people in Iraq are not stupid.

MR: And we don't want to get Saddam Hussein.

MH: No. If we wanted to, we would have taken him out. The Mafia could have tracked this guy a long, long time ago. Why don't they just call up the mob and tell them, "We'll trade you John Gotti for bin Laden." It's so simple; it would take them probably 24 hours and they'd have his head in a basket.

MR: There's nothing to it. With all the intelligence and the smart bombs and the guided missiles and the entire CIA, I'm sure that's not a problem, so the point is, he's a ready scapegoat for our intervention in the Middle East.

MH: Don't forget that Americans have always been deluded into that one-man theory. You know, there's only *one* bad guy. So he was a perfect pick as the one bad guy.

MR: It seems to work as a large-scale campaign.

MH: It's pretty scary. People really don't want to look at it. Last night, I flipped on CNN (I don't know why I do it, maybe just to see what garbage they're putting out) and Ari Fleischer was on, bald-face lying again. He was talking about anthrax and he actually said the sentence (I ran for a piece of paper to write it down)—he said before last month, not one single letter with anthrax had ever been mailed in the United States. Now, I did a story last week on the fact that 30 anthrax powder letters were sent to Southern California in 1999.

MR: How convenient. What's the reason for the lie?

MH: Why tell people this is a new thing? Now, if this was happening in 1999, do you really think it was bin Laden's people sending these letters?

MR: The reason to tell people it's a *new* thing is to connect it with September 11th.

MH: Exactly! I said how convenient. So, all of a sudden it's a new threat. Where are these letters going? Okay, they're going to the press, which is a joke. And it's going to politicians, okay? To me, it was like from the get-go, this sounds like an at-home, home-created, home-grown nut-job.

MR: It looks like the far right to me.

MH: When they hire thugs to go in and beat the hell out of people doing a recount in Florida, I mean, what can you really put past these people?

MR: Nothing.

MH: Then the news is, we sold anthrax spores to the leader of the white supremacist groups. If we'd stop being such a whore, money-based country, where we'd sell our mother to the highest bidder, we wouldn't have the problems we're facing today.

MR: Anthrax has been manufactured here in the United States and sold overseas, sold to the Middle East. We're the producers, but that's the contradiction between capitalism and democracy, or capitalism and freedom, because it shows that if the profit principle is put above all else, we endanger the very things we're supposed to be providing for.

MH: Exactly. I think it was [in] the *New York Times*, their quote of the week, by Bush, who said these terrorists' aim is to upset the global economy and we're not going to allow them to do *that*. It wasn't that they want to hurt our citizenry or the health and welfare of the American citizens and we're not going to allow them to do that. He said they want to stop the global economy and we won't allow them to do that. So, right there, you've got to see where this guy's coming from. It's all about money—and people have to understand that. Whether they're in the World Trade Center, Sears Tower, Disneyland, wherever the hell they are, they're expendable. We're nothing. We're little bugs.

MR: We're basically getting in the way. It's basically as hostages, is the way they might look at us. We've got mutual hostages and the various leaders have mutual hostages and they're able to expend them and use them as threats.

MH: Right. [Supreme Court Justice] Sandra Day O'Connor, this week, had the nerve to say that because of terrorism, we're going to have to lose some of our freedoms in this country.

MR: Which she's been after in the first place.

MH: Don't you think losing the votes of everyone in America by [the Supreme Court] picking a President was a loss of all our freedoms at that point?

MR: We've already had our rights eroded dramatically. Since September 12th, it's been an onslaught on a continual basis. Beginning with the loss of voting rights; then, we continue to lose more rights and effective representative government was gone. All the voice of the political will of the citizens was totally silenced, and now, with this terrorist crisis, we have the rationalization for squelching yet more rights: First Amendment rights, Fourth Amendment rights, etc.

MH: And let's not forget the oh-so-popular Anti-Terrorism Bill. I want to talk more about the connection between what happened in the election of 2000 and what's going on in the world today.

MR: The roots of the connection go back quite a way and I think there is definitely a connection here. We have, basically, the son of one of the most reviled men in the world, in the Middle East, at least, as the President of the United States. Had the election not been stolen from the rightful winner, Al Gore, and the usurper put in his place, perhaps the United States would not have been targeted as such. Remember, it was George Bush, Sr. who bombed Iraq, who mercilessly bombed them. It was George Bush, Sr. who has connections with the rich Saudis bin Laden is angry with, including his own family. It is this kind of criminal cartel of CIA/Bush family connections that really has ushered in a tremendous amount of anger.

MH: I remember during the campaign saying that we've got a lot of people with scores to settle against Bush.

And if Bush gets in as President, don't you think those people are going to come after his son to get back at him?

MR: You see what they did in the extent that they went to steal an election. I mean, they'd do anything. They do this unmitigated across the globe. George Bush, Sr. is intimately involved with *coups* internationally, so that's where they had their practice for the *coup* that they pulled off here.

MH: And through the Carlyle Group.

MR: People are angry about the dictators who are put in place and propped up by the U.S. at the expense of the majority, the great majority, of their citizens around the world. We always have to look for a real motive. I think that is sufficient. It may not be necessary, but it's sufficient.

MH: Europe always has the real news about what's going on in America. The attitude of the rest of the world towards Americans was that we are nothing but a weak bunch of sheep who, when we lost our vote, didn't do anything, so it kind of made us look weak and open to attack because we didn't even fight for our own rights at that time. And then we get a President in office whose father still is in business with bin Laden's family through the Carlyle Group—who won't resign from the millions of dollars he gets paid because they're the "nice" bin Ladens—the part of bin Laden's family that disowned Osama. Yeah, and I believe that *and* that elephants can fly.

Then, you get Bush into office with his millionaire cabinet, who is basically his father's cabinet, who is still hated from 10 years ago, and then he goes breaking all kinds of treaties and gets involved in this star wars thing. There wasn't anything else he could do to possibly piss off any more people in the world than he was pissing off. And then, at a time when he was not showing any kind of global perspective as far as the environment or protecting the planet or human rights, we get bombed. And, all of a sudden, he wants everyone else to help us. Well, that looks pretty stupid to anybody.

MR: We're all of a sudden bi-lateralists.

MH: Now he's getting into bed with all the other countries in the Middle East who are the terrorists of tomorrow. What is he setting us up for?

MR: I think what he might be setting up is a long-term war, like you said.

MH: You have a son who's 14. Do you want him to look forward to getting drafted and going and fighting in caves in Afghanistan when he's 18? Do you know how many people are telling me they're scurrying their sons the hell out of here? One of my listeners asked the question, "Do you think we sold anthrax to bin Laden or do you think it's just some crazies in the U.S. doing this?"

MR: We *did* sell anthrax to Iraq. I'm not sure we sold it to bin Laden directly, but we *did* sell it to the Middle East. We sold to Iraq and, if the reports of our own government are true, these terrorists are multi-national, and might be involved with Iraq, then we may have indirectly, yes.

MH: This week's *Newsweek* actually tells you we sold to Saddam Hussein and North Korea. For $3,600.00, you can buy all the anthrax you want. There is something wrong with that picture. First, we create these deadly diseases. We sell them to people crazier than us. They bastardize it even further, because I understand Russia actually has some designer diseases that totally destroy your immune system and they have no treatment or vaccines. They also have the form of anthrax that doesn't respond to antibiotics. There are so many people in America who yell at people like you and me. If they really knew the truth, that this is what America's been doing for a long time, I think it would change their mind quite a bit.

MR: I think that knowing, like you said, what this wing, or this party, of our government represents to the world, and an immediate demonstration of that upon the taking of office, I think that things just went into high gear in the Middle East. The memory of the bombs in Iraq is still vivid; it has to be and, of course, the sanctions are still in effect. The country that was ranked in the top 10% for children's health and education prior to the Gulf War is now in the bottom 20% from the bombing and the sanctions.

MH: What do you think about Bush's bright idea of all the children in America putting dollar bills in envelopes and sending them to the White House?

MR: I think it's funny and I just can't believe the credulity of some people. It's really horrible to manipulate the sentiments of children in such a way when the policies that are under-girding the entire scenario are so despicable, to take and manipulate the good will of people, especially young and impressionable people.

MH: My six-year-old granddaughter called me and she said, "Grandma, I just put a dollar in an envelope for the children." How could I explain to my six-year-old granddaughter that that wasn't a good thing to do? I try to educate my daughter, but you're a parent, you know what I'm saying.

MR: It's not easy. I think if the reports are right, by the Red
        Cross and the United Nations, there's going to be a lot
        of starvation in Afghanistan.

MH: Cheney said we're going to be out of there by the
        winter, that it should be over by the winter. It's going
        to be over by the winter because everyone's going to
        starve to death. Starved and frozen to death. I saw
        those children on TV at the border of Pakistan and
        Afghanistan. They don't know who's shooting at them
        first. People trying to keep them from the border—the
        Americans, whoever. My heart was breaking for those
        kids. Imagine the horror of living like that every day.

MR: It's unbelievable. I make the analogy that's apt; would
        it be right to bomb the state that Timothy McVeigh
        was from because he blew up the federal building in
        Oklahoma City?

MH: Or all white Christians?

MR: Essentially, that's exactly what we're doing. We're
        bombing a country over supposedly one person's—or
        a network of terrorists'—activities. We have a lot of
        militia people here in the United States, in the
        Midwest, and I don't think it would really suit
        the Midwesterners if we were to drop bombs on their
        states in order to flush out the terrorists who are living
        there. It's just insane.

MH: Yes, it is, but there's more to this than meets the eye.
        A lot of people talk about Afghanistan as being the
        pipeline through to the Caspian Sea where all the
        other oil is, the big oil.

MR: That's been the design, the pipeline through, and
        Afghanistan's the necessary link. It'll happen, I think,
        suddenly on the heels of this entire campaign. By the
        time it happens, the connection between the pipeline

and the bombs will probably be all but obliterated in the minds of most people.

MH: *Especially* if we have the gal who did Uncle Ben's Rice commercials. I always thought Uncle Ben's was the best rice because of the advertising.

MR: I'm not eating that any more.

MH: I know it's not. No, I only eat organic food now.

MR: Back to Rice-A-Roni for me; the San Francisco treat, after all.

MH: Speaking of San Francisco, they had a lot of peace protests in San Francisco. They had a big one this weekend, 5,000 people. No coverage, *again*, in the media.

MR: We found some articles on it, but obviously the mass media are not covering any of this. There were 5,000 there, and there have been huge protests and demonstrations all throughout Europe—London, Paris, many major cities. It's basically gotten nothing, no coverage at all.

MH: I find it ludicrous. I get most of my American news off the *Independent UK*. What the hell is this about? A lot of times, people ask me where I get all that stuff that's on my show. You've got to *really* look.

MR: Yes, you have to dig hard. Unfortunately, it gets branded as "off-news." Because it's not covered by the major media, it can't be true, is often the assumption of a lot of people.

MH: But now that the media are finding their little letter-bombs, their little anthrax powder letter-bombs, they're actually making the news and they don't like making the news that way. It was okay when they were ragging on everybody else, but when it came back to their own studios, they didn't know how to handle it. I find that very interesting because up to until now, I think a lot of these reporters and media stars, who I don't think could really dig up a news story if they *had* to, thought they were invincible, like Superman or Superwoman.

MR: Basically, all they do is read the White House press releases and *that's* what they consider to be the news. It's spoon-fed to them. If the U.S. government isn't telling them what to report, they don't have anything to say.

MH: I've always said that the media, like television, is just a big PR firm for the government. When the World Trade Center blew up, how many times did we see that? It was more often than seeing the body of Kennedy in the Rotunda, which I thought I'd *never* get out of my mind. And then one of my friends said, "If you want to feel better, just shut your TV off. Don't watch it for a couple of days."

MR: Oh, I haven't watched it at all.

MH: You know, that *really* works.

MR: I tuned in last night just to see what is going on out there and it's the same.

MH: It's like a soap opera. It's the same story.

MR: The human interest story is an *endless*, endless parading of fireman. I have nothing against fireman; firemen are wonderful.

MH: But now we've sanctified them.

MR: The whole idea just cements itself into the idea of this jingoistic revenge.

MH: It's mind control. If they keep hammering us with this, we're going to be rah-rah behind this war. This war on terrorism sounds awfully familiar, like the war on drugs and the war on cancer. Those are the invisible wars that never get any better, but continue to raise a lot of money.

MR: Our group is non-partisan. Harry Brown of the Libertarian Party has seven rules on how to deal with terrorism, "What Can We Do About Terrorism?" it's called.

MH: Where can I get a copy of that?

MR: We have it linked on our site. You can go right from our site, from our "Hot Articles." I was surprised. He came out with some very good tenets and some truths about how we should look at this and exactly what the terrorism represents.

MH: You would hear Bush say, "Stay alert. We've got a 100% chance of more attacks, so stay alert," but they don't really give us any how-tos, what-tos, and it seemed that the U.S. Post Office came out with better ideas of staying alert than our government has.

MR: This is more about political policy regarding the strikes and what expectations the citizens should have, and what they ought to know regarding this, and why bombing doesn't work. The question we are asked is, why are people so mad at us? Of course, the *Guardian* has gotten lambasted for their articles on that.

MH: They get lambasted all the time just for having Greg Palast [*see* Chapter 2] attached to them.

MR: But they've been lambasted from some segments of the left for that, including Palast himself. As a matter of fact, he kind of slammed them over that, saying just because we haven't experienced an attack against our citizens, to look at our policies and say that's why people are attacking our citizens doesn't seem very appetizing to our citizens, but nevertheless, we have to look at the policies.

MH: I read an article, and I don't remember *where* I read it . . . but it said if we're *really* going to believe what Bush said—that the rest of the world hates us because of what we have and our lifestyle and yadda-yadda—then, everybody would have attacked Beverly Hills *years* ago.

MR: They want to attack us for our freedom? I don't think so.

MH: They *know* we don't have our freedom because of the election.

MR: They're not attacking us for that, that's for sure. Basically, it's not for some abstract ideals and it's not for some mystified religious thing, either.

MH: And it's obviously not for our computers or cell phones because everyone else has them, too.

MR: I think the mystification of this and to put it all in terms of religion is also one of the false explanations that is being proffered out there.

MH: My feeling is that it's all about money and oil and this global economy that looks to mess everybody over. Otherwise, we wouldn't have these world protests everywhere.

MR: We need to get behind the anti-war movement. We're trying to roll those two movements into one, the opposition to Bush and the opposition to the war. Stand up and remember that's what true patriots have to do.

MH: If it's not clean, why should we be involved in it? And we do have a right to know what's going on.

MR: We're trying to keep people on top of all the news sources that are out there and we collect them all together, with a few original pieces by our people, as well.

MH: A lot of people out there are using their brains. If we're going to have the freedoms that our forefathers died for, lost everything they ever owned for, we've got to be educated about what's really going on.

FOUR

AFTER 9/11 – LET FREEDOM (?) RING
Meria with Nancy Oden and Bob Fertik

This double interview deals with the real and current loss of freedoms in America. The first half of the show is an interview with Nancy Oden,[4] organic farmer, environmentalist and member of the Green Party. Oden tells her first-hand experience with the Maine National Guard preventing her from flying out of Bangor, Maine to Chicago because her name was on a "computer list." They said she tried to resist security, but listening to Oden's story will convince you of the truth of what really happened. Obviously, racial isn't the only kind of "profiling."

The second half of the show is an interview with Bob Fertik,[5] who discusses results of the NORC (National Opinion Research Center) Report. Six out of nine scenarios demonstrated that Al Gore was the winner of the 2000 election, yet with only three out of nine, corporate media spun Bush as the winner. They never admit who won, but we KNOW who lost—the American people. Fertik also discusses voter reform for 2002, as well as the need to sweep out the "Repugs." America is waking up, slowly, but surely. (Interviews taped/broadcast on November 20, 2001.)

MH: I heard Gerry Spence, a defense attorney, on CNN last night talking about how many of our freedoms we are losing in the name of security and how dangerous that is. My friend, Vince Bugliosi [*see* Chapter 1], continues to say, "It's time to start prosecuting the Supreme Court." The voice for freedom is still out there, still alive and kicking for sure. Nancy, would you tell the audience a little bit about yourself.

NO: I've been a political, environmental, and anti-war peace activist for over 30 years, so I'm not 19 any more. I'm an organic farmer. I live on the north coast of the Maine. I am a peaceful person. I mostly stay in my farmhouse and I wouldn't even have a computer if I were not an activist, but I am, so I am in touch with people all over the world. I am also a lead person in the Green Party, USA. That website is www.greenparty.org.

I needed to go to Chicago a couple of weeks ago for a national committee meeting, and I bought my ticket online six weeks before to get a cheap price on Priceline.com. I printed out the itinerary and had my ID and dressed conservatively, no jewelry even. I knew there would be military at the airport and *expected* to be searched.

I went to the airport, walked in the door, and there were 30 National Guardsmen in their "camo" outfits, all carrying machine guns. They don't carry them on their shoulders any more; they are in their hands as, in fact, they're ready. It's incredible. I walked up to the American Airlines counter and the ticket clerk was very nice. I told him my name. He never looked at my ID. No one, at any time, looked at my ID. He knew who I was by sight and I do not look appreciably different from most of the other passengers there. He started typing on his computer. He was on it for a long time. He finally came up with a boarding pass with a big "F" written on it. I asked him what that was and he said that was for search, that I had been picked to have my bag searched.

I thought, "Well, don't be paranoid, because I could be as random as anybody." I turned back to him and said, "This wasn't random, was it?" and he said, "No, actually you were flagged in the computer; you were going to be searched in any case; your name is flagged." So, I thought, "Oh, okay, it still could be random, maybe." I went to the x- ray machine, my bags and I went through, with no beep. I picked up my bags and sat down with the other passengers.

I was just sitting there, and there was one National Guardsman in the room standing where they search the bags at the table. No one else was searched. No one else was flagged for anything. He was a little short guy with a black eye carrying his machine gun. He looked up at the passengers before people started boarding and his eyes looked at my face. He said, "Bring those bags over here!" He didn't call my name, no "please."

He was just yelling at the top of his lungs as if we were in boot-camp or something.

So, I brought my bags over there, but I wasn't fast enough. "Hurry up! Bring those bags!" I mean, really, making a person look like an idiot. Everyone was starting to stare. He never said my name. I put the bags on the table.

One woman was looking through each of my bags and couldn't get a zipper open. It was stuck. I said, "Oh, here." I was determined to be calm no matter what they did because I know that giving these guys authority is trouble. So, I reached over and said, "Here, let me help you with that," and he yells, "Get your hands out of there!"

Now, everybody is getting nervous, thinking, "Oh, my God, who is she? What's going on?" So, I turned to face the guard to say, "What?" and I didn't even get any words out of my mouth. No one could see then because my back was to the people. He grabbed my arm, hung on, and started spouting pro-war stuff into my face about didn't I understand how we had to kill those people before they came over here and killed us? I don't even remember what all he said and I was stunned, but not so stunned that I allowed him to do that.

I pulled my arm away and I said, "You don't get to do that. Please don't touch me."

The first time, I said, "Please," and I said, "I really don't want to hear your views on the war or why you have to kill those starving people in Afghanistan." So, he went to grab me again and I backed off two to three steps and said, "Do NOT touch me."

Meanwhile, they were proceeding with the search of my bags and the guy came over with the wand. He did the wand. Then, they were finished with my bags and I heard the guard say behind me, "Don't let her on the plane." I thought he was talking to himself, annoyed that I wouldn't let him hang onto me. So, I walked all of three feet, and mind you this is Bangor, Maine, a tiny airport, to the boarding gate where the guy was standing there, and he said, "You can't get on the plane."

I said, "What do you mean? You were standing here the whole time. You saw them do the search."

He said, "I know it, but he says you did not cooperate with the search."

I said, "But you saw."

He said, "I know, I know. All right. Look, we'll put you on the 4:00 plane. If he says you can't get on the plane, I can't let you on the plane."

All because of this one little guy who is mad because of an uppity woman who wouldn't kow-tow to his authority and wouldn't let him hang onto her.

I said to the guy, "All right, let's just do this; I'll wait until 4:00. I don't care." The last plane of the day, I could still get to Chicago out of Bangor. So, I picked up my bags and started to go back to the lobby to wait, but the guard wasn't done with me. He looked hesitant for a minute, but he had heard what the clerk said, so he didn't want me to go *any*where. He yelled, "Come with me!"

I said, "Why? Where are we going?"

"Come with me!" he yelled. You could *not* talk to this automaton. I thought, under the circumstances, probably I'd better go and I did. We went down to the entrance by the airport where the airport police station is and he says, "Sit down!" I just gave him a look and I sat down, but I was isolated from everybody, and he found the airport policeman and told him (this is the Bangor Police, who are also under his authority—*his* personal authority—this one little guy, a private, whatever he was) to stay with me.

I had the distinct impression I really wasn't free to leave. The policeman and I were talking—he's a local guy; so we talked about people we knew. The next thing, we look up and here are six National Guardsmen with their machine guns at the ready, marching in kind of a formation toward me and I thought, "What?"

MH: Did you happen to get that guy's name who was nasty to you?

NO: I didn't, because I was in the moment and I wasn't thinking of problems. I looked at the lead guy, who was a sergeant or something, and I said, "What *is* this? All this just for me?"

MH: How threatening *are* you? Tell me what you look like! You must be pretty threatening, as a middle-aged, organic farmer from Maine. Can you *get* more nerdy than that?

NO: I know. I'm 5'6". I have slightly more insulation than a lot of people do, but we need it up here for the winters. You know, my natural insulation, also known as f-a-t, but we need it here, it's cold.

MH: Are you white; do you look white?

NO: I was dressed in a long, dark skirt with a matching jacket, a turtleneck, and a coat, of course. It's going into winter here. Neat brown hair, white skin, blue eyes, brown hair combed back with a barrette. A little gray at the temples, you know, because I'm not 19. Totally respectable-looking person, which I am.

MH: A lot of people are under the impression that white people are not being stopped at airports or considered terrorists and that is why I wanted to ask what you look like and are you white, because that reporter in Sacramento was white also.

NO: That's right, and a lot of people want to feel comfortable by saying it must have been something she did. They want to make sure they aren't threatened, but they should understand that in Germany when the Nazis started rounding up the leftists and the Jews, people said, "Oh, well, I'm not one of *them*," and so they didn't worry. But eventually, of course, it went to all kinds of people so you couldn't even meet on the street corner. You couldn't even be with more than one or two people standing on a street corner; no unions; no nothing. No speaking out.

This is what happens if people don't speak out when these things *start* to happen. Anyway, I am perfectly respectable and that is why when they came towards me, the whole situation was ludicrous. I was never afraid because I'm a white person in this country and I don't *expect* anything bad to happen to me for no reason.

MH: And an organic farmer. How harmful can it be unless, of course, they thought maybe you had some pesticide residue on you.

NO: The thing is that they *knew* better. The women barely searched my bags. It was just cursory. They didn't search me. I had clothes that had pockets. I had a coat that had pockets. They didn't actually really search me. We knew what this was about. He knew me by sight; he knew my politics; and some people think he was trying to incite me, to provoke me into doing something so they would have an excuse to arrest me on a felony charge because it is a federal felony to not cooperate with one of these security searches. I've never been arrested.

MH: Maybe he had that black eye from his wife and maybe he was taking it out on any woman who came along.

NO: That's what I am wondering.

MH: If he was *my* husband, I'd probably want to give him a black eye. So, what happened after all these other National Guards came all around you?

NO: I looked at the lead guy and I laughed a little and I said, "This is ridiculous. What *is* this all about?"

And he said, "Well, we understand you didn't cooperate with the search."

I said, "Of course I did! You can't *not*; it's against the law to not cooperate. They did my bags; they did the wand. The only trouble was this guy here grabbing my arm and insisting on spouting his views into my face in a loud voice so, of course, I pulled back, as *any* woman would, if a strange man grabbed her. It's instinctive. You don't even think about it. You pull your arm away and you step back and say, "Please don't do that," or whatever you say.

So, he looked at the guy and said, "Well, he told me he only hit your arm."

NO: I looked at him and said, "Oh, and that would have been okay?" This guy may be a bank manager in his real life, I don't know, but I think he has some sense of when people are telling the truth and that his guy had messed up. So, they went away. He said, "Wait here," and they marched away.

A few minutes later, they called the policeman over and told him to tell me, which he did, that (I mean they had to do something, they'd made such a fuss) I was not to be allowed to fly out of that airport that day on any airline. So, I said, "I have to go and get my money back," if I'm going to drive or do anything—two days to Chicago from here on the northeastern part of Maine up here by New Brunswick, Canada.

I went over to American Airlines and it was the same guy. He was very sympathetic, but he said, "I'm not allowed to give your money back."

I said, "I can't get there unless I get my money back. I don't have extra money. Besides, if you don't give my money back, I'd have to buy a ticket cash today full-fare at the Boston Airport or something [five hours away, by the way], pay their parking, pay $400.00–$600.00 round-trip," which I didn't have.

The policeman escorted me to the door because I had been banned from the airport for that day. I asked the American Airlines guy, "What about tomorrow?" and he said, "I don't know."

So, since then, I have gotten hold of the airport manager (that's the City of Bangor). They told her [the airport manager] to tell all the airlines not to allow me to fly out of there and, by the way, gave my name to all these airlines as someone who did not cooperate with the security search, which, of course, I had. Now, I don't know. My name may be in every airline computer in the world saying I didn't cooperate with a security search.

MH: So this is a "nice" way of grounding whatever and whomever the government thinks is a dissident.

NO: That's right. They can refuse to let me fly *any*where, if that's true, but I have to find out. The ACLU [American Civil Liberties Union] is discussing my case and they wanted to know what did I want from this. That's one of the things I want to know, if I'm in all these computers.

MH: With the way the airline security is right now, I wouldn't really mind too much not being able to fly. That's just a joke.

NO: That's true, except if you have to go to North Carolina, which I do, for a meeting in March, or California, occasionally, is a little hard to drive in a 17-year-old car.

MH: Do I remember reading that your hotel room at the end of your trip was also canceled?

NO: Oh, yes, that's another thing I keep forgetting about. Somebody called and said they were me and canceled the hotel room, but three other women were sharing that room. It was in a hostel, where you have four to six people in a room. Three other women got there the next day and they were told I had called and canceled the room, which of course I never did. I was furious, but it's like one of those things to say, "Nya-nya, look what we can do."

MH: Talking about nya-nya-look-what-we-can-do, I have gotten a few articles from different listeners basically slamming your story as an untruth because of your association with the Green Party. Now that my listeners have actually heard you, if they are somewhat alive, their own intuition can tell them whether or not you're telling the truth, and that you're just a regular, decent person.

NO: Of course. But there was a huge, internal split in the Green Party this July [2001]. There was a group that was trying to get us to vote ourselves out of existence and give them our name and our website. They were very indignant that we wouldn't do that, and they are bitter and angry. But they didn't have the votes. They lost this internal split and in July, almost four months ago now, they split and formed another group, which is not doing well. They thought they would somehow see if they could do us a little more harm here and to me, especially, as the primary leader who wove our way through this split and managed to stay political without personal attacks all this time.

When they split, they tried to make it appear that they were us. We are the Green Party, USA, the original Greens from 1984, and now they decided to call themselves, five days after they lost the split, the Green Party U.S. So, it's GPUSA and GPUS, which we spell, I'm being naughty here, G-PUS. I told them when they did it. I said, "This is crazy. Do you realize that now you are going to have to answer for anything we say and do, and vice versa, if you try to appear to be us?" I am a leader of Green Party USA.

MH: Nancy, wasn't the Green Party originally started for environmental changes?

NO: Yes, that's right. And that's still *my* primary focus. I work mostly on trying to stop the use of pesticides and toxic, industrial chemicals. Before the Green Party existed, I was also a social activist, active in the anti-war movement in the late '60s and the women's movement, and with all of the movements for social justice, I've been involved with over the years.

MH: Now, this is the same Green Party that backed Ralph Nader for presidency?

NO: Well, we both did. Both Green Parties, so to speak. That group had a different name then. We both supported Ralph Nader. Nader, in fact, has a special place in his heart for genuine activists. I've run for office several times. We use it as a forum to build the independent movements, the anti-war movement, the women's movement, the People of Color for Civil Liberties Movement, all of the movements, that's why we run.

If I happen to get elected on the principles that I run on, which, of course, are on the website, www.greenparty.org, we will know then that people are in the middle of serious change and they are ready for serious change by the time they start electing people who say the things that I do.

MH: One of my listeners said, "Screw the airlines and the fascists. Why not use the Web or a phone conference instead of traveling by air?"

NO: I agree, in most cases, except when you have something important to discuss, the discussion can get fairly intense. Discussing things in person often is the best way to do things, but maybe we can all get one of those little eye things that sits on top of the computer so you can actually look at one another.

MH: A lot of companies now are using video conferencing. Let's face it, it's cheaper and it's safer, especially after what happened September 11th. A lot of people are realizing they don't need to be in an office away from home working.

NO: Maybe we *should* look into that, but we should not have to do it *because* they are denying us the right to fly. We should do that because *we* want to do it, not because we have been denied our right to travel.

MH: When do you think you are going to try flying again, Nancy?

NO: Not until I have to go to North Carolina in March and, even then, if I'm able to ride with someone who has a better car than I do, or if I can figure another way. Maybe there are trains from Boston down to North Carolina, or something. I will certainly look at every other means possible before doing this again.

        What we have done, meanwhile, though, is start a new group called the Bill of Rights Defense Committee, and our website is going to be up within the next few days. I had hoped we would have it up by today, but it just didn't get done. We are going to have a secure site on it, too, and these things take a little longer. The website is going to be www.billofrightsde-fense.com. People can go there and we will have there not only the stuff on my case, but there have been people who have been treated worse than I was, and we will have other cases on there, too; proposals of what people can do. People can post comments and ideas. It is going to be a big meeting right on the Web.

MH: I posted the Bill of Rights on my front door. I think people should be doing that on their doors and on their cars rather than flying the flag, or do both together.

NO: I carry it around with me all the time. I have for years. It's on our website. If people want a nice print-friendly version of the Bill of Rights, it's on both this new site, when it gets up, and also on www.greenparty.org. You'll see it by scanning down an inch or two and it's in red in one of the sentences there, Bill of Rights, and you can click on that.

MH: You tell me what threat Nancy is to anybody in this government. But, if you were listening to yesterday's show, then you also know this is now the new defini-tion of domestic terrorism in this country, according to the brochure I read by the FBI. This is not an iso-lated case, so we don't really need to just say, "Oh, that's because she was with the Green Party." How about that reporter in Sacramento? I read that story awhile back. I think we are going to see more and more of this because we have some two-day-trained National Guard people full of themselves, who want their 15 minutes of fame, or to do their little imitation of the Gestapo, trying to touch and feel and fondle, or push and shove around middle-aged women, who just want to get from one place to the other.

MH: I have a new guest with me. This is the "second sit-ting," we'll call it. Bob Fertik is with democrats.com. I saw in your newsletter today that you have been get-ting quite vocal about the stolen election these past few days. I'm not exactly Ms. Shyness myself. We were talking on Thursday about the NORC [National Opinion Research Center] Report and the fact that it really showed that even though media spin has said that Bush won, some media spin said Bush *and* [former Vice President Al] Gore won. What do you want to say about it?

BF: To us, it's clear that Gore won. There's no way to confuse the facts. There were nine scenarios the newspapers examined and in six of them, Gore won. It just so happens that all six of those scenarios were the scenarios where they counted *all* the votes. The three scenarios that Bush won were scenarios where they *didn't* count the votes. Since elections are supposed to be about counting the votes, not about which team has the lawyers who have the best connection with the judges, there's no way that history is going to look at the election of 2000 and not conclude that Gore won the most legal votes. If it weren't for the ballots that were all screwed up in their design and the machines that didn't work well, Gore would have won by as many as 50,000 votes.

MH: And let's not forget that Gore did win the *popular* vote. That's a little something most people want to forget about, but how can you forget about it when you look at the America we are now living in?

BF: There are so many important points there. Let's say you're of the belief that, well, it was so close in Florida that it was effectively a tie. If you're looking at the situation impartially, and you say, "Okay, Al Gore won the rest of the country by 540,000 and Florida is tied." So, who do you give Florida to? The 25 electors? How about splitting them down the middle?

Then, you'd have a fair solution and that way Gore wins unless you're totally convinced that Bush is the only *possible* President, which was the position of the United States Supreme Court. But if you look at it in any fair way, Al Gore should be the President.

MH: Of course. How do you feel about the fact that Al Gore is not only taking a backseat on this, but actually took a real job?

BF: We all have to support our families.

MH: I thought maybe in the private sector he'd see what a *real* salary is like and decide to stay there, but a lot of people have written different scenarios on what would be happening today if Al Gore were President. People have to really look at the fact that we are quickly becoming a fascistic-type country. Even the *Moscow Times* said that. That is a scary thing. When I read that little blurb in your newsletter about the *Moscow Times* saying fascism is creeping into America like the chill of an autumn morning, I was astounded.

BF: Russia is now a more democratic country in some ways than we are.

MH: I learned that when I was in junior high school. It was a hard thing to tell people that. Nobody wanted to hear it. Where do you think this whole NORC Report is going? Do you think it's just going to get buried now?

BF: It served its purpose. The media intended to validate George Bush's victory and intended to exonerate the Supreme Court. That was their objective. Even though the facts didn't support that, they went ahead and did it anyway. You would be surprised the people I talk to, who ought to know better, who say, "Well, but didn't the papers conclude that Bush won?" And, then, I have to explain to them, "Well, the headlines did, but the articles didn't." They accomplished their goal, but are we going to get over it? No.

Here's what's going on. The polls taken since the election have asked, "Do you think Bush *really* won or did he steal the election or did he win on a technicality?" Since the election, these polls have barely budged. Half the population—the half that voted for Bush—thinks that Bush won. The other half that voted for Al Gore thinks Bush either stole the election or won it on a technicality. So, those people have not forgotten and they will *not* forget, and guess what? We are not going to *let* them forget.

Democrats.com is planning a couple of events to celebrate the first anniversary of the *Bush vs. Gore* decision. We are doing an event in Washington, D.C. on December 10th [2001] at American University, and we are doing one in New York, hopefully, at Cooper Union at the Great Hall on December 12th [2001]. What we are going to do is go over the facts, what really the election results proved, and what the *Bush vs. Gore* decision was all about. We are going to talk about where we go from here and how we make sure the Republicans don't steal any more elections.

MH: I think that's going to be a hard one unless we get some major voter reform out there. But you know, like Bob Kunst of the Oral Majority will say, how can we have voter reform when we haven't even counted the votes from the *last* election?

BF: Well, it's a good question. There is election reform legislation before Congress. They did a study nationally—MIT and, I think, Cal-Tech—and they found that 6 *million* ballots out of 100 million that were cast were not counted in the last election nationally. So, this isn't just a Florida problem. We had tremendous problems in New York City counting the votes during the mayor's race. There is a need for a national solution and the Democrats have been proposing legislation and the Republicans, of course, refuse to even discuss the topic so we've got to get election reform, we've got to get money so the states can upgrade their voting system.

Every precinct in the country should have the second-chance technology so if you cast a vote and there is something wrong with the paper you hand in, you get told, just like an ATM machine. Some counties are upgrading to touch screens where it beeps at you if you get it wrong. Why should we not make use of that technology? That needs to be done. The Republicans need to get on board. The Democrats need to push this issue harder.

MH: I agree. I know Vince Bugliosi [*see* Chapter 1] recently came out and said it's more than time now to start prosecuting and pushing hard on the Supreme Court.

BF: We're all for that, too. A number of Democratic parties out on the west coast have passed resolutions calling for the impeachment of the Supreme Court Five. We have a whole website devoted to that at www.democrats.com/supremecourt and we're keeping track of all of the counties that are doing this. We are encouraging *all* of the counties throughout the country to do this. This notion that the Supreme Court's decision didn't affect the outcome is ludicrous. We don't know what would've happened if they had counted all the votes. The election was so close. The popular theory that the media are presenting is that, since the Florida Supreme Court only ordered a count of the undervotes, the 60,000 under-votes, and didn't order a recount of the 120,000 over-votes, and Gore's victory was really in the overvotes, Gore would've lost.

The *Orlando Sentinel* asked Judge Terry Lewis what he would have done. If you remember, after the Florida Supreme Court ordered the statewide recount, they put the state courts in charge of that, and Judge Terry Lewis ended up the one who had to actually administer the election. The Bush lawyers were telling him he needed to include the overvotes. When he was asked about it a few weeks ago, he told the *Orlando Sentinel* that he probably would've included the overvotes. There is no way of knowing. All we know is that the votes were not counted, 175,000 votes were not counted, and that is because five Republican members of the U.S. Supreme Court were determined to put their man, George Bush, in the White House. They didn't care what the laws were; they were just determined to appoint him.

MH: A lot of people are pretty pissed at the Democrats for not having stood up, especially at the recount or the count at the Electoral College. When the Black Caucus was looking for one senator to knock down that Florida situation, they couldn't get any backing. What do you think of that?

BF: About 14 members of the House stood up, and they are our heroes, led by people like Al C. Hastings, Maxine Waters, Jesse Jackson, Jr., and they were will-ing to fight for the 175,000 disenfranchised voters in Florida. We were very disappointed that no senator was willing to step up to the plate, but Washington is a strange place. Once you get elected into Washington, you get put under tremendous pressures, and these senators didn't want to appear to be standing in the way of the Bush presidency.

They didn't want to take on a Don Quixote-type battle to tilt at windmills. They didn't have the votes to stop the 25 electors from being accepted, and they just didn't want to fight a losing battle. I think that's something folks should remember the next time these candidates send them a letter and say send me money.

MH: That's what I did. You don't even want to know what was in my return letter, but it was pretty strong. The other thing is that you've got to look at why is it then that these anthrax letters are going to *Democratic* senators? My own personal feeling, and it's not like I have any proof to this effect, but I have thought from the beginning that this whole anthrax thing is a home-grown nut. They think the latest is they found a letter in [Senator Pat] Leahy's office. It's kind of interesting when you look at it; people really wanted to follow where these letters are going. I should think that would give them a profile of the person putting together this anthrax crap.

BF: If you look at what's been going on for the last 10 years at abortion clinics, where anthrax letters—*allegedly*, anthrax letters—have been sent for the past 10 years, dozens of them, and naturally because these are women's health facilities, the Justice Department didn't really take them all that seriously. The first place to look is the anti-abortion terrorist movement, which has resulted in the death of a number of clinic doctors and staff, not through anthrax, because none of those anthrax letters were ever *really* anthrax, but there is this terrorist mentality in the anti-abortion movement that led to the sniper murder of Dr. [Barnett] Slepian in upstate New York and the bombings of clinics and the use of butyric acid around clinics. There are people out there who believe they are justified in murdering people because of the anti-abortion cause. The people who do that are, in my mind, likely to be the ones to put anthrax in a letter as a way to go after Democrats, as you say, Tom Daschle, Pat Leahy. That seems pretty apparent to me.

MH: A few weeks back, Ari Fleischer was on CNN and he actually said the bald-faced lie that before September 11th, these letter bombs never existed, never went through the post office. Abortion clinics were targeted and there were a lot of letters sent to Southern California in 1999 that the FBI had traced. Don't people get that this whole Administration lies right to our faces? I think there are a lot of people in America who are really asleep and into the whole mesmerizing drum of CNN and Fox, just listening to the lies that we are being told constantly.

I don't know if you've seen it, but yesterday, I got a copy in my grubby little hands of the latest FBI brochure on domestic terrorists. Even being a loner is considered a sign of a domestic terrorist. Anyone who is an animal rights activist is now considered a domestic terrorist, according to this brochure. I was shocked. This is America. This is the country I was born and raised in. It's hard to believe what's going on. Anyway, Greg Palast [*see* Chapter 2] had said the NORC Report was destined to fail from the start and they really weren't counting votes, they had a whole different system of putting things together. Do you agree with what Greg said?

BF: We had hopes, maybe unrealistic, that the fact that the credibility of the nation's leading newspapers was on the line here would lead them to do an honest job. They could've come out and said, "Look, it was just too close to call," because even the scenarios where Gore wins, it's between 40–170 votes that he wins by. He wins, but it's very, very close, so you know you could give them the break and say, "Well, it was too close to call," but they didn't even choose to do that. They just chose to twist the outcome to make Bush appear to be the winner. So, when people say that was their intention from the beginning, it's kind of hard to disagree with that.

MH: Don't forget that report was supposedly ready to present to the country before September 11th. Then, all of sudden, September 11th happened and they were going to delay indefinitely letting anyone know who won because they didn't want to hurt our wartime President's legitimacy. Just that fact alone lets you know it was all bullshit. Because if Bush would have legitimately won, that would have been on the front page of every paper in the world, let alone in this country, because that would have played right into corporate media's hands; that would've been perfect. Just the fact that they delayed it this long was, "Oh, let's see what other kind of lies and fairy tales we can tell the public and make it look right."

Then, what happens when this was supposed to be released again, we have that plane crash in New York. You know, we have a hell of a lot of "coincidences" in this country, don't you think? Most people say, "Meria, oh, come on," and I say, "Well, I don't really think engines and tails fall off a plane because of a few birds or because they caught somebody's wake." It's whenever there's something big that has to come out, it seems something bigger happens. Did you see that movie *Swordfish?* Everybody in this country should see it. It demonstrates that a lot of what goes on is really misdirection, and I think when it came to this election, it was nothing but misdirection. What is going to happen to make it different for people to actually *want* to vote in 2004? What can we make happen?

BF: We're thinking about both 2004 *and* 2002. Next year, less than a year from now, the House of Representatives and a third of the Senate are up for re-election, as well as a lot of governors' races. It is *very* important that we just make up our minds that we are going to sweep all Republicans out of office in the next election at all levels of government, and why? Because the Republican party at all levels of government stole the last election in Florida.

It wasn't *just* the Supreme Court, it wasn't *just* the Bush campaign. It was the governor of Florida, Jeb Bush. It was the elected Republican secretary of state, Katherine Harris. It was county election officials, people in places like Seminole and Martin counties, where the Republican election supervisors received *thousands* of defective absentee ballad applications. They invited the Republican operatives to sit in the office and fix them illegally. They called up and said we're not letting you in. So, it took an effort on all levels of the Republican party to steal that election. Therefore, we should punish the Republican party at all levels, vote them all out of office.

We also need to register more people to vote. Only half of Americans even bother to vote, and that is understandable. If your votes don't get counted, why should you bother? So, we've got to register millions of new voters and we've got to make sure we have people at the polls to help those voters, to make sure their votes *do* get counted, so when they close the polls and declare the winners next November, the Democrats have won by such a big margin, even the Republicans can't steal the election.

MH: Then something also needs to be done and said about the Republicans' hired hands and hired guns and thugs-for-hire, trying to stop people from voting, and even trying to stop the voter recount. I interviewed the person who was working for the Democratic party on the recount, and he was telling us how those thugs just busted that up. People are going to be afraid to go vote. I understand there is a little town in California where the mayor was defeated because the guy running against him actually had people with guns threatening the voters at precincts; and [he] forged ghost votes, and was sending non-residents to the poll. What has happened here? Is it like winning at all costs in America? Is this what we're getting down to?

BF: The Republican party is probably a criminal organization for the way they engage in election activities. Certainly, the thugs that shut down the Miami recount, that was criminal activity. The whole stuff that went on before and during the election, that was criminal. We've made a list of about 60 crimes that were committed in Florida to steal the election. You've had Greg Palast on, so you know all about the felon purge, which was criminal, and people need to be prosecuted and sent to jail because we have election laws in this country. If the people who break those election laws get away with it, then they are going to keep breaking them.

MH: That's what people need to understand. If it doesn't change, what's the point in going out and voting again? People have to get active and they can't leave it for the next guy. For all you people who are listening, if you're not on Bob's newsletter or actively involved either in democrats.com, the Oral Majority or one of these other groups like Voter March, then don't sit back and complain. It's time for you to get some action going and be responsible for something of what's going on.

BF: People are starting to wake up about the assault on our civil rights and civil liberties by [Attorney General] John Ashcroft. The stuff he is doing is just so beyond anything people could imagine a U.S. government would do and, of course, it's couched in the need for the fight against terrorism. We should step back for a second and say, "Look what we're losing. Look how our civil rights are being thrown out the window." If the lawyers can't have a conversation with their clients without the government listening in, we don't have a criminal justice system any more. If we can round up people and put them before a terrorism tribunal, a military tribunal, where they don't have the ability to have an appeal, there is no rule of law in America.

Terrorism today; tomorrow it'll be Democrats. That's why Nancy Oden's story is so important. We have to take action when they do these things because we have to let them know we won't tolerate it. This goes back to what Reverend Martin Neimuller said about the Holocaust. First, they came for the Jews and the gypsies, and when they finally came around to the Protestants, there was nobody left to defend them. We can't let any one group of people be targeted, and I don't care what label they've put on them. Over 1,000 people are in indefinite detention. Why? Because they have dark skin. Because they come from an Arab country. We can't let that go on. The Justice

Department refuses to release their names and release the charges they're being held under.

MH: But a lot of people don't know that. Those people are only allowed one phone call a week, and that's when they're supposed to be trying to get an attorney, so you know that means they're *never* going to get an attorney. I don't know about you, but if you've ever tried to call an attorney, you're certainly not getting them on the first phone call. And they're only allowed one personal call a month. That's crazy.

Again, if you look at Nancy Oden, or that reporter in Sacramento, these are people who are white, U.S. citizens, born and raised, and they're *also* getting their rights slammed. Like I told Nancy, "Cheer up. I wouldn't be caught dead flying on a plane now." Even when Bush, under duress, passed the airport security laws, they're not going to go into effect until the end of the year and they're only limited for three years. Why do you think he did that? Because he's gone in 2004. In three years, when he's not President, he doesn't care.

The information in your newsletter [www.democrats.com] is invaluable. You had some really interesting stuff this week on the Bush Administration lining the Afghanistan Taliban with carpets of gold. You just don't know which story is going to wake up that one person who is still hesitant.

FIVE

WHERE DID THE MADNESS ALL BEGIN?

Meria with Howard Winant

Howard Winant,[6] a Professor of Sociology at Temple University, is the author of *The World Is A Ghetto: Race and Democracy Since World War II*. Among the issues discussed were the noticeable absence of the U.S. at the World Conference Against Racism [WCAR] in Durbin, South Africa in September 2001, and why racism is alive and well in America, perhaps owning up to the genocide of the Native Americans, import of African slaves, internment of Japanese-Americans during WW II, and the current treatment of Arab-Americans. The disenfranchisement of the "non-white" voters in the 2000 election is also discussed.

Racism has been, and still is, prominent in all parts of the world. Why and where did it begin? What can and is being done about it? How does the World Trade Organization [WTO] figure into the poverty of "darker" nations? Winant states that because 42% of the "founding fathers" were slave-owners, the wording of the U.S. Constitution was carefully crafted, and still carries through in the disenfranchisement of former slave states in the South's voting rights for non-whites. Racism is built into our governmental structure, and is the foundation of the "haves" and "have-nots," globally. Are we color-blind in the U.S.? What is the "Vietnam Syndrome" and how does that play into the disinterest in foreign affairs (war) of the average American? Have we made *any* progress at all in the battle against racism? Winant has some interesting opinions. (Interview taped/broadcast November 28, 2001.)

MH: Howard, would you like to mention a little about what you do and who you are?

HW: I'm a Professor of Sociology at Temple University in Philadelphia [Pennsylvania]. I would also say that I'm a long-time activist coming out of the civil rights movement and out of a long-standing concern for matters of racial equality and social justice.

MH: My audience may or may not think it is relevant, but I thought I would mention that at least by the picture on your book cover, you look like a white person, so it's not slanted at all. It's not a hate book by any means, but I can tell you it's loaded with facts. It is my understanding that you were at the conference against racism in Durbin, South Africa in September.

HW: It was in late August, early September, before the September 11th event, in Durbin, South Africa—The United Nations World Conference Against Racism.

MH: How did you get to go there? Were you invited?

HW: I was part of the delegation. There were really two levels to that conference. One level was an official conference of the member nations in the United Nations. The second level was the so-called non-governmental organization level, or NGO level. Those are groups that are involved with the issues, but are not official governmental organizations. I was part of the delegation to the NGO conference. As people will probably know, the United States officially withdrew from participation in the conference.

MH: Why do you think the United States did that?

HW: Of course, different explanations have been offered, but the one I find most convincing is that there is a certain kind of defensiveness on the part of the United States, reluctance to admit complicity, or responsibility, for the long-standing history of racial oppression that the United States has been involved in and that in some ways it was founded upon. Since a central question in the conference revolved around the techniques the world should employ to overcome racism, the U.S. was concerned about culpability issues.

MH: When you talk about culpability issues, do you mean like in the past, against Native Americans and black Americans?

HW: Certainly. I would say the two central questions for the U.S. are the genocide of Native Americans and the fundamental, foundational involvement of the United States in the African slave trade. In both of those areas are questions of crimes against humanity, which is essentially what the conference was attempting to deal with and in large measure, to recognize. Now, I don't think you can overcome crimes of that magnitude or events of that magnitude by any action, but there was a certain openness, or an effort on the part of many delegations to the conference, both the official delegations (particularly the African ones) and many of the NGO delegations, to raise the issue of reparations and restitution. That takes many different policy forms and political and economic forms.

I think, in a general way, it was that specter of having to confront its own dark past that the U.S. was fleeing from, [that] was the reason it withdrew. There were also the issues of Zionism, racism, anti-semitism, treatment of the Palestinian people, which were highly-charged issues and which the U.S. gave as its official reason for not continuing to participate. Central as those issues are, I don't believe they were the *real* reasons for the U.S. to withdraw.

MH: What about the current history in the U.S., such as the disenfranchisement of the black community in the vote in 2000; the racism that I feel is still very much alive and, unfortunately, kicking in this country? And, now, with the racial profiling of Arab-Americans, I should think that would be enough to keep America away.

HW: These are nice, small topics that you are raising for me to discuss.

MH: I don't mean to put you on the spot, but after reading your book, you proved, beyond a doubt, that these kinds of things still exist.

HW: You're quite right. First of all, in terms of the present situation, the present dynamics of racism in the United States, I think it's very important to recognize how much continuity there is between present instances of discrimination, exclusion, restriction of democratic rights, and, most centrally, the right to vote, and the tremendously embedded history of racism in the United States. It's not coincidental that in the Florida events of November 2000, the last presidential election, people were targeted so extensively for disenfranchisement.

We have to remember, and few of us will be unaware of the fact, that the access to the franchise on the part of black people and, particularly, in the former slave states, the states of the South, has *always* been tenuous, and has *always* been a major source of conflict and repression. There was a century or so after the formal abolition of slavery, formal emancipation, in which attempting to exercise the vote was enough to get a person lynched in many, *many* cases. The continuity is particularly evident there, but there are many other ways in which we can link the present processes of discrimination, the issues of violence, the police violence, the profiling, many of the issues you were naming, to long-standing dynamics of racism.

MH:	A lot of people like to say that racial profiling or discrimination is gone in America. I don't see how anybody can actually say that, because I don't see that things are really that much different than they were say, in the '60s, especially if you're white, and white according to the description by who-knows-who. One of the things I remembered reading in your book was when the Italians and the Irish came to this country, they were not classified white. Being an Italian-American, I used to find that very offensive, but a lot of people don't know just how lily-white whoever the powers-that-be require people to be, to be considered white. Where did this all start? Where did this supposed superiority of the "white race" start?

HW:	Again, these are complex issues that I do address in the book in a great deal more detail than we can discuss here, but the logic of racism, the dynamics of race, are really associated with the rise of the modern world. We tend to assume that racial classification, racial categorization, of human beings is something that has *always* been there, but it really hasn't. Before the rise of Europe, the onset of the European empire and the circumnavigation of the globe; before the internationalization that in many ways founded the modern world and the setting up of European empires, conquests and so on, there really wasn't a concept of race, *per se*. There were religious differences, and ethnic or national differences, but these were cultural issues not linked to the body, not based on people's appearance, or at least not fundamentally so. Therefore, ideas of who could be a citizen, who could assimilate, who could be afforded full rights in a given society, were much more open.

The Roman Empire, for example, which was *definitely* an empire, was based on slavery and was highly oppressive and dominated a great deal of the classical world; but there were no racial distinctions, at least not racial distinctions in the way we think of them today. It's really with the rise of modern Europe, sort of at the time of Columbus, if you want to just pick a moment, but of course it wasn't in one moment that the idea of race and racism was first raised on a world scale. It was raised because it was needed on the part of the conquerors and dominators, the oppressors, to classify their subjects.

MH: Don't you also think it was needed on their part to justify their treatment of aboriginals wherever they landed?

HW: Absolutely. That's another very important point that you make. So much bloodshed, so much exploitation and suffering were involved with the onset of the European empire, even the conquerors needed to rationalize and justify it. There were debates among them about what was legitimate, religiously permitted, and so on. Did Africans or Indians in the Americas have souls, divine souls, or were they animals who could be exploited and killed at will — that sort of thing.

MH: I forget which Native American Chief it was who had said when the Pilgrims first landed on Plymouth Rock, "First they fell on their knees and then they fell on the Indians." Although Columbus' first trip, supposedly, had reported he had found a super-race of the most beautiful humans in the world, it's interesting to see that the religious fanatics who came to this country had to classify them as people without souls so they could justify the genocide that went on here.

HW: Obviously these were not simple matters. There were big debates; there were more humane members of the European colonists and imperialists. Religious figures attempted to protect Indians and black people and so on, so I don't think we should see it as a model that's a hundred percent. In a general way, it is certainly true that the racial classification and, as you're pointing out, the justification of that racial classification in a system of hierarchy, of superior and inferior, a natural order of race, was a fundamental part of the creation of the modern world.

MH: If we look at the "modern world" right now, today, even though people say they don't feel it, everybody seems to be a little stand-offish if they come in contact with someone who may look like an Arab-American. So, that kind of racial profiling is still going on here even on an individual basis.

HW: After September 11th, we have reached some new wrinkles in the standard pattern in that we tend to explain most major political, social, economic, cultural events by reliance on the old familiar rhetoric and understanding of race. In terms of racial profiling of Arabs and Arab-Americans, this, again, is a recurrence of similar patterns we've seen in earlier times, most notably the internment of the Japanese-Americans during World War II, the seizure of their property and the placing of the entire Japanese-American population of at least the western parts of the United States in concentration camps without any due process whatever.

MH: The same thing that's happening now with these Arab-Americans that are locked up.

HW: Something *very* similar going on. At this point, people are not being confined; they're not being incarcerated as the Japanese-Americans were. More than 50% of the incarcerated Japanese-Americans, by the way, were American citizens and there was never any due process, never *any* charges brought against them. It was highly problematic in terms of any constitutional issues. Very late in the game, under the Reagan Administration, 40 years or more after the event, minimal reparations were made to the Japanese-American citizens, many of whom had not survived long enough to collect. Even that didn't make up for what they had lost.

Up until now, we haven't seen actual wholesale arrests, but we have seen *retail* arrests. More than 1,000 people of Arab descent are being held on very uncertain charges. We're not even certain about who all the people who've been picked up are. I believe I saw in the paper just this morning that [Attorney General John] Ashcroft has released a very limited list, like a hundred names of the over 1,000 people who are under arrest, and the charges against them are also not all listed.

MH: From what I understand, they are mostly immigration charges.

HW: They're immigration, credit-card fraud charges. Obviously, these particular issues are merely the excuses for holding these people. I was reading also in the paper this morning that in the state of Michigan, rather than arrest people of Arab descent, they're going to write everyone a letter asking them to come in voluntarily for an interview. In other words, trying to skirt the edges of what is constitutionally permissible, but at the same time, what *is* the process of selecting these people is strictly a matter of descent.

MH: I don't think there are too many people in America who actually see that that is terribly wrong.

HW: We're in kind of a war fever, a fever of patriotism. I can understand how this happens to some extent. I don't think it's totally illegitimate to oppose terrorism or to mourn or regret the loss of life of the attacks that happened on September 11th. But in terms of the way we process this, in the way we organize our response to this, it's very important that we defend democracy and equality, and justice. These are, unfortunately, the first things to go when there's any sense of crisis. Worse than that, is that the military situation going on right now is, in many ways, used as a political excuse on the part of the administration to accomplish things they couldn't accomplish by other means. They intrude on people's rights that they could never have gotten away with under normal circumstances.

MH: It goes back to why the U.S. wasn't at that conference. If we don't learn from the past, we're doomed to repeat the past. It's not looking too good for the United States right now as far as democracy goes, when the average citizen, regardless of your color, is losing freedom and rights every day since this happened.

HW: It *is* a difficult situation. I don't think we're seeing that much of a movement against this situation yet, but in the long run, we will. I hope I'm not being too optimistic to say people in the United States do not accept very easily a loss of rights. And I think something that is called the "Vietnam Syndrome" exists in the United States, the reluctance to engage in large-scale military intervention abroad after Vietnam, after the horrors of that war, the loss of life, and the tremendous movement that had to be organized to end that war and that intervention.

It does seem to me that there's a strong legacy of that movement and other civil rights movements, and the allied movements for democracy in the United States, that that legacy is alive. We're a little confused now, we're a little uncertain about how to mobilize and organize because the attacks of September 11th were such a shock. But, in the long run, I have a certain faith that the American people will not put up with restrictions on their freedoms.

MH: A lot of my guests are the people who are actively out there fighting against the loss of freedom, but the majority of people don't get to hear that in the regular news. I really believe if all Americans really knew what was going on, you'd almost have a riot in this country.

HW: There *are* tremendous restrictions on our access to information.

MH: Do you see the world racial situation changing? We talk a lot about America, but what about globally, because it's not just an American problem.

HW: One of the important things I try to make clear in this book is how much the racial situation in America is a part of the world racial situation. When I grew up, and when I was a civil rights person at a very young age, active politically and so on, in the '50s, when I was a kid and in the '60s, when I was in college, I never thought we were fighting a worldwide problem. I saw it as a U.S. problem. I think we've come to understand more in recent years and in recent decades how much the racial situation in the U.S. was connected to the world as a whole, how much the civil rights movement was interconnected, the black movement was interconnected, with the anti-colonial movement around the world, just to pick one example of many.

I think there have been changes. The world racial situation, like the U.S. situation, is changing with all the continuities we were talking about previously. I wouldn't want to say there has been no improvement, that there haven't been significant victories for peoples of color and democratic movements around the world. What we have to understand is that none of these victories come without a price and one of the prices is the ability of those in power to regroup, to say, "Well, see, we *can* make reforms. What are you guys still complaining about?"

The whole argument one gets in this country now is about how now we can be color-blind, now we don't have to worry about race any more because we've passed civil rights legislation, people can vote, etc. What are you guys complaining about? It's the whole reverse racism that's placed against efforts to achieve affirmative action or inclusion in college admissions or in workplaces or to desegregate still segregated neighborhoods. All of that, I think, is the price we pay for actually having made some gain through the blood, sweat, and tears of the movement we went through in the 1960s and the whole post-war period.

There *has* been improvement, without question, but it's come at a price. A lot of what the book is about is trying to compare in different national settings, in different countries around the world, what that price is and what the emerging patterns of racial inequality and racial injustice are, in both in the United States (again, the color-blind thing, etc.) and around the world. I look at the South African situation, the situation in Brazil, which is often not recognized as the blackest country in the Americas and the second blackest country in the world after Nigeria. I also look at Western Europe, really the European Union, which has been totally transformed in the post-colonial era into a multi-racial area.

It used to be that in the colonial period, although there were some black people, some Asians, and so on in England and France and Germany, etc., the racial divide was between the mother country, so-called, and the colonies and, you know, the "wogs," and "kaffirs," and "coolies," and "niggers." [They] were out there; they weren't in here—they weren't in London or Paris or Frankfurt or Madrid. These are some of my comparative cases, but many others can also be examined.

MH: We're talking about racism and democracy, not only here in America, but globally. This really *is* a global problem. Who is responsible for continuing this racial inequity and how can it be ended?

HW: The first thing to realize is that racism, racial inequality, racial injustice, are not only a matter of people paying a price and being denied their rights and opportunities; they're also a matter of something paying off for certain people. This is something we often don't recognize—that racism works, that it reserves privileges, opportunities, access to scarce resources for those it favors, as well as hurting those it doesn't favor. So, if you look at patterns of unemployment or in access to education or healthcare, all the different areas in which racism operates, you'll see that it not only hurts some people, but it helps others. If it didn't have a pay-off in this sense, it would not continue. That is a very important thing to recognize.

Often this is not recognized. Often, there is a kind of invisibility about how racism assigns privileges to people; basically, that it assigns privileges to whites. I have lots of students, working-class students, white students, for example, who don't think of themselves as racists, who don't have prejudiced attitudes, who associate and are friends with black and Latino colleagues, other students who live in the dorms, share their classes, who would be horrified to find out they retain a set of racial privileges. Yet, they do. This is a major topic we have to talk about. It comes up in terms of where a person is going to live, what expectations of service a person has when he or she goes to a hospital, how one deals with the police, how one *views* the police. Are they there to defend and protect you and offer services or are they there to harass and possibly do violence to you?

Many different sectors of our lives are affected by this. It's a complex issue, just in terms of what keeps it going and what interests it serves. Another thing that's *really* important to say, that's not so immediate, is how built into the structure of our society racism is, and not just our society, but all around the world. I think using American examples makes sense in a discussion like this. When we think about how much the whole way our political system is organized, it's based on race. If you look at the Constitution of the United States, how much the founding fathers had to wrestle with the issue of race. They never wanted to mention race, but they built it in in numerous clauses of the Constitution, if we realize that 42% of the founding fathers were slaveholders and the ones who weren't slaveholders, were involved in enterprises—shipbuilders or traders or business people—that were deeply involved with the slave trade.

With these kinds of things, you begin to get a sense of how deeply embedded racism is in the whole founding of the United States. And, again, this would be something that would apply equally to virtually any country in the world. Even in countries that we don't ordinarily think of as racially structured, it would be true for them.

MH:　The comedian, George Carlin, does a whole skit on racism. One of the things he sees as the solution to it all is that everybody should have sex with everybody until we all blend into one color. *Newsweek* had an issue with a cover that was really just about that. It was the "new Americans," the young people, and all the different mixes of races within one child. I mean, they had some kids in there who could be six or eight different "races." Not even the strongest political mind or racist can actually stop the blending of the races. It seems as though people under 30 are much more open to that than people of our generation.

HW:　I hope that's true. I think there's some truth to that. It's a funny thing to say because I'm in my 50s and, to me, the civil rights movement, the black movement – Dr. King [Martin Luther King, Jr.], Malcolm X – were crucial figures of my college years. So I kind of take it for granted that that whole period caused tremendous effects in our society. The question of how deeply that legacy has run, how deeply it's remembered and recognized, how much it will grow and change and develop with subsequent generations, I think that's something we still don't really know much about.

Certainly through popular culture, through the music, through hip-hop, through television, there's been a tremendously rich encounter with the dynamics of race that has happened during and after the civil rights movement. I think that has had a lot of effect on young people, without question. Even though our society is still very largely segregated, there is more race-mixing now, more integration now, than there was in the years before WW II. Universities, for example, as exclusive and racist as they are, still have to accommodate a great number of students of color whom they didn't have to, previously. All of these things have to have some effect, so there's absolutely room for optimism. It's also important to recognize that the race-mixing thing has always been around and it can play out in a lot of different ways.

It's interesting to think that we could have some kind of hybridized society and culture in which everyone was everything. But that's never happened before and I don't think, on a sort of a biological level, in terms of human reproduction, it will ever happen. If that's not going to happen, if we're not going to have a sort of mestizo culture, then we have to recognize that racial classification is still going to play a big role even if people are more mixed than they were in the past. And, by the way, when you look at a mestizo culture – I talk about Brazil, about Mexico – the fact that a culture is racially mixed doesn't mean it isn't simultaneously racist, that it doesn't value the lighter skin, the blonde hair, etc., over darker skin; that it doesn't value the European over the non-European in terms of appearance, cultural value or honor given. If you look at Mexico, you can see the disparagement leveled still today at the indigenous population.

MH: It seems the indigenous population suffers wherever they are, from here to Australia and back. It doesn't really matter.

HW: The fact that almost everyone is mestizo in Mexico, is some combination of European and Indian and, by the way, there is a significant black heritage in Mexico, too, doesn't prevent a kind of hierarchy and condemnation of the Indian parts of people's heritage. There's no question of that.

MH: I'd like to let America off the hook for a few minutes today. This has been going on in many other countries, it almost seems like since the beginning of time. Are there now significant efforts to overcome racism? Do you find that the conference, the WCAR conference, was a sincere effort to overcome racism?

HW: Definitely. In terms of the WCAR, yes, there was a sincere and I think, a successful effort in many different ways despite the reprehensible behavior of the United States and some unresolved conflicts that were going on, which you have to expect in any UN or world gathering. It's a tremendous opportunity for anti-racist activists and analysts, resource people on race, of which I consider myself as well, to come together, learn from each other, share information and make contacts. I learned so much in this conference and I'm someone who has studied race and racism for decades; but that doesn't mean I don't have a lot to learn.

I learned about "Roma," for example, what people call gypsies. They reject the name "gypsies." They are millions of people spread out all through the world, but particularly in Europe, and they face all kinds of discrimination. I got a much better perspective on indigenous peoples all over the world, but particularly in the Americas. Indigenous movements are linking up and forming much bigger and more complex organizations, offering assistance to one another not only through conferences like the UN conference.

It's conferences and opportunities to get together that make such a difference for them. I learned about groups you normally wouldn't consider as racially oppressed, but you have to rethink it. For example, there was a tremendous presence in the South Africa conference of the "Dalit" people, which is another word, the preferred word, these people use. We often call them "Untouchables," people from India. There are more than 250 million Dalit in India. India is an enormous place of about a billion people.

The Dalit comprise the lowest caste of Indians. People have always said, "What's racial about that? That's a matter of caste. That's a matter of economic and cultural differences," but it's not really. Again, it becomes something that's visible, that's classified. It's called caste, but it looks like race. And if it looks like race and walks like race and smells like race, you start thinking of it as race, so these people were pointing out all the different ways they were discriminated against, that the anti-caste legislation, the minor reforms that have happened in India, while they've accomplished something, have not overcome the problem. In all of these ways, the conference was extremely useful.

This conference also pointed to the link between the "haves" and the "have-nots" of the world. This is something that is so much overlapped with patterns of racism we don't often think about it. When they protested in Seattle, students and trade unionists and ecology people, they were protesting against the World Trade Organization (WTO) and the system of exploitation it involves, like sweatshops throughout the world in the underdeveloped parts, the debt crisis that exists for these people. I didn't realize before going to Africa and to this conference, how much the burden of debt on Africa impoverishes the people there. The national debt that different countries in Africa owe to the IMF (International Monetary Fund), to the World Bank, and to the big private lenders, the big banks, Wall Street, and all that. It's in the hundreds of *billions* of dollars.

MH: So, that's another way of keeping that "race" down.

HW: The important thing to recognize is that they've *already* paid back the money they borrowed, but because there's so much interest charged, the debt has not really been significantly reduced, even though they've paid back everything they ever got from those banks.

MH: But they can't get past the interest.

HW: It's a burden, like being a sharecropper, like being a peasant on a world scale. You know how a peasant, a sharecropper, might get burdened by debt to his landlord. They can *never* get out of it. I think we have to recognize there is a tremendous racial dimension to this on a world scale, the world's "South." The darker countries, the darker regions of the world, are being exploited by the world's "North."

SIX

LIES, SECRETS, AND SUICIDES
Meria with Linda Starr

Linda Starr[7] is the Assistant Editor of *Online Journal* and a friend and associate of the late Jim Hatfield, author of *Fortunate Son*. Among the many topics discussed is Hatfield's book about George W. Bush, which was banned and *demanded* to be BURNED by the Bush family, as well as Hatfield's subsequent suicide pressure exerted by the powers-that-be. Starr discusses the Republican defections due to the perceived insanity of the present administration and loss of rights in the U.S., the Republicans wanting to repeal the Posse Comitatus Act that gives the military power over civilians without any consequences for their actions (can you say, "Nazi party"?), and how it must be stopped. Starr also discusses the desire of President Bush to "coronate" Daniel James as head of air space security, a man who should be facing criminal charges for falsifying records. Was September 11th a true wag-the-dog? There have been many comparisons with Pearl Harbor and beyond. (Interview taped/broadcast on December 4, 2001.)

MH: Would you like to tell the audience a little about yourself?

LS: In addition to writing and editing, I do some of the investigative research for *Online Journal*. When the Editor, Bev Conover [see Chapter 8] has a question about something a reporter has written, sometimes

I will vet the information just to be sure it's absolutely factual. We try very hard to be as correct as possible.

MH: You certainly put out a tremendous amount of work. I've used a lot of it on the show because I think it's pretty cutting-edge. What got you involved in all of this?

LS: It's kind of ironic. At one time, I was a Republican. I became more and more concerned about the way the party was moving and about the extremeness of the Christian Conservative Coalition. When they began to try to criminalize private conduct, I felt like that was going too far. A combination of things happened, but just prior to that, I became alarmed because I found out that during the Reagan-Bush Administration, they had diverted one of our military defense satellites to do nothing in the world but track Princess Diana at the request of the Royal Family so they could get dirt on her. They knew the Prince and Princess were separating and there was trouble coming down the pike. I thought that was outrageous.

MH: We live in a world of illusion, that's for sure.

LS: The mainstream media have decided they are going to control what everybody thinks and the information they get. Bless Al Gore's heart. He sure caught it for George W's claims that Gore said he invented the Internet, which is not what happened. Al Gore claimed to have secured the financing that gave us the Internet that we have today. Bless him for it because if we didn't have it, I don't know what we would do for information.

MH: It really is the only place where you can get real information or real news. People ask me, "Where do you get this news from?" and it's certainly not from the *Arizona Republic* newspaper.

LS: If you think about it, back in the '60s, people used to get information from the underground news. I think that's the only place a lot of information was available.

MH: So the Internet is the *above*-the-ground news.

LS: It's a little more mainstream than the underground news of that day because we are able to reach more people.

MH: Now, thanks to you, I was actually able to get a copy of the book *Fortunate Son*, because I thought it was impossible to get. You were kind enough to tell me about Soft Skull Press and the fact that they had copies available.

LS: The first paperback version is exactly identical to the first hardcover that Martins [St. Martin's Press] recalled, except that it has an index in it, which I did, and the second one does have updated information. The information that is in the first one, not all of it is in the second one because of a settlement in a lawsuit agreement. Both books are worth having and pursuing. If anybody sees them anywhere, for heaven's sake, pick them up because they are limited edition printings.

MH: What's the difference between the first and second books? I know Mark Crispin Miller [*see* Chapter 13] has quite a bit in the book that I have discussed. Am I missing anything really juicy or important?

LS: There are juicy things in both books. Things that were taken out pertaining to the settlement of a lawsuit that prevented the first version from being distributed in Texas have very good information and there are even indirect links to the person who brought the suit, and the Bush family. Because of the settlement, they agreed to take certain things out, so

Jim added some things to the second version that Soft Skull published that are juicy. I hope people get it because I would not be able to do it justice to sit here and just list the things off the top of my head.

MH: I really didn't know the severity of St. Martin's Press caving into that kind of pressure that the book was actually suggested to be burned.

LS: They *demanded* that. They wanted the book burned. They wanted it recalled. The way I understood it is that "Poppy" Bush had six lawyers after St. Martin's and St. Martin's, of course, came out with this drivel that they were burning the books. Jim found out they did *not* burn the books because of me. I found out here in Texas that they were bringing truckloads of them into all the second-market stores, brand-new. And because of the work I did, calling bookstores around the state and country, I found out they were just releasing them to the second-market so it would look like they didn't have sales. They claimed to have burned them, but they did not. And Jim took that information to his lawyer. I don't know what they ultimately did with it, but he did find out they didn't burn the books because of my research.

MH: I reported on the story that Jim Hatfield had committed suicide a few months back.

LS: I became pretty good friends with Jim. He used to joke that I was his biggest defender and a whole PR company rolled into one person. My father used to have a saying that even a chicken can kill you by pecking you to death. Well, they pecked Jim to death. They told him two years ago; I was told by Jim, that Clay Johnson [a Dubya crony] said they were not done with him after the recall, when they found out that the book was going to be republished. And they weren't. Every time he turned around, they destroyed everything he did to try to make money. Every book deal he had was destroyed and they didn't murder him, but they "killed" him.

MH: When you talk about "they," who are we talking about? Are we talking about the Bushes themselves?

LS: Yes. The Bush "regime," the Bush "crime family," you name it; that's what I call it.

MH: It's a sad state of affairs, but I'm starting to hear that story about a lot of other people, too, who have spoken out pretty freely against this Administration. All of a sudden, somebody gets shot in the middle of the night while they're supposedly getting served a subpoena after midnight, or these mystery suicides, etc. It's a very strange country we're living in.

LS: I will say this, in the course of my research about them recalling the book, I found out that several bookstores (one in Colorado), had received a memo from St. Martin's saying it was *illegal* to sell the books of a convicted felon, which we all know is a pile of poop because Oliver North and *all* of the Watergate people had books that sold. When did it become illegal to have First Amendment rights in this country, I'd like to know?

MH: When Bush got into office, and his friend, Johnny Ashcroft or, as some people refer to him, Herr Ashcroft.

LS: We have little sayings that we put on the bottom of our signature line of our e-mail. Some of them are "Hail to the Thief," "Coward in Chief," instead of Commander in Chief, various things like that, but the things they are doing to take our rights are just impossible. I have cause to pause to wonder about some events since 9/11.

MH: If you have somebody who is suggesting banning and burning of a book before he's even in office, could you imagine what else they want to do?

LS: Oh, yes, I *can* imagine what else they want to do. George Bush came to San Antonio on August 29th [2001] to speak before the American Legionnaires National Convention here and they had been removing people to so-called "First Amendment Zones" or "Free Speech Zones," where they could not be seen or heard protesting.

The lawyer I had working on our behalf who works closely with the ACLU and is a First Amendment Rights expert also happened to represent one of the local police union organizations and let word be known that if they removed us, there was going to be a lawsuit and we were going to slap them with some stuff legally. They did not come and say one word to us. They patrolled around us, they walked around us, they looked at us distantly, but they did not remove us. At the time, we thought that was the reason why. Now, I'm wonder[ing] if there weren't other possibilities.

We do know that the Bush Administration did know at least as far as three months in advance that there was going to be an attack on America. We have information that came from other military intelligence groups in different countries that warned them as recently as a week before the attacks that something major was going to happen. They did not step up any security or take any actions to prevent the attacks of 9/11. In the wake of the way they reacted that day and the conduct they exhibited, I have very strong feelings that they were complicit by negligence, at the very least, if not actual conspiracy involvement.

MH: When are heads going to roll for all these FBI, CIA, yadda-yadda for letting this one slip on by?

LS: In fact, the FBI was told to lay off the investigations of the bin Laden family right up until the 9/11 attacks. Then, they let the members of the family that *were* in this country leave the day after the attacks, as well as the Saudi royal family members that were here. Stories being leaked out of Europe, primarily England, suggest the Bushes are actually directly implicated because of Poppy's close relationship with the bin Laden family who have now been proven to be not so distant from Osama bin Laden as they initially claimed, that he's actually complicit because of business with the bin Laden family via The Carlyle Group, as are Dick Cheney and Colin Powell and James Baker III.

MH: I remember during the campaign when people were calling for Bush, Sr. to resign from The Carlyle Group specifically for that reason.

LS: When the U.S.S. Cole was bombed, this came up. What also came up were some points that Jim put in *Fortunate Son*, the fact that the brother of Osama bin Laden had been one of the original investors in Arbusto Energy, which was George Bush's first oil company, his first independent business venture that eventually transpired several ways and became Harkin Energy. He should have been in jail for insider trading on that deal, too, but they've been protected and covered up. They knew Osama bin Laden first denied that he had been guilty of the bombings of the American embassy in Tanzania and, yet, when a lot of Americans were killed and other people, later on, [he] did admit it; so they knew. I think they are spinning this business about how he refuses to be taken alive. He's told his bodyguards supposedly to kill him if they were going to take him. I think that is just bull. I think they have no intention of taking him alive.

MH: They don't want him to be able to talk.

LS: That's right, and if they have these secret military tribunals behind closed doors, then the American public cannot find out how involved the Bush family is in the World Trade Center attacks and the Pentagon attacks. I think it's to cover themselves because they do not want normal, traditional rules of American criminal jurisprudence to expose their involvement. That's my sincere belief and it's my constitutionally-protected right to say so.

MH: So far. You know the new definition of terrorist is anybody who talks about the Constitution too much?

LS: Yes, that's what we've been hearing.

MH: I actually saw the brochure. I was shocked.

LS: They say we're supposed to trust that they are going to be fair about exerting these rules and that we are supposed to trust that they are not going to expand them to include American citizens; but I'm here to tell you, if they think people like me are going to be quiet, then they are going to have to arrest an awful lot of American citizens. I would pit my pedigree up against George Bush's any day of the week.

MH: Yesterday, I saw [Homeland Security Director] Tom Ridge announce that we're under another warning threat. They don't know where, what, when or how, but they came out and gave us this big, useless warning. What do you think of that?

LS: Isn't it interesting that they now know the anthrax strain being sent to all these newspeople and, primarily, Democrats was an American strain?

MH: I think they knew that from the get-go. I don't know if you're familiar with Dr. Leonard Horowitz, but I've had him on the show and he's a super-intelligent, credible man. He wrote to the FBI, repeatedly, long letters about anthrax, because that is one of his specialties. He said they say they're following up every lead and no one even answered his letters. My feeling is, they already know about it, so they have no use hearing it from anybody else.

LS: They also don't want us to know the names of the people they're detaining or any information about them. When the 9/11 attacks first happened, they were all hot on this insider trading on the stock deals where there was a put on the American Airlines stock and the other one, millions of dollars were made in those deals, which remain unclaimed. But when they found out the third highest man in the CIA was involved in those profits, they suddenly dropped it out of the media and there has been no further pursuit of that.

MH: And then there's also the story of Building No. 7, which housed this supposedly private, secret little place of the CIA, which was fully engulfed before the towers even came down. I remember the early-on stories about the bombs in the buildings. Even the firemen were reporting that, and there's another story that seems to have gone away.

LS: I don't know how we are able to get all the information we're able to get out. They are trying to pooh-pooh us off as being some kind of subversives or lunatics or troublemakers or whatever, but information is still surfacing. Even though they are trying to discredit the messengers carrying the message, they're really not doing anything except making themselves look like they're trying to cover up something. If you remember back during the campaign of 2000, everybody tried to get the DOD [Department of Defense] records of George Bush or his records in the Texas Air National Guard back in 1972.

I have a friend who got quite a bit of it that gave very strong indicators that George Bush was AWOL [Absent Without Leave], but we couldn't get anything specific, any disciplinary documents. The reason why is that Daniel James, who was the Adjutant General of the Texas Air National Guard and in charge of everything at Camp Mabry, covered everything up for him. And his reward is that he is supposed to now be made Director of the Air National Guard for the entire country and, incidentally, in charge of all of our air space security.

He has multiple lawsuits that have been filed against him by individuals for sexual harassment, anti-semitism, discrimination, four or five of these lawsuits that are just terrible. He and George Bush have been directly implicated in a criminal fraud against the government for falsifying readiness reports and, yet, he's been nominated by George Bush to be put in charge as Director of the Air National Guard.

People who want to object to that, I suggest they call the Senate Armed Services Committee staff or Gary Leeling at (202)224-9339 and tell them we do not want a criminal put in charge of our national security air space. This is absurd. This guy should be going to jail. He shouldn't be getting a reward appointment. But, of course, that's the way everything in the Bush Administration is.

MH: Everything is pay-back with him. Pay-back or blow-back.

LS: In the Florida election, they are trying to say he actually won in the NORC Report, but that has been skewed. We know, in fact, Al Gore won no matter how you look at the recount issues and analyze it. If you do it with the parameters that the court put on them, Al Gore won by any definition of winning. They tried to put a spin on that and say he did not win. In addition to that, our friend [attorney] Phil Berg, who, you remember, was actually one of the observers down there in Florida and witnessed where the Republican canvassing board admitted to having altered over 300 ballots by putting white oval stickers over the other names and, in some cases, re-marking the ballots for Bush. And nothing has happened. Katherine Harris and all these people counted those votes. I want to know *when* there are going to be some criminal charges come out of these ballot alterations.

MH: The last I talked to Phil Berg, I understand he was putting together some kind of petition to disbar the Supreme Court and I also understand Vince Bugliosi [*see* Chapter 1] has figured there's been enough time since September 11th to mourn America and now to move forward with trying to impeach the Supreme Court; so hopefully, these things will get moving.

LS: I want to clarify that about Phil. Phil is going to file grievances and complaints for disbarment on three of the members of what I call "The In-Supremes," Justices Scalia, Thomas, and O'Connor, in their states where they have passed the bars. Scalia has passed in more than one state. The reason is, all had serious conflicts of interest. He's not just going after anybody who voted against, because that's not the concept. The concept is that these three had a serious conflict of interest, should not have even sat in on hearing the case, and certainly should not have handed down a ruling. The fact that they did so makes it a conspiracy to interfere with the proper election process, and I think that's criminal in itself. That's why he's filing against those three and not the five, because it is an ethics canon they violated by the state bar associations and also by the Judicial Code of Conduct.

MH: The FBI and CIA were kept so busy tracking the Clintons' whereabouts, they didn't bother following up on the leads to the event of September 11th.

LS: They absolutely would *not* cooperate and it really makes you wonder whether they had anything to do with it. It's like they just deliberately set out to rape, torture, and murder democracy in this country and then subvert it into what they want it to be; but we're not going quietly away. We're not getting over it. We are keeping it in the public eye. We're getting more and more converts every day; more and more people are becoming alarmed at the actions of this Administration to take away our rights.

MH: And a lot of them are Republicans.

LS: That's right. A lot of them who are converting because they see the abuse. Even [Representative] Bob Barr and our sector are alarmed by their actions, so what does that tell you, as right-winged as most of them are?

MH: I know the new thing that Ashcroft came up with, the FBI now sitting in on religious meetings, was a big blow to a lot of people. I've heard them say, "That's it. Where does it end?" Unfortunately, it's too bad people have to wait until a specific issue hits *them* before they give a damn, but I've been saying it on the show all along, sooner or later this Administration is going to do something to piss *you* off and then, you might not have anybody behind you.

LS: Like that old saying, "They came for the Jews; they came for the blacks; they came for the non-mainstream religious groups; and now they're coming for me." At what point do we put our foot down? When they take the first group or when there's too few of us left because they've taken *every*body?

MH: I also understand that out of sheer disgust, a lot of FBI agents have just walked off the job. I think even the director has said, "So long," because they felt their hands were tied, they were lied to, and a lot of them told Ashcroft "we are not going to do what you want us to do to American citizens."

LS: I understand there is an FBI agent [R. Wright] who has even filed a personal lawsuit about the things they have demanded they do that are considered illegal and a violation of people's rights in this country, and the agent refused to do it. Some interesting things have been coming out of this 9/11 business that gave them the excuse they needed to end the protesting because they said we were subversives and *maybe* we were terrorists and *maybe* we're this and *maybe* we're that. It seems to all be bogus. It seems they cannot stand the microscope looking at *their* actions because they know they stink. That's why George Bush had to cover up for Poppy by hiding some presidential records.

A memo was released when Bill Clinton declassified a lot of the records the CIA had on [former Chilean dictator General Augusto] Pinochet from Chile, when they had the takeover from [former Chilean president Salvador] Allende, and they did all that stuff down in the Chile election. Poppy Bush was implicated in quite a bit of it, as was [former Secretary of

State] Henry Kissinger and several others. They have to cover up their criminal actions. They have to cover up their involvement in Iran-Contra and how they used drugs to finance that through [former Marine Lt. Colonel] Oliver North. One of the things I used to taunt the Republicans with on the message boards was that as soon as [former President Ronald] Reagan kicks the bucket, we are going to come and carry Poppy off in chains, four-point restraints, and put his butt in jail. That used to just send them into a fever.

MH: What do you think about the fact that Poppy Bush was over in the UK this week helping with the celebration for the mourning of the Britons who were killed in the World Trade Center?

LS: George Bush, the one I call "Dumbya," keeps talking about how they want to go after the evildoers, that they want to seize the assets of the people conspiring with the terrorists. I want to know when they're going to seize the assets of Poppy and other people who were involved in the profiteering off of this, including the third highest guy in the CIA, who they *know* profited off stock manipulation. I want to know when are they going to start seizing *their* assets?

MH: If we're going to go after the "evildoers," there are plenty of them right here, so what are they waiting for? How will they arrest themselves?

LS: I don't know. I want to know when is he going to quit hiding Dick Cheney? What is it they don't want him to say? Information has come to me, which if I had to prove it in a court of law right today, I could not do this—but many people who have been combat pilots have told me the flight that went down in Pennsylvania was shot down out of the air, that the debris pattern was consistent with an airplane that had been shot out of the air and it was *not* consistent with one that had merely exploded and crashed.

MH: Exactly. They found pieces of that plane within a six-mile radius.

LS: And they said, also, that the day of that crash, American Airlines had told its employees the plane had been shot out of the air by the military. Right after that, the next day, they started saying, "Oh, no, we didn't shoot the airplane out of the air." Yet the theory is, the reason why they have made heroes out of the passengers is that they had actually retaken the plane and actually *had* control of it, but they shot it out of the air anyway—and Bush is the one who gave that order. Dick Cheney exposed that on *Meet the Press* that Sunday after the attack. He said the one order that Bush gave that day was to shoot planes out of the air that did not try and land. Now, I will bet you dollars-to-donuts that is *exactly* what happened and they're horrified because they know if they release those black boxes, that's what is going to prove that they did. They knew about it and did it anyway.

MH: How come we never get to hear the stories in these black boxes?

LS: They keep claiming they were damaged. Black boxes are designed to withstand the types of abuse they got in those plane crashes. How come we're able to recover black boxes from *other* plane crashes that are every bit as bad—and not *that* one?

MH: Because it's only when it's convenient. You know, a lot of people are comparing what happened on September 11th and since to that movie, *Wag the Dog*. What do you think about that?

LS: I think it's not only a case of wag-the-dog, I think they *created* this because they were desperate. Jim Hatfield told me repeatedly in our private conversations, and we agreed about this, that George Bush had to do something desperate to get people behind him because there were too many questions about his illegitimacy and about the things they were doing. They *had* to do something to silence the protesters and dissenters. They *had* to do something to take away our rights so that anybody who would protest would be considered a traitor. The only thing that we could compare it to was the attack on Pearl Harbor.

He said it would have to be something *that* significant to stop all of what has gone on and it *still* has not stopped it. It's only silenced some people and delayed the inevitable, but it is going to come to light. I believe they're involved in it. I believe they have no scruples. You remember George Bush is Governor Death. He is Governor Death in Texas and he is all that will be standing between living and dying of the people who are convicted in these secret military tribunals. He will have no compunction about issuing the death sentence on people they want to silence.

MH: And that could be *any*body. It could be the Sierra Club for all we know.

LS: That's the truth. I just absolutely have no confidence in their fairness or anything else. Seeing his transcripts from Yale during the campaign, it gave everybody the distinct impression that they had *bought* that diploma for him. He had such bad grades and must have done so poorly on his LSATs [aptitude test required for entrance into any U.S. law school] that he was rejected by the University of Texas Law School where his own father was our Congressman. They were so bad he couldn't get in, so he had to get a legacy admission into Harvard to get his sheepskin there for business. Then, every business he's been involved in has failed and they've had to have his father's friends come and bail him out.

MH: That is so clearly pointed out in the book. I know there's something you want to talk about because it's timely, which is how the Republicans want to repeal the Posse Comitatus Act and confirm the Daniel James appointment.

LS: First of all, I do want to address the thing about Jim Hatfield. Jim Hatfield knew the Bush family quite well and he predicted any number of scenarios that were significantly reflected in the 9/11 attacks. Anybody who doubts that should read either of the versions of *Fortunate Son*. I would suggest that you get both of them because there are different things in both, primarily the same, but there are different things in both versions. There are things that lead up to the story about Daniel James' nomination as Director of the National Guard, and this is the man who is going to be in charge of our air space security. A man who has been implicated in a story that is being pounced on by *USA Today* where Daniel James is implicated with George Bush of conspiring in a criminal fraud against the government for falsifying readiness reports of the personnel that were on the payroll.

The Senate Armed Services Committee had two generals come and testify to improprieties that have been committed, and possible illegalities committed by Daniel James. They are wanting to sweep it aside and not investigate and stop this promotion. There have to be consequences to criminal acts and I don't think that rewarding somebody with a high-profile appointment is the way to do that. I don't think George Bush should be able to reward people who have committed criminal acts to cover up for his illegal behavior. I think that's just horrible. I think we need to all be calling Gary Leeling at the Senate Armed Services Committee. There's also a Colonel Norman Schaule at Norman.Schaule@Pentagon.as.mil. They need to be stopping this appointment. They need to *not* confirm it. This is as bad as Ashcroft. Ashcroft is a *disaster* as Attorney General.

MH: He's a disaster to the whole planet.

LS: He should have never been appointed. And this man, Daniel James, has multiple lawsuits for anti-semitism, sexual harassment, improperly advancing people who did not have the educational requirements to be made officers. The list goes on and on. He has retaliated against a whistleblower who tried to stop him from promoting people who were not qualified for rewards. The stuff they have done to people is so typical of the way they treated Jim. They tried to destroy the reputations of the people. One person who was an active military member for many, many years did not get confirmed that he *was* active duty military because he was a whistleblower. He was denied necessary medical treatment for a very serious problem that has now taken decades off his life.

MH: Now what is the Posse Comitatus Act?

LS: Posse Comitatus was enacted after the Civil War because of the punitive damages of the federal military against civilians in the South, as in Sherman's March and the burning and pillage of the South. American military officers, Union officers, came into the South and committed rape, pillage, murder, and literally took everything that wasn't nailed down, unless it was buried and hidden. The actions by the military were so punitive, they enacted the Posse Comitatus Act that basically says no American military could ever again take actions against private citizens, civilians.

The Republicans want to repeal that because they know that legally they've got a problem when they put all these military people in all the airports and they're all walking around with guns. They know there are going to be incidents like has recently come to light about the strip-searching in airports—a flight attendant they were strip-searching in a terminal because of some button she had. She was pregnant; she had some buttons or something on her uniform that were making the metal detectors go off. I mean, that's assault by contact.

MH: And then what happens if they decide to put this military in the streets blocking roads and doing all kinds of other things?

LS: At least with police, most of them have some kind of training. They understand about legalities and they understand the parameters of what they can and cannot do. Sometimes they do violate the laws, but we have consequences we can impose upon them for that. The Republicans want to remove all consequences so the military can act as an extension of George Bush's personal army.

MH: Doesn't it seem a lot like the Nazis in Germany?

LS: Absolutely. In fact, we made many correlations. Jim and I talked many times about that, about how this is *exactly* the way Hitler came to power and the things he did in the '30s that were so horrific against the Jewish population.

MH: And then yesterday or the day before, when I learned about Ashcroft wanting to allow this FBI spying on religious groups, I talked to one of my friends who fought in WW II and he said that was the last thing Hitler knew he had to do in order to take over in Germany. In order to do the evil Hitler did, he knew he had to infiltrate and destroy the religions. My friend said this is like a nightmare for WW II people because it's like seeing the same thing happen all over again, except this time it's happening here in America.

LS: People keep saying, "Well, in 2004, we can get him out." We won't be *able* to get him out because we will no longer have free elections. If we do not start voting in 2002 for the Democrats and boot the Republicans out of there, giving a clear signal to Washington that the American people are not going to stand for this, we are sunk. I'm afraid we will not have free elections by 2004.

MH: That's some of what I talk about with Bob Kunst who's running for governor of Florida. Jeb Bush has Florida so sewn up, it's like who's to even say you guys are going to be able to *have* an election? Here you had somebody in as governor who four days before September 11th had basically brought out the troops.

LS: A friend of mine explained to me that there are major differences between state martial law and federal martial law. Under federal martial law, there are a lot more procedures that prevent them from doing a lot of things they are able to do under *state* military militia law. There are too many indicators that they *did* know and all this stuff they're saying about how they didn't know is purely bogus. There have been many proven lies that Ari Fleischer has told. The White House and Air Force One were *never* under attack. They *know* that's not true. They also know the Clintons did *not* pillage Air Force One.

MH: I see Ari Fleischer on TV and match him up with the real news and I say, "What a bald-faced liar."

LS: They all lie.

MH: And there's only one American casualty in Afghanistan? Are they kidding us or what? Are we *really* supposed to believe that this CIA guy was the first casualty we've had in Afghanistan? How much of what's gone on in America since this stolen election is the result of the passivity of Americans over the stolen election?

LS: Everything they're doing is because people did not take to the streets and justice did not demand the removal of the "In-Supremes" who voted partisan instead of by the law. Everything they have done is a result of the fact that we are not standing up and saying, "No, we are *not* having this. Democracy is alive and well in America even if you don't like it. We're going to do things by the law, not by the way you want to enact a regime."

MH: When I had Mark Crispin Miller on the show, he made some good points. Unfortunately, it was close after September 11th, so we were a little toned-down in the interview. He did ask, "What's the point of us going to Afghanistan and fighting for freedom if we don't have freedom in this country? What are we fighting for?"

LS: I love George Bush's comments about people who are installed as heads of countries who are not elected. It's pretty bad when Americans have to get our information from European media sources. They have such a stranglehold over the news that's being reported here and the only people who are reporting the truth are people like us at *Online Journal* and those at *American Politics Journal*— I know Doc Dave Gonzo [Gene

Gaudette] pretty well. We work together quite often and cooperate with each other and Greg Palast.

MH: Greg Palast [*see* Chapter 2] was one of the first ones to get trashed in Florida trying to break the stolen election story.

LS: I've got news for them. He has the smoking gun; the memo that proves what their intent was in the voter purging role.

MH: He's got a lot of guts, that's for sure and, you know what? A lot of us do. *Online Journal* does a great job. That is without question of a doubt. Luckily, people who are online can get all this information.

LS: Well, Bev [Conover] [*see* Chapter 8] has the story that the Barrick goldmining lawsuit forced Greg [Palast] to remove from his American website because he is an American, but works for the *London Observer* and the *Guardian* over there. But *Online Journal* is one of the few places where you can still get that story.

MH: I remember when I had Greg on, I told him I would post it on my site if he wanted. I think it's crazy that people would allow the Net to be used that way. That's a long-reaching arm from England to America to have him take it off his American website.

LS: Bev, as the owner, publisher, and editor of *Online Journal,* is somebody who is *not* going to be intimidated that way. If they want a fight, they'll get a really nasty one and we've got a whole group of lawyers who have privately said to us they will represent and defend *Online Journal* if the government were to come after us. The government would be *very* foolish to do that.

MH: Where do you think this whole mess is going? A lot of people talk about One World Order. Do you see any of that in this?

LS: I think George Bush and his father have ambitions to turn this into a dictatorship because they want to take over the world. And I definitely see their hand in all of this business with the bin Ladens and Afghanistan and the oil pipeline. Although George Bush is so stupid, he just gave all those rights to [Russian President Vladimir] Putin when he was there with him.

MH: That's because he "saw Putin's soul."

LS: He looked in his eyes and he saw his soul. He found criminality there.

MH: All he's managed to do is make Russia and China real tight against us, which I see as a major, major threat to the United States.

LS: He's got the philosophy that if they don't like what he's doing, he'll just nuke 'em.

MH: I find myself telling the rest of the world that most Americans are not represented by this Administration. We shouldn't all be judged by our military cabinet. During the campaign, I thought if Bush gets in, we're going to be in war and in no time flat. Sure enough, ba-boom, here we are. And now I understand he's got his peons planning the best way to attack Iraq. He's already getting ready for the next step.

LS: Saddam Hussein was a CIA puppet and they are all in bed together. The corruption by this occupying administration is just despicable. I have news for them. A lot of Republicans are very concerned about the things they're doing to evaporate and violate our rights, and to undermine the Constitution. They are losing, not gaining support. I do not believe that 90% approval rating. I think that's been totally puffed up because when we first started one poll shortly after the 9/11 attacks, asking if people approved or disapproved of Bush, I saw he had a 63% disapproval rating when they were saying he had a 90% approval rating.

MH: If they're going to lie about the election, they're going to lie about everything. My father used to tell me if somebody lies in small things, they're going to lie in big things, too. That's just the way that it is.

LS: And they don't have consequences that will stop them. A friend of mine is really hot on this business with 9/11 [at findtruth38@hotmail.com]. He has actually done an interview on a Toronto [Canada] station this morning and is trying to organize everybody into demanding an inquiry into 9/11, whether they are Canadians or Americans or Americans living abroad or people who have been affected or impacted by this. He has a whole list of sites that provide people with information. He asked me if I would make that little announcement that he is trying to coordinate and organize an effort to demand an inquiry into the 9/11 events and all this stuff that's going on because there's too much information and there are too many indicators and implications that this administration is involved in this to some degree. We don't know to *what* degree.

Bin Laden met with a CIA station chief in Dubai [United Arab Emirates] seven weeks before the 9/11 attacks when he was supposedly wanted by the CIA. So, bin Laden was treated at a U.S. hospital.

MH: Someone said if there wasn't already a bin Laden, America would have to have made him up. People have to use their brains. If they think one guy was responsible for what went on or some poverty-stricken people living in caves with a few pop guns could have pulled that off, then they've been seeing too many movies.

LS: A group came here from London in October [2001]
        and interviewed me with a film crew for a documen-
        tary about Jim Hatfield and the Bush family. I gave
        them quite a bit of information and they were very
        happy. The Hatfield story is not going to go away. The
        theft of the election is not going to go away. We are
        not going to get over it and we *are* going to keep on.

SEVEN

DID WE VOTE FOR OIL WARS?
Meria with Dave Chandler

Dave Chandler,[8] the Publisher/Editor of the online newspaper, *Earthside*, wrote the article, "Gore Won: Why It Matters." He ran for Congress on the Green ticket in the 2002 election. In this interview, Chandler discusses the "war" in Afghanistan, with one in Somalia maybe next, as well as India vs. Pakistan and Israel vs. Palestine, all taking cues from our President. What international enemies have we created by pulling out of several treaties? Chandler discusses our position as a world leader now being emulated by "wars on terrorism" initiated by other countries, and America's position as "Globo-Cop." He also discusses the loss of civil rights in America, starting with the disenfranchisement of ALL voters by the Supreme Court in 2000, and the important aspect of this time- and money-consuming "war" on the environment globally.

Chandler postulates how Gore would have handled 9/11, whether America would have pulled out of the Kyoto Treaty (Gore penned some of it), the Germ Warfare Treaty or the Anti-Ballistic Missile Treaty, all creating many more global enemies of the U.S. The world is running out of OIL (the Number #1 cause of war), yet nothing is being developed globally to replace it. Will it take bread-lines and soup kitchens in America for us to wake up?

We have more homeless and hungry in America now than ever before. The events of 9/11 did not help, nor the collapse of Enron, and these could be just the beginning. The whole world knows better what is happening here than do most Americans, thanks to the media spin trying to keep us ignorant of facts so we will continue working and churning out taxes. (Interview taped/broadcast December 20, 2001.)

MH: Dave has an environmental and political website, which I found through Aaron Cohen's unbelievably great newspaper, *The Democracy Chronicles*.

DC: I'm speaking to you from a suburb between Denver and Boulder, in Arvada, Colorado. We've had a lot of growth out here, which has been a big issue for us environmentally—the sprawl. It's hard to fight that.

MH: It was my opinion several years ago that Boulder was a perfect example of growth with the environment in mind. Has that changed?

DC: No, I think they've done a pretty good job. It's made some of their neighbors unhappy because Boulder has made some tough decisions to purchase a lot of open space around their community. It's not all positive. That's meant some spill-over into growth in some areas, some residential growth, but as far as Boulder's concerned, they've preserved their quality of life.

MH: They have, from what I understand, one of the best models of living in harmony with the environment than probably any city in the country. A few years back, I was involved in a Save-the-Mountains campaign here in Arizona. They called in the "founding fathers" of Boulder to teach Scottsdale how to do it here. This is the land of just mow-it-all-down. They call it scrape-and-rape the desert here. After a wonderful presentation and everything they did, everything they talked about. Scottsdale rejected it, because it's all about money here in Arizona.

DC: It's about money here, also. Boulder made some tough decisions, but they've also demonstrated by making some of those tough, pro-environmental decisions, contrary to a lot of the doom-and-gloomers about growth, that it's a very prosperous, upscale community. It's the difference between long-term vs. short-term planning and Boulder has planned longer-term.

MH: I had a few choice words for the members of my Save-the-Mountains team, and I said, "I'm outta here."

DC: It's the desire of the developers vs. long-term quality-of-life decisions.

MH: You had a good article. Right now, I'm simultaneously reading three books. I'm reading [Jim Hatfield's] *Fortunate Son* [*see* Chapter 6], [John Nichols'] *Jews for Buchanan* [*see* Chapter 9], and Molly Ivins' book [*Shrub*]. Your article fit totally in line with why it matters. It wasn't about Gore vs. Bush. It was about *everybody* in the United States losing their vote.

DC: The commentary is on my website, which would be at Earthside.com/Chandler-commentary.html. I wrote this in response to the Consortium final vote count, which, of course, the mainstream media wanted to slant (because we were involved in the so-called war), to say that Bush would have won anyway. Of course, if you went to the *Los Angeles Times* website (I think it's still available), and clicked on the details of the vote count, you would have found if the votes had been counted the way the Supreme Court *itself*, in its final ruling, would have mandated if they had allowed enough time (instead of an hour or two before they shut it down), Gore would have won by several hundred votes. That's the bottom line. Gore got more votes in Florida than Bush.

MH: That's very clear in John Nichols' new book. He actually has in there the overvotes that they talked about until we all wanted to throw up. He actually has copies of at least a half a dozen representative overvotes. I think anybody who has any vision left, even in one-half of one eye, can see that they were very clearly votes for Gore.

DC: Even the Consortium, the *New York Times* articles about the last unofficial vote count, indicated and had to concede it was clear that more and more people intended to vote for Gore than for Bush. I can understand the problems of what we were going to do with the butterfly ballot, but this is where I lay the onus back on the Bush people and their desire to win, even at the sake of degrading our democracy, because they had choices they could have made at the time in November and December last year [2000], to pursue the avenues they pursued. And the avenue they pursued was to purposefully not count all the votes.

MH: I've been pretty on top of this story, but what I see in John's book, which I haven't seen anywhere else, is in so many different counties, how many tens of thousands of votes more Gore got that were thrown away.

DC: That's why this commentary I wrote put the decisions the Bush campaign made last year in the context of this so-called war on terrorism that we're fighting and involved in now, and why what happened in Florida matters. Because what Bush did in his campaign undercuts the moral legitimacy of what we're asking other people around the world to now involve themselves in.

MH: You keep calling it a "so-called war." I'm not going to let you get away with that one. Why don't you explain that to us?

DC: It's not a declared war so, in a technical sense, it *is* a so-called war. The Constitution says the Congress has the right to declare war, and they haven't done that. They passed a resolution allowing Bush to use necessary means for us to go after the terrorists, but it's not a declaration of war. My feeling about this is that the Bush regime wants the PR, the feeling that we're fighting World War II again. This *isn't* World War II and there are a lot of differences, obviously. There was a lot of talk after September 11th about Pearl Harbor. I saw a photo on television taken on December 8th, which was a Monday, the day after Pearl Harbor was bombed. There were lines around the blocks throughout the cities in this country, with people wanting to sign up at the recruiters to fight; to join the Army. Nothing like that, of course, happened after September 11th. In fact, it's quite the opposite. There has been no increase in recruitments.

MH: So many mothers have said, "My son's outta here if they think they're getting him."

DC: This is being billed as a war as kind of a propaganda ploy to give this the *aura* of World War II, that this is somehow in the same league as that.

MH: A righteous war.

DC: And, of course, it isn't. For one thing, Bush doesn't have the mandate from the UN or Congress, as I see it, to pursue this in other places once the hard work is done in Afghanistan.

MH: They've already announced that Somalia is next.

DC: Increasingly, we're seeing that and on the front page of my website every day, I track more of the warmongering that we're hearing out of the Bush regime. It's Somalia. It's Iraq. Yesterday, apparently, the United States fired on an Iranian oil-tanker. What's that all about? They're, of course, claiming it was mistaken identity. They thought it was an Iraqi oil-tanker. I find that suspect.

MH: We hear about all these mistakes. What? Are we *really* that stupid? You've got a five-year-old kid who could make fewer mistakes than our Army, on a computer game bombing something.

DC: It demonstrates a contradiction that we're so proud of our smart bombs (you know, that can blow to pieces single, specifically identified individuals walking around on the ground), but it was mistaken identity between something the size of a super oil-tanker?

MH: A floating football field. Oops! We missed.

DC: I see that increasingly happening, as well. Remember before September 11th, the consensus was starting to build that the Bush presidency was tottering. It was failing. The economy was in bad shape. He was having trouble with the Democrats in Congress who were starting to put up a fight. After September 11th, everything changed. Some of that should have happened. There should have been *some* changes. As this thing wears on, I think, people need to open their eyes and see the Bush people increasingly exploiting this for their own political advantage.

MH: I read in the *New York Times,* I think, that there are more *new* homeless people in New York and the rest of the country than ever before, people who always had a home. They call them the "working homeless."

People who have jobs or they got downsized or whatever, who could no longer afford to have a home. When did we hear these kind of statistics before? It was during the *first* Bush regime and now we have the same situation, but *worse*.

DC: Crime statistics, which *had* been declining, have now leveled off. That's a function, of course, of the economy, but I think it's also this general feeling the Bush people have brought to the leadership of the country, which is more of a kind of a [former President Ronald] Reagan pull-yourself-up-by-your-own-bootstraps theory. You're on your own.

MH: The only people who are benefiting are the rich, the rich Republican people who have the brown nose from reaming it up Bush's butt during his campaign, and people are starting to see that. One of the stories that's really giving me great pleasure is that Kenneth Lay of Enron, who was in-like-Flynn with all the big boys in D.C., including [Vice President Dick] Cheney, now is seeing them all turn their backs on him. He's odd-man-out because of the Enron crash. They're all scared to death that they're going to be exposed as having been part of it.

DC: They *should* be scared. I saw in this morning's paper that Kenneth Lay resigned from the board of directors of a major pharmaceutical corporation. I suspect that wasn't a voluntary resignation. I understand at the White House, the word is, "Kenneth who?"

MH: Everybody was all helpless and hapless over this situation going on in America. My mother used to say, "The bigger they are, the harder they fall." That guy is a perfect example of it. I still believe this whole move towards Nazism in this country is going to collapse on top of them. I think they are going to push the people so far and then the people are going to say, "Screw this. It's time for a new Constitution. It's time for a new America."

DC: That could happen and what I see in Bush himself right now is hubris. He's clearly very pumped-up right now, thinks he's won the war in Afghanistan, striding the globe like a Colossus, but I can already—and the news indicates this as well—begin to see the seeds of the pride that goes before a fall. This warmongering and saber-rattling towards Iraq is a prime example. I have no doubt that just like Afghanistan, if this country, with its massive military power, decides to topple Saddam, it can be done in fairly short order, but [Russian President Vladimir] Putin has clearly said he thinks that's a bad move. The British, although they're a little wobbly about it, have great concerns about it. The United Nations has said that's a bad move and I think the big question is, as bad a man as Saddam is, in the last 10 years, what has he done to us?

MH: Nothing. He wrote a couple of romance novels. That's as far as I know.

DC: And that's important. This was my concern about Bush being installed in the White House in the first place. One of my concerns was, it puts perhaps even legitimate foreign policy concerns in a bad light. Is this a Bush family grudge?

MH: The question has been, "Is he going to go in and finish his father's unfinished business?"

DC: That's exactly what it looks like, since there isn't any evidence offered, as of today, that links Saddam or Iraq to this kind of terrorist activity that's been going on. You have to have a link or it looks like it's settling old scores.

MH: In one of the Bush books I read, it said that Bush's biggest fear was ever repeating his father's mistakes. They say that whatever you fear, you create. All the things he *didn't* want to recreate of his father's, supposedly, are exactly what he's dealing with now.

DC: He's been so concerned about alienating the more conservative and right-wing elements of the Republican party, which is why he's taking some of the hard-line anti-environmental positions and some of the pro-Christian right decisions, yet this assault on rights in this country in the name of fighting terrorism, has created some very strange bedfellows in some ways. When you have [Representative] Dan Burton and [Representative] Bob Barr, from the hard Republican right in the Congress saying the same thing as what the ACLU and some Democrats like Senator [Pat] Leahy are saying, you've got to perk up and say, "What *is* going on here?"

MH: He's got Congress screaming at him from both sides, saying, "Hey, wait a minute, this isn't a monarchy," and he doesn't care for that kind of talk because he thinks he gets to do whatever he wants.

DC: My problem with the Bush involvement in politics, it's what I disliked about his father and I don't like about him as well, is this sense of entitlement. The Bush men were bred to rule and that has a smack of monarchism to it. I think that's why he dislikes that comparison.

MH: Did you know that after George Sr. and Barbara moved out of the White House, went back to supposedly a regular life, it was the first time they found out that pizza stores deliver pizza. Barbara Bush thought that was so "quaint." People in America look at these people who *try* to come off like your regular home-boy,

Joe Blow down the street, but they didn't even know until after his presidency that pizza gets delivered. I think it was Molly Ivins who said George Jr. was born with a silver foot in his mouth. I loved that one.

DC: The family has a long history of this kind of, coming from his father and even before then, an economic, political power elitism. I don't think they're in the intellectual elite by a long shot, *any* of them. I guess my disappointment, to some extent, in the American people at this point is that they fell for this.

MH: Because they ended up with good media spin, actually making it seem like it was wrong that Al Gore was intelligent, has some class, and some knowledge of foreign affairs. They actually made it seem like he was *wrong* for being intelligent.

DC: And there has been some independent media analysis already done of the 2000 presidential campaign that clearly indicates there was an institutional bias against Al Gore, in spite of what the right-wing and the Republicans like to say about the so-called liberal media. I don't think that ever existed. I think it's fallen by the wayside, particularly as the electronic media superstars have risen up that economic ladder. They're not dirty white-collar grunt journalists any more. These are people who are pulling down hundreds of thousands, if not millions, of dollars a year, these reporters and anchors, but they don't have any class any more. They, I believe, increasingly identify with the kind of Republican Bush rhetoric view of the world. And that's why I think, to this day, when you turn on the television to find out what's going on around the world, the media and CNN, of course, particularly, have become a branch of the Bush regime.

MH: Robert McChesney [*see* Chapter 10] has several books out on the media spin and how it's killed democracy in this country. All my foreign listeners tell me they're in a constant state of fear watching the United States; no matter where they are. They could be in Italy, they could be in the Czech Republic. And the fact is, Israel and Palestinians are mimicking us. India and Pakistan are ready to go to major war; have already begun it. And what are they saying? "We're going after terrorists they same way the United States did."

DC: Already in the space of three-and-a-half months, Bush's rush to war, instead of considering alternative action, has done exactly what you just said. You hear [Israeli Prime Minister Ariel] Sharon and [Prime Minister Atal Bihari] Vajpayee in India parroting Bush's words, and it's put us in a real bind. We're in a real bad situation.

MH: Because now we're Global cop. A lot of these countries have nuclear weapons and they're not going to give two damns about what *we* have to say if they get pissed enough at their neighbor to blow them off the face of the earth. Let's not leave out China and Russia, who made a pact together, in the event we pulled out of that ABM Treaty, which we did. And North Korea saying that all bets are off, "You come after us for war and we're going to retaliate with war."

DC: The mainstream American media right now offer absolutely no perspective.

MH: Most Americans don't know how close we are to getting involved in a massive nuclear war.

DC: And this is what I find distressing right now with what's happening to our culture in this country, in light of this terrorism and the anti-terrorism legislation. There almost seems to be an attitude that it is more patriotic to live in ignorance. That you're not being sufficiently patriotic if you pay too much attention to what's going on in the rest of the world.

MH: But what's going to happen if America takes a huge hit and everybody starts dying by the hundreds of thousands? Are they going to say, "Oh, you should have told us"?

DC: This is what you would have hoped we would have learned from Vietnam: the more secretive you are, in the long run, the more it undercuts all of what you're trying to do; because we haven't been told the truth and we haven't been prepared. Yet the Bush regime is falling right into that same trap. They want to control the news.

MH: And they want everything to be in secret.

DC: In keeping this information from the American people, they're, in the long-term, going to undercut themselves.

MH: So many times I've said on my show to my listeners world-wide that not all Americans even *know* what's going on, and not to blame all of us, that there are *some* of us who are awake, but we don't get told anything.

DC: The wonderful thing about the Internet is that you can find all of these stories in the foreign press and you can get a clearer picture of what is actually happening. There are just scores of English language Internet newspaper sites where this can be done. I try and go through those sites every day as much as I can, read the stories, and pull the best and most important ones and put them on my front page. I think I know what's going on.

MH: People who listen to my show say it's like a lifeline for them: "Where do you get all this news?" First of all,

I spend 10 hours a day on my computer, but most of the news is gathered from overseas sources. We're not going to get any news here. The only thing we're obsessed with in this country is who's banging who. And we're banging the whole world right now and most people in America don't know that.

DC: I have found that although the Labor party in Britain and [British Prime Minister] Tony Blair have become a little bit too toadyish towards Bush, the British press seems to have a more vigorous approach to finding the news than our own newspapers in this country. Even the *New York Times* and *Washington Post* have not been doing as good a job at ferreting out the real news you find in the British newspapers. *The Independent*, in particular, has done a marvelous job reporting on some of the atrocities that have been perpetrated by the Northern Alliance, our "friends," in Afghanistan. You don't read any of that in the American press.

MH: Of course not. They had an article just a couple of days ago, I read it on the air, about how angry the people in Britain are against Tony Blair. But when you hear our news, they make it seem like Tony Blair is this purveyor of hope for all of England. The British people are pissed to the gills and this article was about them asking us why aren't we saying no to George Bush? They say, "You need to stop this man," and they look at what's happening here as nothing but a horror.

DC: If we take a step back and look at this somewhat objectively, which is hard for all of us to do, we should look at all the saber-rattling and warmongering the Bush regime is doing around the world. North Korea, Somalia, Sudan, Iran, Iraq, the Philippines. This is the globe.

MH: This is the whole world.

DC: It's not World War II, because it's much more serious than World War II if this thing goes out of control, and wars have a propensity to do that. But Bush is setting us on the precipice of a global war.

MH: And *no* one is our friend. We've lost *all* of our allies by him pulling out of the Kyoto Treaty, pulling out of the ABM Treaty, the Germ Warfare Pact. I mean, I don't know what is left for him to pull us out of.

DC: And the world is such a different place than it was in the 1940s. India and Pakistan have nuclear weapons and because of this great technology that gives us the Internet, it has also given rogue nations and terrorists the ability to create all kinds of weapons. That's why I question this rush to war that Bush got into. I believe this was a perfect situation where you needed (the term has been maligned in the past) "police action," international police action.

MH: This was just an act of terrorism. It certainly wasn't a declaration of war and no one *really* has taken credit for the attack on the World Trade Center.

DC: It was mass murder. It was a heinous crime and it should have been treated as a heinous *crime*.

MH: A lot of people are comparing it to that Reichstag fire in Hitler's time, in 1932, which ended up being a wag-the-dog by Hitler, as an excuse to go in and invade Poland, and set up a military state. I love New York (I grew up in New York, I spent my whole life there) and the Twin Towers, I mean, forget it, when I saw that, my heart almost stopped, but we have to be reasonable. Those were two *buildings*. That kind of stuff happens in Israel and all over the world every day. For us to go out and just declare open warfare on the rest of the world over that is insanity.

DC: I would have certainly preferred to see us, the United States, put together some sort of international tribunal; perhaps a special kind of international tribunal.

MH: Isn't that the same thing that [Yugoslav President Slobodan] Milosevic is now being tried under? Why not have done the same thing for whoever was behind this?

DC: I think the response is disproportional.

MH: This is *totally* out of control. You take that and then throw the crash of Enron on top of it, with our economy going down the tubes, realize how much money it's costing us to bomb empty caves in Afghanistan every day while our American people are living on the street. There's more hunger and more homelessness, they said, this Christmas in America than ever before.

DC: I think we'll see that increasing. I certainly look at the economy and that's another place where the mainstream media (if you look at CNBC or Bloomberg Television) are painting rosy scenarios with a vengeance.

MH: Here in Arizona, one of the biggest employers is Motorola. Motorola has been slashing jobs like crazy, another 9,500 people are slated to be let go. You've got to start thinking, you're going to have states collapsing, one at a time.

DC: I think Enron is the tip of the iceberg. I'm very concerned. There are a plethora of websites that give you the economic news behind the superficial economic news. It's interesting that what the Federal Reserve has done with all these interest cuts has pumped so much into the system that the dot-com bubble may have deflated; but we've got a money-supply bubble. What I think is fueling the stock market with the little it's gone up recently is all this money that has been put into the economy by the government. It has no place to go. It's false. It's not based upon production. It's not based upon earnings and profits. It's conceivable that we're headed toward a big fall.

MH: The "D" word. They didn't want to admit to a *recession*, but they *did* admit that the recession was legit in March, which was six months before September 11th. I think we're going to see a depression in this country, which is something we really haven't seen since the '20s.

DC: It's very possible. I think that could happen.

MH: It's very scary to think that here we are, everybody wants to go and rebuild Afghanistan, feed the children, and that other photo-op that Bush used getting our kids to send a buck apiece to the kids in Afghanistan (what a joke that is), when we have people here who are starving. We have people here who are in the street and every drop of that bomb, how many people could that money house? How many people could that feed?

DC: Even on the security issue, there's an article that's the top story on my website today from the *Economist*, "America the Unready: Preparations against Another Terrorist Attack." What our first priority should have been was securing our own nation. That has fallen by the wayside in large measure so Bush and his pals can get pumped up with testosterone and go and bomb all these countries. It costs a lot of money.

MH: What happened to the big homeland security? I mean, what have they done? There's an article in last week's newspaper about how the one thing that is selling like wildfire in America is guns. One of the people who bought a gun said, "Well, as far as I'm concerned, Tom Ridge can protect our shores, but I'm going to protect my doors."

DC: I've never been particularly pro-gun, but I have to tell you this. I grew up in Wyoming and I grew up around guns. I'm not frightened of them or anything. I have problems with "gun nuts" who seem to see the gun as the solution to *every* problem that ever would come down the pike, but I think it may be time for liberals and progressives to consider it right now, with this mounting fascist kind of mentality emanating out of Washington, that it's a right in the Constitution. It's only a matter of time before this Administration, in my opinion, will try to find ways to take guns out of the hands of people.

I don't want people to misunderstand me, I'm not believing the gun is the answer to a lot of problems, but it's your right. In a time of increasing chaos, you have to figure out ways to survive and protect yourselves.

MH: It was also written in the Constitution that there's a right to bear arms, to keep your government honest, to protect yourself against too much government, especially if they're going to start questioning any American citizen who speaks out against this Administration and locking people up who are in environmental groups, etc., under the guise of terrorism.

DC: That's why I would encourage anti-gun people and liberals and progressives to perhaps re-evaluate their position a little bit, at this particular time.

MH: I say, "Why should just the bad guys and the crack-heads have the guns?" If every decent citizen in America had training, actually took classes, to know how to handle a weapon and everybody knew you had a weapon in your house, what do you think that would do to the crime in this country? Those are the things that have been tested throughout the years. One town where everybody's armed and trained and one town where they aren't. Which one didn't have any crime? It was a simple test. Of course, the one where everybody was armed had zero crime. That's one thing I'm sure a lot of my Democratic listeners will probably have a little tiff with me about. I lived my whole life in New York and never had a need for a gun before.

DC: I'm not trying to be an alarmist, but I think the situation is such now that we have to re-evaluate how we're going to survive in this world with the potential of further terrorist attacks or renegade action by the Bush regime that will set off a chain of events they have no way of controlling.

MH: Or the fact that now anybody can just bust into your house without a warrant and go through your stuff.

DC: The thing to consider overseas is, we're so dependent upon foreign oil. There's no way we're not going to be dependent upon foreign oil. All it would take would be for one terrorist attack in Saudi Arabia that will send the price of oil up $100.00 a barrel and what will that do to the United States and our economy? We'll be in a desperate, desperate situation.

MH: But why? Because we have refused for decades to go to an alternative fuel.

DC: And those chickens are going to come home to roost. In the big picture, that's what I think a lot of this is all about, is we are running out of cheaply produced oil. We will reach the peak of production of petroleum, worldwide, according to some experts, as soon as next year, according to others, maybe as late as 2010. That's not very far away. What do we do then?

MH: You mean, when there's nobody left to bomb and there's no oil left to bomb for? This is something environmentalists have been talking about for decades. I've been involved in the environmental movement for decades. Here in Arizona, we have sunshine more than 300 days out of the year. Yet, there is no solar energy happening here, very little. It's ludicrous. Then, of course, you get a couple of car manufacturers that put out hybrids, but if they're not big gas-guzzling SUVs [sport utility vehicles], nobody wants to buy them. Until the American public realizes that all these wars have been about oil and trying to steal what doesn't naturally come into our country, we're just going to keep paying the price. Unfortunately, it looks like the price we're going to pay is going to be our children's future.

DC: People should not be deceived right now because the price of oil is down. There are a lot of different reasons for that and September 11th is one reason. Because demand has gone down so much, there is excess supply. This is short-term. I read in the paper today that the prices have bottomed out and they are already starting to go back up some. That is something we're going to have to deal with because even if you installed solar on homes in Phoenix, solar doesn't run an automobile.

MH: You can use wind power; you can use alternative types of fuels. Some farmers discovered there is some kind of grass they can grow that they actually make fuel out of, and they're using it. Why aren't we putting all this money we're wasting on war into these kinds of inventions that are actually working? There were kids in California who figured out how to harness the power of the waves in the ocean and they're getting electricity off that.

DC: And time is wasting, even by some of the best estimates. If we launched a massive program now to find alternative energy sources, it would take us 10 years. Yet, this is one of the other tragic things about the Supreme Court's *coup* that put Bush in the White House. You could not even imagine putting a *more* wrong person into the position.

MH: He's an enemy of the environment. I tried to tell people that during the campaign. I told people if Bush gets into office, we're done. Humankind is done. I paid very close attention. I'm sure you saw *The Omega Report* by those 6,000 scientists on their timetable of how many years we have to turn around the destruction of the environment. We only have three, and Bush will be in office for all of that, so it's not going to happen.

DC: Every day that goes by is now a lost day that is going to lead, unfortunately, to a decline in our prosperity and our way of life. I would encourage all your listeners to visit a website that has almost all of this information. You can get to it through my website by clicking on my "End of Oil" page, but it's Dieoff.org. The name of the site is BrainFood. This fellow has done an excellent job of compiling all of this information in one place.

MH: Another good site like that is LoveEarth.com. I don't know if you are familiar with Mark Elsis [*see* Chapter 14] who has that going on. He also has *The Omega Report* published there.

DC: I see a growing consensus among those who are willing to take a real hard-nosed look at where we are, environmentally and with resources. Our timeline is growing short.

MH: And this politics is only creating more of a delay. All this war and all this waste of time and money and killing of human beings, we really don't get that we're on the verge of extinction. It's almost like maybe we'll beat the time clock before we totally destroy the environment, but maybe we'll end up blowing ourselves to pieces before that.

DC: With my understanding of the world oil shortage that's coming and global warming, what happened on September 11th was just a magnification of what might happen. If an event like that had occurred 30 years ago, it wouldn't have had the same repercussions. For people who take the time to read and study and understand, September 11th has all the feelings of when the Archduke was shot that led to World War I. No one had any conception that that one little event would have led to one of the worst conflagrations the world has ever seen, and massive human suffering—because of the poison gas that occurred during World War I. This is my historical analogy that I see with September 11th: that it has set off a chain of events we simply cannot seem to be able to control. I get so upset with the Bush people, of course, because they seem to be feeding right into it.

MH: People don't get that September 11th *could* have been used as the beginning of world peace. People could have just taken a big long breath, come together, and said, "Let's find the bad guys without blowing half the planet up." You saw the outpouring of love and generosity of people the world over for those victims.

DC: It is my belief that if Al Gore had been duly installed as President, as he should have been, it would have been dealt with differently than the way Bush has done it. With the experience in foreign policy that Gore has, not just the people around him, but he *himself* has, I believe Gore would have taken another approach.

MH: He certainly wouldn't have pulled us out of all those treaties.

DC: He wouldn't have done that and he would have taken the horrible event of 9/11 and turned that into a catalyst to say we have to re-evaluate the way we approach the rest of the world. We could have made lemonade out of lemons and I think Al Gore is that kind of a guy. I think we would not be having these visions of "Apocalypse Now" if he had been installed in the White House as he should have been.

MH: A lot of people take offense at that one. A lot of people who were on Gore's side are a little ticked at him because he's done nothing to come out in the past year. My feeling is, what else could the guy do? They made him look like a sore loser before he even "lost" the presidency to the Supreme Court. If he were to come out and say anything about this Administration, my feeling is, who knows, maybe he'd end up being killed. This is the kind of world we live in.

DC: He *is* in a very difficult position, although many of us are in a difficult position who have decided to offer an alternative point of view.

MH: He's got to be looking at this world situation and saying, "Holy crap, this is all the stuff that for the past 20 years of my life I've been warning people about." It goes beyond when he was Vice President. He was the guy who said we need to take the environment into consideration. He helped pen the Kyoto Treaty. There are a lot of things he would have done right because he understands the need for alternative fuel, but he wasn't a corporate little boy. He wasn't the corporation's big friend. Even the unions turned on him, but what are the unions doing now? They're all bitching and moaning over the Bush Administration. I was crying, begging and pleading before the election. I said, "Please, this is the last chance we are going to have to vote where it's going to matter to the human race, not just America." I said that if we don't put the stop on this clock for environmental destruction, it doesn't matter, we're going to be gone. We're going to be dust.

DC: There are so many tragic things about what happened December 12, 2000 when the Supreme Court did what they did—even for genuine small-"d" democrats and small-"r" republicans. You can read the Constitution, you read the Declaration of Independence. This is what still surprises and disillusions me about true conservatives. I don't believe true conservatives can accept what the Supreme Court did. In fact, a lot of conservative court scholars believe what they did was wrong.

MH: I agree. My son had just turned 21. This was his first presidential election. He waited his whole life to go vote for President. The kid said he was whistling "The Star-Spangled Banner" on his way to the polls. When he sat and watched that whole thing, he had the same attitude of every young person in America. "Why did I vote? My vote didn't mean anything. Why did I bother?" What are they going to do to get people back to the polls if that, indeed, was what they want anyway?

DC: I think it was a tremendous blow to our democracy. And as we find out more and more that we're not being told the truth, that 9/11 is being used for political advantage of one particular party, the disillusionment and cynicism will set in as the economy declines because of the manipulation of corporations like Enron, the shortsightedness on the environmental scene that won't recognize that the oil era is drawing to an end.

MH: What's it going to take? Getting back to soup kitchens and bread-lines?

DC: We're going to lose a lot of the wonderful things we've had in this country.

MH: This isn't the America I grew up in and it's not the America I want for my grandchildren.

DC: I think things have changed and some of it started during the Clinton era. It's been progressively getting worse. There have been more indications of decline and decay in the culture. I don't know if it can be turned around.

MH: I think it can certainly be improved. I'm not giving up until the fat lady sings, or until the fat man shuts up. That's my reference to Rush [Limbaugh].

DC: I do what I do and you do what you do.

MH: And there are thousands of us, tens of thousands of us all over the planet, doing the same thing, pulling together. The best way to change the world is to just let people know what we know. I know that takes a strong fearlessness, especially under this current regime.

DC: Knowledge is power.

MH: I think if every American out there knew what we know, or even half of it, they'd be up-in-arms. They'd be flipping out.

DC: The Internet gives us the ability to acquire that
        knowledge.

MH: Whenever Bush talks, he says we're brave and we're
        strong. He never says we're intelligent. That really
        bothers me. I know it's almost Christmas, but what
        better time of the year to start a whole new way of
        living and thinking?

DC: To your listeners, stay on the Internet and find out
        the truth.

MH: My number one thing is always the environment.
        If you think politics have nothing to do with the
        environment, then you've really got to wake up. If we
        don't worry about the environment, then politics isn't
        going to make a difference.

EIGHT

LEARN FROM THE PAST, OR REPEAT IT

Meria with Bev Conover

Bev Conover,[9] the Publisher and Editor of *Online Journal*, reports that her online publication receives over four million hits a month—and for good reason. Conover and her staff are not afraid to put out the news and opinions of "the people" without the corporate spin. Conover discusses the stolen election and the disenfranchisement of ALL voters in this past election. She discusses Operation Northwoods, how it was tried in Cuba while [John F.] Kennedy was President (he said a loud "No" to its use), and how it could have come into play on 9/11.

Problems facing the few remaining public broadcasting stations and real journalists and how to raise awareness/support are discussed by Conover, as well as the still lingering suspicions surrounding the death (murder?) of Lori Klausitus (what did she know?), the supposed "new" voting machines in Florida, and why people who use the free speech afforded in the Constitution are considered un-American. Other topics discussed are the Army of God's ability to dictate from death row while innocent true patriots are getting arrested—and why it is important for Americans to LEARN our history and develop longer attention spans. (Interview taped/broadcast on January 2, 2002.)

MH: One of my listeners wrote in about an article in the news this week naming the four women "who shape and sell media words, images and ideas for the Bush Administration." The listener said the four women who *should* have been nominated were myself; my guest,who is Bev Conover, the Publisher/Editor of *Online Journal*; Carolyn Kay, from MakeThemAccountable.com (I have had Carolyn on my show); and another woman whom I haven't had the pleasure of meeting yet, but I will find her, Hypathia [www.e-thepeople.org].

My listener said, "I nominate these women who would be far, far healthier for this country in leadership, but would also prevent this country from degenerating any further because they each, with integrity, tell the truth instead of shaping, coloring, changing, tinting, retouching, restructuring, fabricating, and manipulating images and facts as the others have been trained to do for the public to consume for their own self-centered, exclusive right-wing war and class consciousness agenda. These women working the false and manipulating image for the Bush Administration to dupe the public mind must be themselves outdone, out-reported, overcome, and overthrown by the journalism of the new media of integrity carried in the minds and hearts of the likes of Meria, Bev, Hypathia and Carolyn. God bless."

BC: I think one of the saddest things is how all of us who take what we do very seriously, and basically are devoting our lives to it, have to go around with hats in hands, begging, to get financial support, while the other side gets checks from SCAFE [Schlumberger Center for Advanced Formation Evaluation]; they get checks from the Coors family; they get money from foundations. There is something wrong.

MH: There *is* something wrong with that picture. I think for you, as well as for me and a lot of other people I've interviewed, this is our passion. I don't know how we can stop ourselves from doing what we do.

BC: It's not a matter of us looking to get rich. In my case, *Online Journal* needs investigative reporters, even freelancers. Investigative reporting is a very expensive proposition. You could work on a story for months and if you are an honest reporter, you follow the trail. When you get to the end of the trail, you may find out nothing is there, but the reporter still has to eat.

MH: We live in a society in America where the media is fully owned and controlled by corporate America and this Administration. They've got plenty of money. This recession isn't going to hit the millionaires and millionaire Republicans in this country as hard as it's hitting the average person.

BC: Up or down, they make the money.

MH: This "war" is making a lot of people a lot of money.

BC: A friend of mine, Juliet Terzieff, is a freelancer. She covered a lot of the war for CNN International, the war on Kosovo. She just got back from Afghanistan. She told me last night that she's off to Pakistan. Juliet's hand-to-mouth, too. She picks up jobs wherever she can. I can't pay Juliet. I'd love to be able to pay her. I'd love to be able to pay a Greg Palast [*see* Chapter 2]. It's good, in a way, that we're all separated. If they take one of us down, the others can go on. I've been approached by several people in the last few weeks, "Oh, why can't we just combine everything together?" There are several reasons for that. Each of us has a different voice. There are things I won't publish and I'm getting very hard-nosed about it. I don't want to see any wimpy stuff, especially about the September 11th incidents— *horrors*. I don't want to give any accommodations to the other side. We are in a war with them. This is a war of words. I got an e-mail last night from a [Florida] county Democratic chairman.

To give you a little background, back in September [2001], my husband and I spent at least 20 minutes with this man, trying to get him to talk to the county elections supervisor. A woman who purports to be a Democrat went to the Republican county commission, asking to buy or lease touch-screen voting systems. Touch-screen voting systems are the worst possible things. They leave no trail. Even if they spit out a piece of paper, you don't know what is being recorded by that computer. She went to the county commission and they said, "No, we don't have the money. We'll go for an optical scan system." That's a little bit better. At least you have something you can go back and look at. She went back to the commission a second time and cajoled them into going for it at an additional cost of $4.5 million that they don't have. Add that to the first $1.5 million they were going to spend for optical-scan. I sent him an e-mail and I said, "Dear Chairman, how could you have let her do that?"

He e-mailed me back, with the usual response of politicians about how you don't understand and we are trying to rebuild the party in this county and I have no control. Hardly a month later, he sends out an e-mail that the Democratic county executive committee was going to give her an award for getting these touch-screen voting systems. Last night, I get another e-mail he sent out to everyone and in that e-mail, he wants us to go to an affair this month where General John [K.] Singlaub [Ret.] is going to appear, something to do with a World War II memorial. He didn't make it clear, since I thought the one in Washington had been taken care of, whether this is something the local veterans want. I sent him an e-mail saying no self-respecting Democrat would be caught dead in the same room with John Singlaub. John Singlaub has a very, very checkered past. He was OSS [Office of Strategic Services]; he was a founder of the CIA [Central Intelligence Agency]; he was involved with the Contras; he was involved with the Afghan freedom-fighters. He also heads up the United States Council for World Freedom. That organization is so far right-wing, even the John Birch Society will have nothing to do with him. And this comes from a Democratic chairman?

MH: Many of my friends locally who are being solicited by Democrats for money are also equally disgusted. That is another discussion we could have—where have the Democrats been? They've laid down for this stolen election and it doesn't seem to be getting much better since.

BC: I have three theories. One, they can't give up the money (some of them). Two, some of them have been threatened, God knows with what, but use your imagination. I think the anthrax attack business got out of hand. I think the people who did it didn't think it was going to be this bad. And, three, the rest of them are just dumb. Going back to these voting machines. The company involved is Sequoia Voting Systems of Oakland, California. Their senior regional sales manager, Phil Foster, has been indicted by a Louisiana grand jury on a charge of conspiracy to commit bribery. It seems he was involved in an $8 million scam with the Louisiana election commission with Jerry Fowler, who I believe is now in prison. It had to do with parts for lever machines and kickbacks.

The CEO of the company, Peter Cosgrove, said, "This is all nonsense." Meanwhile, my county, Palm

Beach County, Tampa, and Indian River have all opted to go for this company's equipment. The last I heard, Pinellas County was saying they were going to look closer at this company. What's wrong with this picture? Are these people all that stupid?

MH: I don't think it just comes down to people being stupid. I think people don't do their homework any more. I don't know where people grew up or what their learning skills were that were taught to them, but my parents taught me at a very young age to investigate and question *everything*. I think people just take things on face value. "Oh, well, here's a nice company. Okay, let's do it." They could have Hitler behind it and not know the difference.

BC: I think I was born asking, "Why?" I've asked that all my life. Why this, why that? Who makes these rules? Who says?

MH: Who are the "they" that everybody always refers to? Something a lot of people might not know is that you are an award-winning journalist and that you also worked with regular media as a newspaper editor in corporate news.

BC: I only had one experience in corporate news and that was enough.

MH: What made you decide to jump to creating *Online Journal*?

BC: We were in the middle of the Clinton debacle with Kenny Starr going after him and the whole Whitewater thing. I kept getting angrier by the second and I happened to meet Jane Prettyman online. She was an editor, as she put it, at "the old *Esquire*." At that time, she was running a website called thereal-newspage.com. The website right now is called

Americanreview.net and all the information is still there. It's a wonderful website. Her focus was on media reform. Jane and I struck up a relationship, and we were exchanging e-mails back and forth. I told her I wanted to do something because I couldn't take this. She kept encouraging and persuading me. I kept thinking about it and formulating it.

Finally, on September 5, 1998, I did it. I was amazed at the response. My readership kept going up every month. Then, something happened toward the end of August 2000. I had gone to Europe that spring with a friend. Starting in August 2000, all of a sudden, the numbers just started to mushroom. I had said to some people my gut feeling is that they're going to steal this election. I wondered how many other people had that same feeling. Then, in March 2001, I got invited on C-Span. I forget how many minutes they gave me. The host wasn't Brian Lamb that day. The host was not very happy with me. The numbers after that were just phenomenal—and it hasn't stopped.

MH: What do you figure your average numbers are?

BC: I'm getting about four million hits a month and growing.

BC: I just watch them bounce. I am now reaching into every continent on the planet. I had some fellow in Tehran sign on, would you believe it?

MH: Every now and then I get a new country and I add it to my listener list. Sometimes, I can barely pronounce the name of it.

BC: The only way I can keep track is because my readers insist I also set up an e-mail mailing list and from those, it'll disclose where they are.

MH: There are a handful of exceptional news sites online and *Online Journal* is one of the best. It seems like you're one of the first, also. I know a lot of my listeners check out *Online Journal* because they all barrage me with news every day from 25 different sites and I get a lot of your stuff.

BC: I don't know which of us is the oldest. *American Politics Journal* [www.americanpolitics.com] has been around, going back I think to 1986. I know when I met Jane Prettyman, she had been at it for four years. Jane's focus was strictly on media reform. There are excellent materials on her site. If you want to know who's who and what they're up to, you go to her site. Another excellent site I always check out for who owns what is the *Columbia Journalism Review*. You keep hearing about your dear congressmen as they give the cable industry more and more, and now they want to muck with the satellite industry so that we have all these choices. That is a lie. Look at who owns all this stuff. A&E is owned by the biggies; Discovery is owned by the biggies. We don't have choices. We have the same corporate media in different clothing.

You made a remark in your program yesterday that I found absolutely fascinating. It had to do with the World Trade Center and why there were so few people there on September 11th. You've heard of Operation Northwoods? Have you gone through that with your listeners? If you have, I'm not going to do that.

MH: I've touched on it.

BC: James Bamford [*Body of Secrets* and *The Puzzle Palace*], who writes books about the National Security Agency, stumbled across Operation Northwoods on a Freedom of Information Act request. Operation Northwoods was cooked up, I think in 1961 or so, by the Joint Chiefs of Staff, which [General] Lyman [L.] Lemnitzer headed at that time. The object of this was to create incidents of terror in this country, in Guantanamo [Cuba], even pretend that an airliner went down to blame it on Castro so the American people would go to war with Cuba. When [President John F.] Kennedy heard about this, [former Secretary of Defense Robert [S.] McNamara initially told him no immediately. Kennedy had a fit. Lemnitzer was immediately removed as the Chief of the Joint Chiefs. All of these documents were supposed to have been destroyed to spare the Joint Chiefs embarrassment. Bamford's latest book comes out in April [2001] and what do we have in September [2001]?

MH: It looks to me like another Operation Northwoods.

BC: It's possible.

MH: I grew up in New York City and I was in and out of the World Trade Center many times, especially when I worked downtown on Maiden Lane. I know the amount of population in those buildings on any given day, especially during the week, at 9:00 in the morning. The fact that, first of all, the figures were so grossly exaggerated, actually more than doubled the amount of people who actually were lost there. There's a big difference between 2,945 and 6,000. At that time of the day, given the figures, already this thing stinks.

BC: They keep discovering, as time goes by, more and more companies that told their employees not to come in that morning.

MH: I understand there were also some e-mails and traces of Instant Messages found that were sent to people one or two hours before, that the buildings were going to be bombed. There are journalists in New York who said they were not allowed on the sides of the buildings. They were only allowed to cover them from a certain angle and they said at that time to whoever was running that operation, "What are you guys hiding? What do you *not* want us to see?" Typical New Yorkers are certainly not the type to just retreat and say, "Oh, okay, I won't go there."

BC: The reporters at the Pacifica station in New York, WBAI, encountered the same thing. Eustis Lead, who was the general manager at that time, put out an edict that they would not discuss this. He's gone now.

MH: I know Pacifica on the West Coast, the station manager, I believe it was, went in and actually slapped one of the women while she was broadcasting because they were forbidden to do any news on September 11th.

BC: That was in New York and was, I believe, Amy Goodman.

MH: How insane is that? This was the biggest story since the stolen election.

BC: Pacifica has gone through how many years of agony now? I'm hoping, for their sake, that they have won the battle because the board that took it over tried to sell off the assets and turn what was left into just another commercial music station. Regardless of whether you agree with Pacifica's political view or not, it was disgusting that no one else in the major media stood up for these people.

MH: I understand they were broadcasting from their parking lot. They were getting physically assaulted on the job. How crazy is that? What happened to free speech in America? There are a couple of words that are huge in the news—the corporate news, should I say—this past year. They are actually grinding these words into my nerves already. I wanted to just throw the words at you and see what comes up for you. One of the words I've noticed over and over again is "unprecedented." Have you noticed how often "unprecedented" is in the news today? It's like everything that's happened since this stolen election is unprecedented.

BC: Are you aware that when [former Speaker of the House] Newt Gingrich took over GOPAC (Republican campaign training organization), he published a little booklet that was passed out to the membership? It was a booklet of words you use on Democrats and words you use on Republicans. Frank Bozell is the man who coined the phrase "liberal media." Go all the way back to when Kennedy was killed. All you had on the news was what a "sick people" we were. I didn't pick up a gun and kill John Kennedy, but we were a "sick people." We lost our innocence in the middle of that one. We are in a propaganda war. You laid out so nicely in your piece yesterday, all the things that have been buried by this total focus on September 11th.

MH: It was all a smoke-screen. Everything important got swept away and, believe me, as an ex-New Yorker, I am *not* downsizing what happened at the World Trade Center.

BC: What happened at the World Trade Center was heinous, but it was a *criminal* act. It was not an act of war. You cannot make war on an idea.

MH: I didn't see it as any different than the Oklahoma City bombing.

BC: Interestingly, Osama was "our" bastard, just as Saddam [Hussein] was, as [Fidel] Castro was, until the day we turned on him.

MH: You can't sleep with somebody one day and then the next day, all of sudden, make him the worst person on the face of the earth.

BC: [Former U.S. President and founding father Thomas] Jefferson understood that you had to demonize your opponent. When he wrote the Declaration of Independence, he didn't put the blame on the Parliament, which was the problem; he put it all on poor old George III. This is an *old* propaganda method. I've said to people, "You know, it's reallynot good to be a friend of the Bush family because when they don't need you any more, you will be thrown to the dogs." This is not to say that Saddam is a *nice* guy. Osama is not a nice guy. Osama is a crazy fanatic. I caught a documentary the other night called "Soldiers of the Army of God." The Army of God has no head or tail. We can't get our hands on anybody.

MH: They did find the one guy who was a member of that who was sending out anthrax to all those abortion clinics.

BC: The documentary proves it is a lie, that there is no organization. They have a white rose dinner up in Washington every year for all their members who have gone to jail or prison for bombing abortion clinics or killing abortion doctors. One of their members, Paul [J.] Hill, who was a Presbyterian minister, who killed Dr. [John Bayard] Britton, is sitting on death row. I am not a fan of the death penalty, but the man is sitting on death row for what he did. From death row, he is sending out word to the rest of these people to go out and kill abortion doctors, workers, and so forth. What is the difference between those people and an Osama bin Laden?

MH: Either you're a homegrown nut or you're an imported nut. That's the difference, which is *no* difference, as far as I'm concerned. What's really interesting is, these Army of God people are allowed total freedom of speech and journalists in this country are not. Does anybody see something wrong with that picture? There was a young boy who was trying to get on an airplane with a book that didn't comport with current public opinion, and he was not permitted to fly on the plane.

BC: How about all the people, which I wrote about a week ago, who have been paid visits by the FBI and the Secret Service on tips that they're harboring "un-American material"?

MH: How can that be un-American and things like the Army of God or most of the entire Christian Network not be considered un-American?

BC: Maybe one of your listeners abroad can give us an answer to this question. Have you ever heard of anybody being called un-French, un-Italian, un-British, un-Canadian?

MH: I never have.

BC: But if we speak out against the propaganda being spewed at us day and night, *we* are "un-American."

MH: And how do they define "American"? By somebody who's totally mind-controlled by the media, a couch potato who just follows like a sheep?

BC: If you go back to the '50s, this was the name of the game at that time. With [former U.S. Senator Joseph] McCarthy and all of them running loose. You know, "un-American."

MH: They were madmen. We could take this even further into: why is it that we don't have more women in power in this country, not only in this country, but all over the world?

BC: We have a big problem. I'm of the opinion that there is a deep streak of anti-intellectualism in America and especially with all the emphasis on sports. We talk about violence in movies and violence in videogames, which is absolute nonsense. The kids are sitting there and they're watching *real* violence on the playing fields, with the sportscasters going, "Oh, gee, look at that. Isn't that great." We don't connect to that. If you think back to the '60s, remember the cry of academic freedom and the students of that era decided that history was irrelevant? Florida is a state that has no requirement for history, to graduate from high school.

Americans do not know their history. Many Americans think the world began the day they were born, and they've got a five-minute attention span. They are in denial. A friend of mine made an observation recently that you've got to be careful when you shake people's centers. You can relate that to when the Soviet Union fell and all those people who had devoted their lives to so-called communism, they were lost. (Of course, the Soviet Union *never* had communism, they just had plain old totalitarianism.) Their centers were just shattered and they could not face up to the fact that they had spent their lives living a lie. I think this is the problem here. The recent events are a play for global corporate domination.

MH: And whether people call it a One World Order or the IMF [International Monetary Fund] or whatever they want to look at it as, it's obvious what's going on all over the planet.

BC: I told my cousin, "You know, we've been trying to tell you this for years," and she said, "Oh, yeah, you've always been gloom-and-doom, but it's not in the local paper."

MH: For many years, I've been out there advocating for the environment, and for truth, justice and what I like to call it the "humanitarian way" because I don't believe truth and justice and "the American way" is necessarily truth and justice. People have told me the same thing, "Meria, you're so doom-and-gloom. Why do you talk about this?" Blah, blah, blah. But the day after September 11th *and on* September 11th, I cannot tell you how many of those same people called me and said, "You were right." And I said to them, "I didn't *want* to be right. This was *never* about being right."

BC: No, it's sort of a curse.

MH: It *is* a curse. I tried to explain that to my sisters who have what I would call *normal* lives. This is like a virus I have. I've been born with it and I can't shake it. I still want to know the whys and wherefores of everything. The day after the stolen election, when we had a president who wasn't elected, I really got the impact of that.

BC: We had a president who was not elected, but he was *selected* by five Supreme Court justices. They disenfranchised every person who went to the polls. The only thing that counted was their five votes.

MH: All I know is that day I knew that whatever illusion I had about America as my country, I lost, and I felt like I had lost my country.

BC: You are not alone.

MH: I found that out from a lot of my listeners. I was like one of those TV evangelists throughout that whole campaign, saying, "Listen, I'm not saying [former U.S.

Vice President] Al Gore is the second coming of Christ, but he's the last chance we have."

BC: You cannot know how much time I spent arguing with Greens [members of the U.S. Green Party].

MH: I predicted what we'd find ourselves in with Bush. And now that people are experiencing it, it's like, "But what are *you* going to do about it?"

BC: I made tee-shirts that say, "If they steal your vote, the rest doesn't matter." Journalists have to get the word out. As I explained with regard to investigative reporters, even if the reporter winds up with just enough to sustain himself, it takes money to get documents. It takes money to make phone calls and if a reporter has to travel to get something. One of my contributors (and all my writers are volunteers, none of them get paid) has been trying since August to get some information. He put in an FOIA [Freedom of Information Act] request to the Pentagon for all the materials that pertain to the military absentee ballots. He told them he was a reporter for *Online Journal.* They were not going to give this to him unless he paid. Now, we are talking in excess of $1,000.00.

MH: How do they justify that cost?

BC: I can't right now give you the convoluted reply they sent him.

MH: In other words, they want to make it as difficult as possible for anybody to get to the truth.

BC: I sent a letter myself requesting this same information back in October [2001], sent it certified mail, return receipt requested. We have heard nothing. I have not even gotten the signature card back. I was in the post office a few weeks ago and I mentioned this to them.

First, the clerk says to me, "Well, I don't think the Pentagon accepts certified mail." I told her she had sold it to me, so what did she mean? She said, "Maybe I'm wrong; maybe it's the State Department. Bring the receipt in." I got another e-mail from this reporter last week, a reporter who works for one of the print magazines. He also put in the same request. Now, this man is very experienced at FOIA requests and he told my reporter it was the worst package of stuff he had ever gotten. It was worthless.

MH: This Administration's intention is to hide all their tracks. This is the most secret administration we've seen in a very long time.

BC: They *have* to be, otherwise George's daddy would be on his way to prison.

MH: And they keep giving us all this crap that it's in the name of national security. *Everything* is national security. I haven't seen anything done *really* in the name of national security. Start with the airlines on down, what have they done? Nothing. By the time they finish arguing over what they're *going* to do, who knows what could happen?

BC: All of this security nonsense is to make people feel good, to give them a false sense of security. The only thing it is there for is to hassle *us*.

MH: *We're* the ones who are being punished.

BC: The men who got aboard those planes on September 11th did not buy their tickets at the last minute, did not pay for them with cash, did not buy one-way tickets. There was nothing to indicate what they were about to do.

MH: How about the passenger list? None of them were listed on the passenger list. None of them had seats on the plane. Every plane recorded fewer people on it than were actually on it if we supposedly had all these hijackers onboard. And, then, of the people who were using their cell phones to call home, not one of them identified these people as being of a foreign nationality, nor did they say they were being mistreated in any way.

BC: There are a lot of puzzles to this whole thing. Even if these guys took their little box cutters and hid them under their belts, which would have obviously set off a metal detector, then we would have wound up with, "Oh, well, it's the belt, go through."

MH: This past weekend in Florida (Florida's so famous now since 2000), this guy arrived, after changing planes twice, with a loaded gun in his carry-on. How does that happen? And they still give you the crap that you're supposed to feel safe about flying.

BC: One of my cousins flew down from Chicago about two weeks afterwards, and I was wondering if they were going to shut the airports down. When we took her back to the airport, we were on the people-mover. As we were going by, I glanced over and there was this pile of unattended luggage. Meanwhile, the airport is crawling with so-called security people.

MH: On that plane from Paris to Miami, they did stop to arrest the guy with the bomb in his shoe.

BC: Why didn't they just continue on to Miami—they had the guy strapped in the seat, with doctors shooting valium into him—instead of hassling the passengers for 15 hours in Boston?

MH: Because they have to continue to create fear to justify their war effort.

BC: And people are falling for this.

MH: But then they let those passengers shop in the duty-free stores while they were laid over before they got back on the plane and didn't get re-checked, so they could have picked up *any*thing in one of those duty-free stores.

BC: I remember as a kid, my mother had a glass knife. I think it was a cake knife. It was as sharp as any metal knife I've ever seen. So what does this mean? They're not going to pick up a glass knife if somebody's got one in the luggage. Now, they've taken all the food away from the passengers so they don't get little plastic knives.

MH: What happened to the big promise of a sky marshal on every plane?

BC: My husband has nothing against flying, but he objects to the maintenance and, now, of course, you've got this other thing going on.

MH: Last month, you wrote an article and said we have a sociopath in the White House.

BC: I also do RadioLeft just about every Friday and I said it there, too. I do believe the man is a sociopath.

MH: Anybody who has done their homework and read the books that are out, especially the one that was banned, [Jim Hatfield's] *Fortunate Son* [*see* Chapter 6], knows that. It's too bad what happened to Jim, but he was a typical case of being harassed and railroaded.

BC: There's a lot more to that and, here again, we need an investigative reporter. It is very possible that Jim did kill himself, but if he did it, he was pushed to it.

MH: What I think a lot of Americans need to realize is while they're so quick to jump on the bandwagon to call us all anti-Americans, unpatriotic, a lot of people already have given their lives trying to uncover truth.

BC: I think it's more than Jim. We have the strange death of Lori Klausitus here in Florida.

MH: That story just came across to me from somebody who wants me to pursue it. I've been very interested in it and I said, "Send me the documentation and stuff that you have." But I understand her parents are not really interested in pursuing it. There are those who get out there and just start threatening people. Al Gore, who I knew was a powerful man, and who wouldn't take crap off of anybody, just went off quietly. I thought, "What kind of threat did this guy get?"

BC: I had been working with a group of ordinary citizens who, basically, have turned themselves into an investigative team. And they investigated the whole Klausitus death. Florida has a peculiar medical examiner with a checkered history. He's been kicked out of Missouri for falsifying autopsy reports. He put down that this woman had some kind of a cardiac arrhythmia, which caused her to faint, to hit her head on the desk, which caused a hematoma, and she died, except when they finally got their hands on the autopsy report, she had multiple skull fractures and one that was seven inches long.

MH: And that was in a congressman's office.

BC: Right here in Florida. I don't think there was anything between him and Klausitus, but what did she know about the election? Her husband is involved in a military "project," shall we put it that way. What did she know there? I mean, we just don't feel that her death was necessarily accidental.

MH: Look at all these so-called coincidences. Remember all the coincidental deaths after Kennedy was shot? The American public is lazy and they would rather accept something that makes no sense at all than to have to do their homework.

BC: [Ohio Congressman] John Kasich, who was the darling of the Republicans, decided not to run for Congress again; Gary Condit and Chandra Levy; [U.S. Representative] Joe Scarborough's aide, Lori Klausitus. Now, those three men were tight friends.

MH: Nobody seems to make that connection.

BC: And, then, we have Jim Hatfield's death shortly before the death of Klausitus.

MH: I get reports online from time to time that there are actually agents, FBI and CIA agents, who have also disappeared from their families.

BC: And now we're having scientists disappear—one, they finally found his body floating in the Mississippi.

MH: They left that to the local police even though his body basically floated into the next state. They decided to leave that to the local police because the FBI is supposedly checking every possible lead, which you know is bullshit. We've never gotten a definition of the word "terrorist," which means we all are terrorists.

BC: If we're not with them, we're against them, but that's an old Bush family trick.

MH: And, then, there's the U.S.A. Patriot Act, which is *really* ridiculous. Look at how much Gestapo techniques have come into play since 2,950 people died at the World Trade Center.

BC: *We're* terrible if we use the "F" word: "fascist."

MH: Then, call me terrible.

BC: And you're even worse if you use the word "conspiracy" because you know conspiracy theorists are *all* nuts. Yes, there *are* nutty conspiracies.

MH: I think it's a well thought-out plan. A lot of people in the service looked at the September 11th thing and said it was a very high military intelligence coup. They said there's no way anybody could have pulled that off on their own.

BC: One of my writers, James Higdon, is a lawyer. He and I had a number of exchanges in regard to conspiracies. Jim wrote a piece, which I think explains it beautifully. It was called "A Primer on Understanding Conspiracies." You can find it on my site under "Special Reports." It's a very enlightening piece. It gets rid of all the nonsense that you have some large group of people who are all involved in this—a cabal, holding secret meetings.

Jim explains it as a wheel and only the hub knows the game plan. Folks wittingly or unwittingly are packed toward the hub. If a spoke goes down, you replace it. Then you've got the rim. It's beautiful. This thing really should be spread as wide and far as possible, because Americans *are* in denial.

MH: We're on the verge of World War III here with nuclear power. I think it's time for America to start waking up and saying, "Maybe we *did* piss off some other people in another country by doing something nasty."

BC: Americans have become nothing but worker ants. And that's not to say the people over there [in Europe] don't work, but it's so different. At the cafés, you don't see people getting drunk. You don't see their kids tearing up the place.

MH: We could do 12 shows on why I think that is—the difference between us as a society and the rest of the world—but Americans can convince themselves very nicely, through Bush's help, that these other countries don't like us because we're all doing so well.

BC: In Europe, it's considered gauche to flaunt your wealth. So, they don't do that. You get the ugly American, as in "I'm an American, gangway, here I come." On a one-to-one basis, they like us. They don't like what our government is doing and has done in our name.

MH: As Americans, we support America, but not necessarily Bush or this Administration. I was reading about a man in India who, when they interviewed him about this impending terror on the planet between India and Pakistan, he said, "*All* our leaders are crazy." He said they don't understand any of the common man's plight. I think Americans need to start letting the rest of the world know that we don't agree with what's going on. We got the shit shoveled to us in this election and look at what *we're* going through.

BC: Americans *let* this happen. You know, as [former U.S. President] Harry Truman said, "The buck stops here." We let this happen. Maybe not you and me, individually, but, collectively, we let this happen. Then, I'm sure you get the same e-mail from people all the time asking, "What can I do?"

MH: You can get involved locally.

BC: Jerry Crawford came up with a brilliant idea in a piece he wrote for me last week. I e-mailed him and said, "Jerry, we're in the age of slogans; we've got to come up with a hot slogan for this one." Jerry looked around and told me we can bring the corporations to their knees by only buying what we *absolutely* need. During the election campaign last year, Pizza Hut ran some nasty ads smearing Gore. Gore is no angel. He may be the type of guy who might have been great at governing, but lousy at campaigning. He's got flaws. He's one of the "new" Democrats. They suck at the same corporate trough as the Republicans. We started an e-mail campaign to Pizza Hut and said, "If you don't get that commercial off the air, we're not buying any more of your products." We went after M&Ms, Mars Candy, the same way, for the nasty commercial they were doing.

MH: Somebody sent me an article listing all the corporations that support this Administration, recommending that we boycott them.

BC: If we, just in general, curb our spending. People don't even have to leave their homes to do this.

MH: It's the best way to vote.

BC: Think of all the time that was spent e-mailing, snail-mailing, calling, faxing the White House. I said, "First of all, they have put in blocks on your e-mail. Your mail is going right in the trash. You're spinning your wheels. You're not going to reach them this way."

MH: The best way is through the pocket.

BC: Through the pocketbook. Europeans understand that.

MH: There's no doubt that we are a consumer society. Consume, consume. I, personally, hate to go shopping to buy *any*thing.

BC: I'm not going to criticize if some people do because if we don't buy, they don't make; and then, there are no jobs.

MH: I can understand the concept of just buying what you absolutely need. We do collect a lot of junk in our lives and people really do need to vote with their dollars. It's kind of like all the vegetarian doctors I've had on this show. They say, every time you pick up your fork, you're voting. So, you know, people can do a lot.

BC: Think how quickly in Germany they brought Shell Oil to its knees. They all stopped buying from Shell Oil.

MH: I've been boycotting Mobil/Exxon here for a year now. These global movements are also very valuable. There is a lot people can do without really making a huge effort. I know people's lives are over-scheduled. They really don't have time. The little things you can do really do make a difference when you have several million people doing it.

NINE

CORPORATE MEDIA'S CULPABILITY
Meria and John Nichols

John Nichols,[10] is the author of *Jews for Buchanan: Did You Hear the One About the Theft of the American Presidency?* Nichols is also a well-known writer for *The Nation.* His book deals with the stolen 2000 election and what it means to every American and every citizen of Planet Earth. The disenfranchisement of black people, in general, and in Florida, in particular, is nothing new, but Nichols presents many facts about the laws of Florida regarding the black "race" and the need for REAL reform, not just for blacks, but for ALL the voters of all parties who were disenfranchised by the Supreme Court's decision in 2000.

Nichols shares his research about the responsibility of the corporate media in helping throw the 2000 election from the outset through the web they spin; how Katherine Harris in Florida overstepped her legal bounds (through loyalty to Bush) to stop real democracy; the need for voter reform in America; and the need for people to re-connect and get re-involved in the democratic process or we will LOSE it. A Supreme Court that will steal an election will stop at nothing, as the news since the "election" has shown.

Were Jews *really* for Buchanan in Florida? Certainly you do not believe that. Even Buchanan admitted they were not his votes. Nichols does not espouse one political party over another, but he speaks to the issue of voters "disenfranchised" by the Supreme Court overruling the lower courts, the Electoral College, and YOUR vote. We must be educated and regain our democracy. The whole world is watching. (Interview taped/broadcast on January 15, 2002.)

MH: John Nichols has co-written some books with another one of my guests, Robert McChesney [*see* Chapter 10]. John's got a great view of what really happened during the stolen election and he presented some new points in this.

JN: I've covered presidential politics for a long time and started full-time covering presidential politics in the 1988 campaign, and have done every one since. I'm a believer in our political system. I have more faith in it than a lot of people do, so I write a book like the one we're discussing today not with glee so much as a sense of real disgust and concern.

MH: I looked at all the blurbs on the back of the book, and the one that I have to agree with the most is the one from Studs Terkel, where he says, "This book is sensational. It's the best thing anyone's written on that whole damn election, period."

JN: I didn't start writing the book the day after the election. I waited until well into 2001 so we could see some of the aftermath and look at a lot of the data that began to come out slowly after the theft of the presidency. And waiting that period of time, I think, gave us a lot more information and a lot more ammunition to make the case.

MH: One thing I learned from your book (and we talk about disenfranchisement of the voters of Florida) was just how deep and old those laws are against blacks in Florida.

JN: It's a stunning reality because we like to think of America as a nation that is in a constant process of progress and, hopefully, moving toward better approaches to all sorts of issues, particularly race issues. But the fact of the matter is that Florida was a Confederate state. In the aftermath of the Civil War, people who were associated with the Ku Klux Klan and with the Confederate revolt against the Union used positions of power in that state to place a number of laws on the books that were designed to disenfranchise African-American voters. It was done at the time because the North was forcing Florida to allow African-Americans to vote. They very carefully wove in all sorts of structures to undermine that pressure.

Many of those structures, amazingly enough, have remained on the books. One of them is the law that bars ex-felons, people who have served their time, who have been released and are completely outside of the criminal justice process, from voting in elections. Florida is one of only a handful of states that has such a law. And that law in Florida disqualifies hundreds of thousands of African-American males.

MH: I thought that once somebody served their time, that was it—that was their punishment.

JN: The disenfranchisement of ex-felons—people who have served their time—is really one of the cruelest and most undemocratic and, I would argue, most un-American legislation you can have on the books because it essentially says to somebody, "If you make one mistake—even though a bad mistake—you can never get it right. You can never again be a citizen."

MH: So it's just another way of holding people down, forever.

JN: Remember, this is a state where we *know* there have been tremendous abuses of the criminal justice process. When we talk about "ex-felons" in this context, we are talking sometimes about folks who didn't commit a crime. More importantly, the way those laws were applied in 1999 and 2000 were dramatically more draconian than even the people who wrote them back in the 19th century imagined. The connection of old racist laws with new high technology is a very dangerous thing. What happened in Florida was, they took the lists of voters and they ran them against lists of ex-felons and *possible* ex-felons, not even people who really are.

MH: It seems like all you needed was a possible "black last name" to qualify for that list.

JN: It was certainly very poorly done and we know that thousands of eligible voters who had *no* criminal record whatsoever were either denied the right to vote or were hassled in horrible ways when they went to the polling place. Can you imagine walking into a polling place where you've voted your entire life and being told for the first time you cannot vote because you're a criminal? And you *know* you're not a criminal, but how do you argue with that? And do you know who people in Florida had to appeal to when they were accused of being an ex-felon? They had to appeal to Jeb Bush's clemency committee.

MH: You also said in your book how Katherine Harris' office really pushed hard to put on the pressure to purge a lot of names of "ex-felons."

JN: At a time when Florida was supposedly experiencing some budgetary tightness, the state allocated more than $4 million for the process of purging the names of ex-felons. That's the most money ever spent on it in the entire history of the state. They told the private corporation that was hired to do this purging of so-called ex-felons, to *expand* the parameters. People at the corporation said, "Look, if we do it the way you're telling us, we know that innocent people's names will turn up on these lists of folks being told they cannot vote." Katherine Harris' office—this is undebatable; it absolutely happened—said, "We don't care, go ahead and expand the parameters."

MH: People really didn't know much about Katherine Harris at that point, but I remember somewhere in your book where you said that when Alan Dershowitz went down there, he obviously knew a little bit more about her than most other people did.

JN: He was highly critical of her and said, "You know, look, this woman's a wheeler-dealer. She's a political insider and she's here to attack the democratic processes." Dershowitz was viciously attacked for those statements. He was called unfair. He was criticized by all sorts of top [President George W.] Bush aides, all sorts of Republican governors; and the fact is, he was stating an absolute truism. Katherine Harris is the granddaughter of an old segregationist state legislator down there, a millionaire who was an incredibly powerful player in Central Florida. She grew up in a political family. She knows her way around the processes of that state. She was not a stupid, pretty girl who just worried about her hair or her nails as she was sometimes portrayed in the media.

MH: I think the portrayal of Cruella deVille was more accurate.

JN: She was a dangerous player.

MH: Let's not forget, she was totally out on Bush's side.

JN: She was his state campaign co-chair and she had traveled to New Hampshire during the primary campaign to campaign for him. Her ties to the Bush campaign were well-established. There is no question that in any sort of legal or political context that was legitimate, she should have recused herself from the process. She should *not* have been overseeing that recount and she *certainly* should not have been the person placed in a position of deciding when the count should end, and then ultimately certifying the results. It would be like having the coach of one football team as the official for the game.

MH: I read in your book that they put all the crappy voting machines in the black neighborhoods, or not enough voting machines—and how some blacks were basically stopped on the roads at roadblocks and given fake shakedowns, anything to prevent them from voting.

JN: There's no question that there were all sorts of structural and official roadblocks to African-American participation. It's important to make the distinction there. A lot of the structural roadblocks are the same roadblocks that we have to the advancement of poor folks and people of color in so many areas of this country. Because they come from a poor area that receives poor services, they have less of an opportunity to participate in the political process, i.e., the machines are old, the technologies don't work, the likelihood of a mistake is higher—the structural flaws.

Then, you also had the official flaw. You did have this aggressive purge effort by the Secretary of State's office. You had, in some instances, state patrol officers setting up roadblocks at exits from the freeway that took people to predominantly African-American polling places. Finally, you had some cases where it is clear the ballot design was done, if not intentionally, at least with malignant neglect. The ballots were designed in a way that they were going to produce a much higher level of error.

MH:	I found the ballot here in Arizona to be very screwy. It looked to me like it was an eye test. I had to use my finger and my eye to make sure the box lined up with the name of the candidate. So, it wasn't just Florida.

JN:	All Florida did was offer us a window to a much broader crisis in this country.

MH:	It is a *big* crisis. It goes back to what Howard Winant [*see* Chapter 5] said in his book, *The World Is a Ghetto*, how this is history, continually putting down the darker races. People want to believe in the fairy tale that in America, this has gone away. They need to wake up and definitely read at least Chapter 2 in your book, "Deliberate Disenfranchisement."

JN:	I would argue that it is important to recognize that many of these discriminatory policies did not merely harm African-Americans. They also harmed poor and working-class white folks and others.

MH:	It's harmed the whole country by installing the wrong president.

JN:	And look at the people who suffered perhaps the most horrific form of disenfranchisement: elderly Jews. Many of them were Holocaust survivors. Others, like retired garment workers from New York with long traditions of union activism, many of them immigrants and children of immigrants, who ended up, because of a criminally bad ballot design in Palm Beach County, casting their ballots for Pat Buchanan.

MH:	And I remember Pat Buchanan coming out on TV and saying, "These were *not* my votes. These had to be Gore votes." Even *he* knew the Jews weren't going to vote for him.

JN: Well, of course not. Pat Buchanan, who I happen to disagree with on just about everything, is at least an honest player. I interviewed him for the book and we did a chapter on him. He was frank about the fact that there was no way he could have gotten the number of votes that he did in Palm Beach County. He didn't campaign there. It was overwhelmingly Democratic, predominantly a Jewish and African-American county. It was not the kind of place Pat Buchanan was going to get what he got, which was his best percentage in the nation.

MH: How obvious was that?

JN: The ballot was a disaster, there's no doubt about that, but the crime came about in the aftermath of the election. In the most developed nation in the world, where we can send smart bombs down the chimneys of factories in Afghanistan, we cannot figure out how to rectify a clearly flawed voting process. After it became clear that thousands of Palm Beach County voters had been deceived by a bad ballot into voting for someone they didn't want, and after it became clear that 20,000 ballots were disqualified in Palm Beach County because of the confusing structure of the ballot, once that happened, there should have been some way to rectify the crisis. And, in fact, there is. Florida law allows for a new vote. There was every effort to block a new vote. It was absurd and wrong.

MH: I had two opinions at the time. I said, we throw the state of Florida out totally or we get the whole state to vote again.

JN: I tend to lean toward the second view. I don't like disenfranchising people. It is clear that the results that were certified for Florida were not accurate results. Much better than certifying *inaccurate* results would be to certify nothing. Democracy can only work if it's flexible and it ought to have been flexible enough to have recognized this as crisis and corrected it.

MH: On page 70 in your book, you have an example of one of the ballots that was discarded as an "overvote." It's very clear that the only circle checked is for Al Gore, and the person actually *wrote* "Al Gore" on the bottom where it says, "Write-in," and yet, this was tossed.

JN: 1,800 such ballots were disqualified in Florida, *1,800* of them.

MH: Short of Helen Keller, *anybody* could have told that this was a vote for Al Gore.

JN: I think even Helen probably could have figured it out. When I started working on the research for this book, I began with the sense that something bad had happened in Florida, no doubt of that. But I still probably thought that people like you were just a little too extreme, that you were just belaboring the point to a level that didn't make sense. When I finished the research, I thought the Meria Hellers of the world aren't complaining *enough*.

MH: My mouth is going to keep this one going until who knows when. Let's take a look at what's happened in America in the short one-year time that this un-elected president has been sitting in office.

JN: Remember that the bottom line is, no matter how good or bad a president George W. Bush is, he has no *right* to claim the office. Even if he was the greatest president in American history, the person holding the presidency is less important than the democracy that underpins the office. And when we allow a casual disregard of ballots and of the democratic processes — which clearly occurred when the Supreme Court intervened — we do tremendous damage. I've made this case to Republican friends of mine and argued this could just as easily have happened in the reverse. You could have had a state that was very strongly controlled by Democrats, and Al Gore clearly lost the state, but then through a lot of finagling and wheeling and dealing, they might have turned the process.

I don't think that would have happened, but I'm telling you, in the realm of politics, all things are possible. They have to recognize that the biggest responsibility we have as American citizens is to defend the integrity and honor of this democratic process. When we let it fall apart, when we let it be undermined on one side, ultimately it will be vulnerable on all sides. I strongly believe that Republicans should be as angry about this as Democrats.

MH: I argued that position with a couple of attorneys I had on the show because attorneys tend to see things only from a legal point of view. The one point I always tried to make was if the Supreme Court picked the president, they really disenfranchised *every* American voter, regardless of what party you voted on.

JN: An important fact is that 213 years of American history passed without the Supreme Court ever intervening to settle a presidential election, and we have had much more complicated and contested elections than this one in the past. The election of 1800, the election of 1824, the election of 1860, the election of 1876, all had multi-candidate races and much more confusion than we had in 2000. And, yet, the Supreme Court did *not* intervene. The fact that it intervened at this point, and in the way that it did, was a dramatic assault on the democracy.

MH: We have the right to vote, but our vote really doesn't mean anything, so our democracy is not a pure or real democracy.

JN: We are a democratic republic, of course, and thus, we're not a pure democracy. Our democracy runs on a set of rules, i.e., we have a system in place designed to divine the will of the people and to turn that will of the people into the structure of our governance, i.e., who holds particular offices. That structure, the democratic processes, the rules, were what were attacked in 2000 and the Supreme Court was the one body that should have been at the forefront of defending those rules, defending those laws, and defending those structures. [Vincent] Bugliosi is right when he argues they should be facing charges of treason.

MH: At that time, Alan Dershowitz also came out with a book. I think his was called *Supreme Injustice*. He wanted to back the President for awhile, but then I saw him come back out again when they started talking about losing a lot of our civil rights.

JN: Remember, this is not about backing George W. Bush or not backing him. The problem is this, whether he's a good guy or a bad guy, and no matter who's around him, no matter how strong or weak or smart or dumb they are, it doesn't matter. This is not an attack on George W. Bush to say that he should not be sitting in the White House today. It is an attack on his brother, Jeb; Katherine Harris, his Florida campaign co-chair; Supreme Court Justices Scalia, O'Connor, Thomas; and their allies.

MH: And let's not forget his cousin, who was working for the television media.

JN: John Ellis, who was the analyst for Fox. All of these people abused their positions of trust to place George W. Bush in office. I have much less antipathy towards George W. Bush than I do toward that whole infrastructure of support that put him there. Bush couldn't have done it himself.

MH: Let's look at the fact that right after this election, how Florida really took a beating and the old Jewish people in Florida were called stupid; everybody was making fun of them.

JN: Vicious attacks. The interesting thing is that when you analyze the Palm Beach County mess, you find that the two groups that clearly cast the most votes for Buchanan (unintentionally) were Jews and Haitian immigrants. Those were the two groups that live in those coastal towns in Palm Beach County. These are very, *very* different groups of people, coming from very, *very* different experiences and, yet, they both ended up in the exact same mess. I think what we have to come away with here is the reality as stated by every single expert on ballot design, that when you have this many people — thousands of people — making mistakes, it isn't their fault. It is the fault of the person who designed the ballot. And when you have that situation, when you have a ballot that is so badly designed that it causes thousands of voters, or tens of thousands in Palm Beach County, to either vote for the wrong candidate or to disqualify their ballot, then you clearly have a case for some sort of government action to rectify the situation. You don't just say, "Well, you know, you came in, you rolled your dice, you're disqualified. Your votes don't count." That is an absurd construct in a democracy.

MH: It's becoming un-American to talk against this Administration, but what a lot of Americans don't realize is how un-American what happened to us during that election was.

JN: The United States is in a situation now where in a number of countries we are attempting to tell indigenous peoples, local peoples, around the world, how they should run their democracy. We're about to tell Afghanistan how it should establish some form of democracy. We are currently telling Zimbabwe how that country should hold elections. Maybe we're right, maybe we do have some very good advice on how to do this, but how seriously do people take us?

MH: They don't. They look at us and ask, "What kind of democracy do *you* have?" I've been following the international news and everybody's laughed at us over what happened in this election.

JN: People were shocked around the world. I was recently in London at a dinner with folks from Africa and southern Asia, all over the world. We ended up talking about the book, as is so often the case. Everybody at the table—people well-educated, very, very intelligent people—universally believed that Bush was not elected. They were shocked that that could happen in America.

MH: And that Americans just laid back for it.

JN: I think, in some ways, they were very impressed with America. One friend of mine from Malaysia said, "If something like this had happened in *my* country, there would have been a revolution." We have to, as Americans, be concerned about the fact that there wasn't more of a response because that serves as a very frightening signal. It says to those who would manipulate democratic processes that they can get away with it.

MH: Look at how much of our rights and freedoms and environmental rights are being slammed by this Administration, and still a lot of people are just sitting back and saying, "Well, it's okay. I'm not doing anything wrong, so I don't care."

JN: I think the Bush Administration was emboldened by what happened in Florida. They came into office after this incredibly contested election, but they saw they were able to get away with a lot, in large part because of their political spin. I think they decided from the start that they were going to govern as if they had a huge level of support in this country. And thus, they have taken actions no administration, not even a Republican administration, not even the [former President Ronald] Reagan Administration in the '80s, would have dared to undertake.

MH: They figure if we're going to lie down for a stolen election, we'll lie down for anything.

JN: I actually think that's a very good point. And, to me, an even more terrifying point than the actual result of what happened down in Florida was, again, one stolen election is a bad thing, but the broad sense that elections *can* be stolen, that democratic processes *can* be warped, that the politics of the country *can* be turned to the purposes of special interests or individual interests, once that becomes the accepted reality, we're no longer a democracy.

MH: And who's to say the next election, if there is one, will be any different?

JN: There always will be an election.

MH: But will it become a moot point, an exercise in futility for the voters?

JN: That's the terrifying thing. One of the main reasons why I wrote my book was not to just go over the old ground of 2000, but it was also to, hopefully, get people angry. I want ordinary people to be passionate and upset about what happened in 2000. I do not want them to simply say, "Well, you know, that's what happens." I want people to belabor this issue, to hang on to it, to keep talking about it, because those are the signs of life in a democracy. Those are the reminders that we didn't lose our country. If there's somebody in a church basement or a union hall or just standing on the street with their friend who's ranting on about this thing, there's hope.

MH: Plenty of people are still ranting about this thing. And I think with the dip in the economy, a lot of people who just said, "Oh, everything is fine," may think, now that it's hitting them in their pocketbooks, "Hey, wait a minute, maybe we don't like what's happening."

JN: People who are upset over what happened in Florida ought to remember that George W. Bush has exceptionally high popularity at this moment. The polls show that somewhere between 80% and 90% of Americans think he's doing a good job. That is a reflection of the fact that this country went through a terrible trauma on September 11th. This is a country that is very patriotic and wants to do the right thing. These are people who want to stand behind their leader in a difficult time. That sort of support does not tend to last and presidents who achieve exceptionally high approval ratings usually end up before the end of their term seeing that popularity level disappear.

MH: It's actually very similar to when his father was in office.

JN: I think it is and I think one of the things we have to remember is that by the end of George W. Bush's term, a lot more history will have taken place. If this recession continues and if it deepens and worsens, I think you will see an awful lot of Americans who begin to question much more loudly how the Bush Administration has conducted itself. And they *will* reflect back on what happened in Florida. And they will say, "Well, hold it. These people did a rotten job in office. And there's some serious question about whether they were even supposed to *be* in office." That's where I think we begin to get, hopefully, a higher level of citizen engagement and desire in 2004.

MH: I think what happened on September 11th was horrific, believe me, especially being an ex-New Yorker. However, I think instead of Americans feeling like their president is their daddy who is going to take care of them, what Americans need to do is start taking care of themselves. Start waking up and getting involved on a local level, politically and environmentally.

JN: We really need to reassert a notion of citizenship. Being a citizen is not as easy as a lot of the media seem to want to tell us it is. You're not a good citizen if you put up the flag in front of your house. That's a nice gesture, and I'm wholly sympathetic with it, but that doesn't make you a good citizen. Frankly, I don't even think you're a particularly good citizen if the only engagement you have during every four-year cycle in the nation's history is to go and cast a vote in the presidential election. That's a good thing. I'm glad people vote, but citizenship is an ongoing, daily commitment that we make to this place where we live.

MH: You've got to think globally and act locally. Here, where I live, I'm involved in my local association. I'm on the board there. I want to know what's going on in my neighborhood. I pay attention to what's going on in the state and the rest of the world. It takes a little time and effort, but it also makes you a much more balanced human being to know what's going on and participate in your own world. I mean, it is *your* world, too.

JN: I think that's a healthy thing. I think people feel disempowered and disconnected when they aren't involved as citizens because they see things happening to them that they don't feel they have control over. Citizenship gives us, at its best, a sense of connection and engagement. Ultimately, it makes us feel like we have some, even if minimal, control over the direction of our world. I fear the biggest danger of what happened down in Florida in 2000 is that it suggested to a lot of people that engagement and involvement aren't worth the effort because you're not going to be able to change things anyway. Even if you *do* win an election, if your candidate prevails, the election will be stolen.

That's my biggest fear about Florida. I'm much less concerned about the fact that George W. Bush sits in the White House today than I am about the possibility that tens of millions of Americans will simply give up on the process. I think activists and political folks ought to be really engaged and ought to be really fighting because we *must* make sure that the young African-American, the old Jewish-American, the immigrant, the person who already feels a little wary of whether they have an ability to affect this system, doesn't get turned off altogether.

MH: It's true what the country song says, if you don't stand for something, you'll fall for anything.

JN: And right now in America, we have a power structure in the media and in our politics, that believes the vast majority of Americans will fall for anything, that they can spin their way through any process.

MH: That's another thing I want to talk about, the media spin, especially around the election, or *selection*, of 2000.

JN: One of the nice things in doing a book tour and going around talking to folks around the country is that people have taken my book in much the sense that I and my publisher, New Press, intended, which is that something needed to be said about the election of 2000 that wasn't being said. When you take the parts of this whole process and look at them seriously, you find that the media, the regulators, the courts, the political players, all of the folks who were entrusted with the responsibility to make sure the political processes of this country function, failed in their duties. And when you put that whole package together, you realize that what happened in the year 2000 in Florida was much more serious than just an election and a recount. It was a crisis of democracy that (a) should never have occurred, and (b) *demands* that we, as citizens, get engaged to make sure it never occurs again.

MH: I think it's the biggest crime I've ever seen in America in my whole life.

JN: There can be no question that in a democracy, which this country is and should be, the theft of the presidency must, by its nature, be the biggest crime.

MH: When this happens in other countries, like in some Latino countries, the whole country goes berserk.

The guy gets ousted from office in no time because everybody goes on strike and revolts.

JN: Frankly, that's a very healthy response. In this country, back in 1800, there was a fear that supporters of John Adams might steal the presidency from the duly-elected Thomas Jefferson. The governors of Virginia and Pennsylvania readied their state militias to march on Washington. That's the American tradition. The American tradition is to *not* let elections be stolen.

MH: People need to remember that this country was founded by revolutionaries, by people who really gave their lives for freedom. It is *not* un-American to dissent.

JN: And this country, throughout 200 years of history has, at its best, operated under a rule of law, especially regarding the structure of elections. When we undermine that rule of law, when we undermine those basic structures, we leave ourselves with nothing. If you take the foundation out from under democracy, which is the commitment to follow the rules, you render the democracy non-functional. And I think in this case, especially in 2000, the media bears a tremendous responsibility.

MH: The media spin on this was incredible. What responsibility do you think the media had in this?

JN: I think the media has an overwhelming responsibility, perhaps even more than the Supreme Court. The media is not a political agent. It is not constitutionally defined as such, but it *is* constitutionally protected. Thomas Jefferson, James Madison, and the other founders of this country put in that protection for freedom of the press with a very specific intent. They did not trust partisan players who might become the controllers of the political processes or political positions and they wanted to always make sure in this country that there was a vigilant media (in their case, a press) that would watch, challenge, expose, shine the light of day on government wrongdoing.

I think in 2000, the media failed to live up to that wonderful protection and encouragement that freedom of the press gives them. It occurred in a number of ways. First off, of course, was the absurd calling of Florida for Bush at 2:16 in the morning on November 8, 2000, by the Fox TV network, a call that was orchestrated by George W. Bush's cousin, John Ellis. That was an example of a television network practicing political spin.

MH: It was that old name-it-you-claim-it game.

JN: And they knew when they called the election for Bush on that night, if Bush was the last man standing in Florida, that would help him in the recount that would certainly follow.

MH: Then, they set it up right away that Gore is a sore loser because they've already declared Bush the winner.

JN: Right after that, you have an example of tremendous wrongdoing. My bigger concern with the whole mass media in the U.S. is that they, by and large, failed to follow the first rule of journalism, which is that you be skeptical. You just don't believe what is handed to you. And the fact is, the Florida circumstance demanded *extreme* skepticism. Does anybody *really* believe that Jeb Bush totally recused himself and took his hands off the process altogether? Does anybody *really* believe that Katherine Harris, the state co-chair of the Bush-For-President campaign, oversaw that recount in an impartial, unconcerned way? Does anyone *really* believe that Antonin Scalia, a conservative activist, before he got on the Supreme Court and since he got on the Supreme Court, whose sons *both* worked for law firms that were representing the Bush campaign, was an impartial judge of the Florida result?

These are the sorts of questions that a responsible media should have not asked just once or twice, but should have pounded down the throats of the political players throughout the 36-day recount and judicial process in 2000 — but they didn't.

MH: The media has failed Americans for a century.

JN: That's why I say it's ultimately more important than what the court did. If the media had done its job, the Supreme Court would have been *afraid* to intervene in the way that it did, because they would have known that if they did, they would have clearly been identified, *broadly*, as having stolen an election.

MH: I want to read a quote from your book on page 189, the chapter on Bush's barristers. It's a quote by the U.S. Supreme Court in their ruling in *Bush vs. Gore*: "The individual citizen has no federal constitutional right to vote." So, that means that, according to the Supreme Court, they really don't care about us as people, anyway.

JN: That was made clear from the ruling, particularly Antonin Scalia, who was passionate about driving home that point that citizens don't have a right to vote. Voting is sort of this privilege that is doled out to people on the basis of the whims, really, of political powers and it was *such* a shockingly undemocratic statement. Intriguingly enough, Jesse Jackson, Jr., who's a congressman from Illinois, has seized on it and put forward in Congress a proposed constitutional amendment that would simply say in the Constitution that every American *does* have a right to vote.

MH: The truth of the matter was that the court was intervening illegally. The Supreme Court had no right to do what it did. If anything, Congress should have had the ball dropped in *their* lap.

JN: And this is an important thing because Congress *has* resolved contested elections in this nation's history several times, in 1800, in 1824, particularly in 1876. They haven't always done a good job of it, but they *have* taken that responsibility.

MH: Congress is voted into office by *the people*. We don't pick the Supreme Court.

JN: That's exactly the point. Many people thought, "Well, how could you possibly give the decision in the 2000 election to Congress when it's controlled by people like [Representative] Tom DeLay [R-Texas] and [House Speaker] Denny Hastert [R-Illinois] and [Senator] Trent Lott [R-Mississippi]?" The fact of the matter is, when they tried to impeach [former U.S. President] Bill Clinton back in 1998-1999, those conservative Republicans found that even some of their own members wouldn't go with them over the cliff. The fear of facing the voters was sufficient to cause even conservatives to back off on impeaching Bill Clinton. I believe that had the election gone to Congress, there's a very good chance we would have gotten a better result than what we got from the Supreme Court. Even if we got the *same* result, however; even if they *did* steal the election, there would have been some way to come back at *them* in the next election. There's no way to come back at the Supreme Court, whatsoever.

MH: The Supreme Court has ignored Congress on so many of the bills and laws that they've slapped on through since September 11th. Congress is really not too happy about a lot of the decisions the Supreme Court's made.

If they could do it over the election, they can do it over civil rights or anything else they want to do.

JN: I think the Supreme Court, at this point, has identified itself as a rogue court. They have essentially said, "Look, we're willing to write a whole new set of laws that serves our purposes politically." That is a very frightening reality when you realize the Supreme Court is made up of people who have life appointments and who, essentially, aside from impeachment, which is a very, very difficult road to go, cannot be removed from office. To have them *not* operating along the simple rule-of-law commitments that we would expect of our Judicial Branch is a very frightening thing.

MH: Last night, I caught a little of [Minnesota Governor] Jesse Ventura, who was on Larry King. They were trying to nail him to the carpet. He said, "Listen, as far as Bush and what he's doing on this war, I support it, but as far as what he's doing with states' rights, I'm totally against him."

JN: The fact of the matter is, for years, Republicans have talked about states' rights and they were the big champions that the states ought to have the ability to regulate their own commerce, politics, and processes, in general. What happened with the Supreme Court ruling in Florida was that it turned the whole notion on its head. For purposes of order, i.e., to make sure that everything was done by a certain date, the U.S. Supreme Court can stop a recount ordered by a state supreme court even though the Constitution clearly delegates responsibility for counting ballots and for resolving electoral disputes to the states.

The Florida Supreme Court clearly had the superior legal authority in Florida. The Florida Supreme Court was in a position to resolve that dispute and, frankly, they had done so. They had set up a recount process that, whatever result it produced, that process was sacrosanct. It should have been seen to its conclusion. And for the Supreme Court to intervene and stop it was not only extra-legal, beyond the bounds of law; it was also completely at odds with everything that conservatives have said for 20 years about how things should operate.

MH: And we're all paying the price for it. I don't want to pay the price for it. I don't like where America has gone in the past year. It's a year later, and you've still got people arguing for voter reform. You've got the 2002 elections coming, and nothing's been changed.

JN: There's been very little movement toward reform. That's an important thing to note. The fact of the matter is that half of Americans don't participate in presidential elections. Two-thirds of Americans don't participate in off-year congressional elections. So long as that continues to be the reality, we're going to have an awful lot of powerful political players who are going to figure they can get away with something like the Enron scandal, that they can get away with the campaign finance abuses that occur on a daily basis, that they can get away with doing whatever they want because not enough people will go to the polls to ever hold them accountable.

MH: I've always wondered, even when I was a kid, why is it that every state has a different way of voting? If we're all voting for the same president, why don't we all get the same forms? Do you remember when we were kids in school and they used to give us tests? You got a No. 2 pencil. You knew that you had to do the dot right next to the answer.

JN: It's even more serious than that. In the state of Florida alone, they had 11 different voting systems. So, from county to county, your likelihood of having your vote counted is radically different. In one county, you had a 1 in 100 possibility of having your vote disqualified. In the next county, you had a 1 in 8 chance of having your ballot disqualified.

MH: If people knew that, they'd be up-in-arms, so it goes back to education, which is really why I continue to do this show.

JN: It's an important message. People need to know their vote counts. And that means they need to know that wherever they go to cast a ballot in this country and no matter how they do it, whether on a touch-screen, a scanner, a paper ballot, an old machine, whatever, that the officials tabulating those ballots will make every humanly-possible effort to ascertain the intent of the voter. That did not happen in Florida and, as a result, we have a different president today than we should have.

MH: I think Florida is going to pay a lot more attention just out of paranoia to their next election, at least I hope so.

JN: I fear there will be many different reactions, that some politicians will see this as license to do whatever they want. I think there are going to be a number of political players, even some conservative Republicans, who are going to recognize they can't pull these stunts again.

MH: Just to give people a little hope, I'll give you one of my Mamma's quotes, "The bigger they are, the harder they fall." My feeling is that Enron is probably going to be the straw that breaks the camel's back in all of this. As the economy starts trickling down to worse than it is, I think people are going to start waking up out of necessity because they've all been living in kind of that after-Thanksgiving-stuffed-belly of the '90s. When reality really hits, which I see it's hitting even here in Arizona with a lot of people I know losing jobs, etc., I think people are going to say, "Hey, wait a minute, what happened? Everything was so good just two years ago."

JN: Economic downturns *always* produce a higher level of civic engagement. This is the history of this country and it's sad because you don't want to believe that you need an economic downturn or a period of instability for people to re-engage.

MH: It always has to hit people in their pockets.

JN: If people want to know more about what I'm writing on this, they can come to *The Nation*, which is www.thenation.com. I think that using radio, using the Net, using these tools to get these messages out is important work to do.

TEN

DELIBERATE "DUMBING DOWN" OF AMERICA

Meria with Robert McChesney

How much are we controlled by corporate media? Robert McChesney,[11] journalist, teacher, and author of *Rich Media, Poor Democracy: Communication Politics in Dubious Times*, is also a writer for *The Nation*. He discusses how radio, television, and other media were created by the government and big business without any input from citizens or public debates. Why does this affect you? Because we are all under the "media spell" of what is fed to us as what we "want."

Do you really *want* advertising on the radio? On television? Do you *want* to just have newspapers and "journalists" quote the rich to you as "news," instead of true investigative reporting with facts that affect the everyday person (the "worker bees")? How did the media fail us in the 2000 election? Why does the media think of the everyday working person as nothing more than a consumer? Where is our voice in our news? Where is our voice in what we get bombarded with by the media 24/7? Where is Public Broadcasting or educational media?

McChesney discusses why we do not get foreign films in America any more, and the cost foreign film companies have to pick up just to show their movies in the U.S. global media takeover is real. McChesney presents facts concerning the anti-democratic manner in which communication policy-making is being conducted in the U.S. The media *should* represent and inform the citizenry, yet it does not. Media reform is not an option, it is a *must* for true democracy to return to the entire U.S., not just for the wealthy few. (Interview taped/broadcast on January 17, 2002.)

MH: I think the whole trend throughout your book is to educate people about our media. We've been pretty much lulled into this fantasy of accepting advertisement wherever we go and not getting any real news. You say that we really do need to get some kind of a movement going. So, where do we start?

RM: I think we start by trying to get a sense of what the problem is and how we got where we are. Then, maybe, we can get a sense of how we can move forward. I cover a lot of territory in my book. It's difficult to do justice to it in a short period of time, so I'll just mention a few quick points.

First of all, a core thesis of the book is that political democracy or self-government or a good humane society is predicated upon having a viable system of communication and information that lets people govern their own lives. That's a starting point. That's the core assumption of the American Revolution. That's a major liberal democratic assumption. It's not very controversial. It's taught in every journalism and political science department in the United States.

The second point that I make, and I think it's an assumption and I think it is empirically verified, is that our media system is *not* the result of heroic entrepreneurs duking it out in free markets, where the business that gives the best service at the lowest price wins, and the least efficient producers go out of business and we all live happily ever after. In fact, our media system, especially broadcast radio and television, but including really the entirety of it, is the result not of a so-called free market as much as it is of government policies.

It's government policies that create the nature of our media system, how big the companies are, what they can own, what they can and can't do, so it's a human-made creation. The policies that set up the media system are made in our name, but without our informed consent. Most Americans are completely oblivious to the crucial decisions that are being made every day in Washington and Brussels that determine the shape of U.S. and global media. These decisions are not being made without the understanding of the huge powerful corporate lobbies that really *are* on top of all this stuff and go a long way towards running it.

The third assumption is that the current system we have that's put together corruptly behind closed doors by policy-makers is highly flawed, from the perspective of a free and democratic society. We have a media and communications system that's set up to serve the needs of the largest shareholders and a handful of extremely powerful corporations foremost, and not to serve the interests of the general public. That's a fundamental problem that has to be addressed or we're never going to make progress in this country.

MH: A lot of people don't think there is any connection between the media and democracy. They'll say, "Well, what's that got to do with democracy at all?"

RM: Just *everything*.

MH: After reading your book, I certainly understand that it's everything. I was primarily interested in your chapters on radio. I never knew the history of radio until I read your book. I did regular radio before this webcast for several years and I was still amazed reading about the fact that radio basically was thrown together, never voted on by the people. The people never agreed with the kind of content or rulings that just seemed to be swept through for radio. People in the 1930s were saying they would prefer to have radio without commercials.

RM: When radio came along in the 1920s, radio broadcasting, the initial generation of radio broadcasters, much like the first webcasters of the first websites, the first Internet users, were almost all non-commercial. The first generation of broadcasters from 1920 to 1926 or 1927 of radio, which was the great radio broadcasting explosion in the United States, were not making money broadcasting. It was a non-commercial haven. About half the stations were run by non-profit groups, especially schools and universities. No one really conceived of radio as what it would shortly become.

By the late '20s, it became clear to a couple of massive companies, NBC and CBS, that you could make a fortune by selling advertising and putting on shows that advertisers would produce over national networks—it completely changed radio. When that came along, the commercial system that we now know today, the basis of our modern broadcasting system, was met by a very strong opposition that organized against it. They said, "Wait a second, we need to have non-profit, non-commercial stations. We can't let advertisers run our broadcasting system." And they tried to organize.

I won't keep you in suspense. They lost their battle to change U.S. radio back to a non-commercial area. It's an important fight because I think it shows that when Americans think about these issues, we shouldn't presume they would be happy with the *status quo*. This cuts across the political spectrum. It's my experience today that when most Americans hear that the radio and TV system we have, the media system we have, is *not* the result of a heroic free market, but instead is the result of government policies made in their name, then they say, "Well, gee, then why don't we change it? Do we really *need* 18 minutes of advertising on a radio show?"

People often say to me, "In your works, you describe how powerful these lobbies are, how they get away with everything, how they own the politicians, how difficult it is to change anything. If that's all true, how can you possibly be optimistic? Why do you even go on? Why don't you just throw in the towel and buy a case of scotch whiskey, and kick back?"

I think the optimism I have comes from the fact that when I study these powerful lobbies and look at the work they do, I see the extent they go to keep their work secret. I see how obsessed the large corporate media lobbies are at making sure there is no public debate in Congress. They understand that when the public hears about things like the gift of TV spectrum for broadcasting, at no charge to these companies, valued at between $50 and $100 *billion* in pure corporate welfare, they're *outraged*. I will only get depressed when these companies no longer care about the public knowing the truth, when they just laugh and say, "Yeah, we ripped you off for $100 billion." *Then* I'll be depressed, but until that time, I'll always be optimistic.

MH: I can remember maybe 20 years ago when they were first starting to talk about pay-TV. I remember most people, myself included, said, "I'll never pay for television." Yet, we all have to pay for television now or we don't even get reception.

RM: We talked about digital TV just now and the wavelengths, that's one of the classic examples of the criminality of our communication policy-making in the United States. We're in the process now of switching from traditional, over-the-air, analog television broadcasting to digital broadcasting, using the computer language of the Internet to send digital signals. I think most of your listeners probably know that in using digital technology rather than analog, you have a lot of new options of things you can do that you can't do under analog. One of these would be what we could do in every American community if we wanted to, using the exact same amount of spectrum that currently broadcasts TV signals.

Using digital technology rather than analog, we could probably increase the number of channels in every community tenfold. Most communities get between five and eight channels. I don't know what it is in Phoenix, but here, I think it's four, because I'm in a small town of Urbana [Illinois]. In a large city like Chicago, it might be as many as 10. Using the same amount of spectrum digitally, Chicago could get 100 channels over the air for free. Phoenix could get 100 channels. And then that would be a use of public service, so no one would have to pay $40.00 a month or whatever for cable or satellite.

You could still get an enormous number of channels. That was never an option that was taken up by our government policy-makers when they thought about the transition from analog to digital broadcasting, because they weren't thinking about what was best for the American people. They were thinking about what was best for the commercial broadcasters. And the commercial broadcasting lobby made it real clear that they did not want to use the new digital technology to increase the number of broadcasters because that would be competition for them. That would reduce their power. They, basically, just want to get the spectrum for free and keep the system exactly as it is, even though the technology opens up all sorts of wonderful possibilities.

MH: So it really *is* all about money. Wouldn't it be great if we could get to where we don't have to pay for the garbage we're bombarded with? One of the things in your book is a little bit of history that a lot of people don't realize. Originally, media, whether it was radio or newspapers or whatever, used to do a lot of coverage and stories for working-class people, but now everything is geared towards the elite few.

RM: One of the striking features of the 20th century in American newspapers and journalism, probably media in general, but certainly journalism, has been the disappearance of the working-class and even the middle class in the classical definition. In the United States, in the first half of the 20th century into the 1950s, even mainstream conservative daily newspapers used to have labor editors and reporters. By one study, there were roughly 1,000 full-time labor editors and reporters on U.S. daily newspapers in the late 1940s. It was a standard story. So, when you have something like the Flint [Michigan] sit-down strike in 1937 that established the United Auto Workers and was the start of the modern trade union movement that built up the standard of living for the working-class in this country, it was a front-page story in *every* newspaper in the country because every newspaper had labor editors. It was an important beat because the majority of their readers were working-class people. It was the beat they had to cover. Since the 1940s, the number of labor editors and reporters has plummeted. The position virtually doesn't exist any more. I think we're down to under five full-time labor editors and beat reporters on U.S. daily newspapers, if it's even that many.

MH: Even if they *do* report on some kind of labor strike, like those schoolteachers in New Jersey who went to jail because they were fighting to work with a contract, they always make the people who are on strike look like they're monsters.

RM: That's actually been going on for a long time. That's not new. The coverage in the '40s wasn't necessarily pro-labor—it usually wasn't—but at least it *was* getting coverage. It was an issue. Now, there is simply no coverage at all. In 1989, there was the biggest sit-down strike in American history since Flint in Pittstown, Virginia, by coalminers, and it was completely uncovered in our news media. Finally, the *New York Times* broke a story, and the story they had on the sit-down strike was that a bunch of Russian coalminers from Siberia came over here to show solidarity with their Virginian coalmining brethren.

The story was, "Hey, isn't this goofy, now the Russians are coming over here to help *us* out." But the point I'm making is that labor, the working class, has fallen from view and it's done so for clear and obvious reasons. The first and most important one is that, increasingly, journalism in the United States, especially in the last quarter century and even more so in the past 15 years, has been perceived as something that's pitched to the upper class and the upper middle class, not to the general population. If you watch CNN or CNBC or

MSNBC or read the large major daily newspapers, they're talking to the upper middle class—the affairs of investors, of people making major consumer purchases—as if those are the affairs of the American people, the average American who has a stock portfolio. This is because that's who the advertisers want to reach, that's where the money is to be made, pitching your journalism at that level. The affairs of the great bulk of Americans who are working-class people, who don't own big stock portfolios, pretty much fall from view. This is a very dangerous thing for our society.

MH: Another thing I thought that was pretty scary is how they can, or at least are preparing to be able to, tell your socio-economic standard before they start broadcasting into your home, depending on your neighborhood, etc. In other words, I could be sitting here in Phoenix watching certain advertisements, and some black person living in a poorer city or poorer ghetto will get totally different advertising sent to them.

RM: This is something that's going to be developed much more in the coming five or ten years because that's one of the things you can do with digital technology. Shifting from analog to digital opens up a whole range of new opportunities. With digital broadcasting and technology, you can do 10 signals, where you used to do one. You can monkey around with the picture. The options are almost infinite with what you can do.

The key question for our society is, what values are we going to put in place as we determine how to use digital technology? One of them, for example, would be to make it possible for people to have 100 channels on their television, rather than five or ten, for free. Another option would be to make it so people could avoid having to see commercials altogether very easily, which would be a highly desirable option. The new technology isn't going to be used in those ways because it doesn't benefit the advertisers and the people in power and the policy-makers who are in bed with them. It benefits the mass of people. Instead, what you're going to get is the use of digital technology to bombard people with specific ads.

You can take advantage of it to give ads by demographic groups. You can take advantage of digital technology to insert advertising into programs. If you're watching a game on TV, like the World Series, you can see how digitally they can put advertising in the background behind home plate. This is increasingly how the technology is used, not to enhance the experience for the average person, but to make more money for those in power.

MH: Your book made it even more noticeable to me how much advertising is everywhere we go, including on the benches where you wait for the bus, which I find very offensive and ugly for the landscape—even to advertising sheets in the bathroom stall in a restaurant.

RM: Yeah, it's atrocious.

MH: Has America just gotten so used to it that we don't feel insulted by this?

RM: That's a good question. I don't know if I can really answer it. What happens, clearly, is that people are grossed-out and pissed-off the first time or two they come upon new advertising, but I think there's this profound sense of powerlessness, like there's nothing you can do about it. Over time, you just get accustomed to it and then you almost expect to see advertising everywhere you turn.

MH: I think there's a lot people can do, like (a) complain, and (b) organize. I would say that's one of the strongest messages in your book—for people to get organized and start saying, basically, "We're mad as hell and we don't want to take it any more."

RM: We do need to organize. We can win on a lot of these issues. I think there's a lot of potential. My experience is that once people hear how the system works and understand it's their democratic right to intervene and set up policies that will serve *their* interests, they get excited about it and they want to do it. The biggest problem we face is that most people don't realize it's an area they have a right to and, indeed, a responsibility to organize around.

MH: Most Americans think there were open debates of citizenry setting up all these rules for TV, radio, and newspapers, but obviously that never happened either.

RM: It was a highly corrupt system from the beginning. Powerful money interests did everything in their power to prevent exactly the debate we need to have.

MH: One of the interesting things for me—because I'm a movie freak—was learning about our movie industry in your book and just how powerful and controlling *they* are. I understood for the first time, probably ever, why I can't find a foreign movie anywhere in Phoenix or Scottsdale to go to. I can read great reviews of foreign movies and look for a theater to show it, but it's just not happening here. Do you want to explain to people why?

RM: One of the great defenses of our media system that automatically comes up is, "Okay, even if you don't like the system, even if it is sort of put together corruptly, ultimately, these are businesses that depend on selling their product to the public. They have to give the people what they want. If they don't, they'll go out of business." And it's a powerful defense. The argument is that if you don't like what the media are giving us, don't blame the media companies, blame the morons who demanded it. It's their fault. The fault shouldn't be with the huge media companies that own the film studios and the TV networks and everything else.

It's a strong argument because there's an element of truth to it. The person who runs Paramount Pictures or Viacom or who programs CBS for Viacom or ABC for Disney are trying to put out movies that people want to go to. They're trying to put on TV shows that people will watch. No one's *trying* to put out movies that aren't going to sell any tickets. The problem with the argument, though, is that it's extremely misleading if left at that level. It suggests they're sort of obedient dogs taking orders from the public, which completely misrepresents the power relationship in our media system.

To have what's called consumer sovereignty, where people demand and then get what they want, you need to have a competitive market in economic terms. That means if you're demanding something and you don't like it, none of the five film studios are giving it to you, you have the capacity to start your own film studio and produce it yourself. That's when you have real leverage as a consumer. That's when you have consumer sovereignty. We don't have that in our media system. You have what's called producer sovereignty. Basically, they give you what you want, but within the range of where they can make the most money.

In the 1930s, we had two companies that basically dominated network radio in this country. The vast majority of Americans did not want any advertising on radio, but they couldn't give the people what they wanted then because they couldn't make much money doing it. They could give you what you wanted, but only after they figured out how they could make the most money. Since there was very little competition, they could pull it off.

Getting on to your question about foreign films, the problem with the give-the-people-what-they-want defense of the *status quo* also is that it takes a complex relationship between the audience (the public) and the producers. This defense reduces the relationship to an extremely simplistic one-way flow. People's tastes are developed over time. They aren't born with them. Supply can create demand as much as demand creates supply. If you're exposed to something and you develop a taste for it, then you'll demand it. If you're never exposed to something, you're never going to demand it. We've seen in nations that do a lot of classical music education in schools, including this nation in the past, demand for classical music by adults is fairly high. When classical music education doesn't exist or is very low, demand for classical music, voluntary demand in the marketplace, almost disappears among adults. So, that's how you see the complexity in this relationship.

In nations that put a high premium on teaching literature in schools, like the former Soviet Union or Russia and places in Europe, you see the consumption of novels is much higher by adults. Foreign films is a classic case of showing how this relationship works. In the early- to mid-1970s, roughly 10% of the movies shown in American movie theaters were foreign language films. In a city like New York, Manhattan alone had roughly two dozen theaters that showed nothing but foreign language films. I lived across the country in the 1970s. I ended up in Seattle and there, I think, we had six or seven theaters that showed nothing but foreign language movies in the mid- to late-1970s. Small towns like Champaign or Urbana, where I currently live, might have had three theaters showing nothing but foreign films.

The point is, 10 years later, in the mid- to late-1980s, the percentage of foreign films in American theaters was down to something like 6% or 7%, and it was falling. By the late 1990s or today, it's down to less than 1%. I think it's one-quarter of 1%, maybe one-half of 1%. It's virtually disappeared. Now, by the give-the-people-what-they-want thesis, what this would demonstrate is that starting in the mid-1970s, the American people stood up *en masse*, smashed their fists on the table, and said, "Get those foreign films out of our theaters. We *refuse* to patronize theaters that show those foreign movies." Then, the dutiful movie producers and movie theater owners complied and stopped showing those foreign films that nobody wanted to see. They gave the people what they wanted, and we should all live happily ever after.

In fact, the exact opposite happened. It had nothing to do with consumer demand directly. The real pressure for why we stopped seeing foreign language cinema in the United States came at the theater level. What happened starting in the mid-'70s was that you saw the rise of the multiplex, the multi-screen theater. This revolutionized movie distribution in the United States because the single-screen theater could no longer survive. It went the way of the dinosaurs.

If you're operating a single-screen theater and a megaplex moves in down the street, the megaplex has one ticket-taker for 10 screens. You've got one ticket-taker for one screen. The megaplex has one projectionist for 10 screens. You've got one projectionist for one screen. The megaplex has one popcorn-maker for 10 screens. You've got one popcorn-maker for one screen. Their costs are pro-rated. They can simply undercut you dramatically. You can't compete with them over time unless you become a megaplex. And with that, the whole network of single-screen theaters in this country collapsed in a very short period of time. When videotape came along, that only encouraged the decline. The entire network of foreign language theaters pretty much went under, or had to adapt.

When French or German or Japanese film-makers brought their films to the United States to distribute thereafter, they would have to go increasingly to these big chains, like General Cinema, with 200 megaplexes around the country, and say, "We want to show our movie. Our past movies have been successful. Will you show this one on your screens?" And they would say, "Well, you've got to do like our other films. You've got to be on all 200 screens and you've got to do a huge advertising push the weekend before the release so we can see what the gate will be like the first day." If you don't have a good first weekend, you're going to get tossed out. Gradually, through this process, the amount of money needed was so much higher than it had been in the past, that it weeded out producers. Only the most successful could stay. Over time, fewer and fewer could afford it.

What has developed is that ultimately there was no more demand for foreign language films because people weren't exposed to them very much. They didn't know they existed, so they never went out to *try* to see them. They didn't "want" them. At this point, there probably isn't much demand for foreign language films, but it was because people just stopped being *able* to see them. [In my classes], we'll be talking about movies and [my students] will look at me in amazement and say, "You mean, they really make movies in France or Germany? When did they start doing that?"

MH: I think it was last year when *Crouching Tiger, Hidden Dragon* came out, there was one art theater in Scottsdale, only one, showing it. What really gets me is that until that movie got nominated for Academy Awards, it wasn't shown anywhere else. As soon as it was, it was in every theater known to man.

RM: I think we lose a lot with that. The glory days of foreign films in the U.S. probably were the '70s, maybe the late-'60s. There were wonderful films by Italian, French, German, Japanese directors being shown here and getting pretty wide audiences. The effects of that weren't just that we got exposed to great foreign films; it also meant there was more diversity in Hollywood films. Hollywood films then, with all this international influence, took a lot of chances. The 1970s is now generally regarded as the Golden Age of Hollywood film-making. We had a lot of edgy, interesting *avant garde* films that took chances then that couldn't possibly be made today. And the foreign influence, the global influence, is no doubt a factor in it because Hollywood directors were dealing with audiences that had been exposed to [Akira] Kurasawa, to [Ingmar] Bergman, to [Lina] Wertmuller films. They didn't always have to have happy endings. They didn't always have to have cliché plots.

MH: I read in your book that when the studio saw how much money they made with *Lion King*, they turned around and realized they needed to just repeat the formula. Somebody came up with a title for a movie with no script or anything, and then said, "Write me a movie on it." All that branding and hype, and all the way they were going to market it had already happened just with the *title* of the movie.

RM: Warner Brothers, in the mid-'90s, came up with a plan for a movie called *Space Jam*, which was going to star Michael Jordan, the basketball player, and Bugs Bunny, the cartoon figure. In their marketing plan for the movie, they determined they could sell so much junk or stuff with Bugs Bunny's and Michael Jordan's names or figures on it, they wouldn't have to sell *any* tickets to the movie. They didn't even require that the movie be a success, as long as they just had the movie as an excuse to put out Bugs Bunny and Michael Jordan paraphernalia.

MH: I don't think a lot of people really get that. I've noticed that sometimes places like McDonald's have the toys for the movie long before the movie comes out.

RM: They're closely linked. McDonald's has had a long-term contract with Disney, an exclusive contract where Disney gets to provide the toys for the Happy Meals for kids based on its characters in its upcoming movies in all the McDonald's restaurants in the world—like 25,000 restaurants. It basically means if you're trying to compete with Disney, they've locked in the McDonald's crowd. It gives them a lot of power.

MH: I'm sure many of my listeners are saying, "So what? So what if this is how the movies work? What does that mean to me?" And I think that what my audience needs to understand is, what it means to you is you're in this mesmerized trance, which is just set up to give you whatever *they* want to give you to listen to or see, as long as they can keep you buying their products. That's all it really is about. When I look at old movies, how many times do you say, "They don't make movies like that any more." After reading your book, I know *why* they don't make movies like that any more. The bottom line for movies today is money.

RM: I don't want to romanticize earlier movie-making. A survey was made of all the Hollywood movies from the 1930s or 1940s and they went through all the movies that the Hollywood studios produced (some huge number like 15,000 movies). All these critics reviewed them and out of that whole number, they concluded there was something like only 75 really good movies that stood the test of time. The vast majority of them were banal and formulaic because they were just out to make money. They weren't especially good. So you say, "What does it take to make really good movies? What are the things we remember, the things that really captivate our imagination? When were they produced? What was the criteria?" The '70s is regarded as a high point, and the foreign influence was a tremendous factor there. The fact that there was cultivation and you had an audience that was exposed to more so, therefore, they demanded more, so they were more willing to take chances. It opened the door, then, for film directors to have more leverage to go into studios and say, "Let's take a chance here."

MH: Here in America, when you think of Disney, you think of all these happy little clean figures, etc., but when you think of the fact that Disney has so much control globally and that a lot of those cute little toys are made in sweatshops in Third World countries and the kind of oppression that a lot of these studios do, changes the picture a bit. Reading about what seemed to me, basically, to be American studios blackmailing European studios into playing our movies to a quota system, I found very offensive.

RM: That's been going on for a long time. It's going on still today. With regard to global media and the global situation, an important tendency or trend that's taken place in the past 10 or 15 years has been the rise of the largest media companies in the world to be trans-national companies. If you look at the top eight media companies in the world (seven or eight that really rule the rest), they own all the U.S. TV networks, they own all the major studios, they own four of the five companies that sell 80% of the music, they own tons of TV stations, they own the satellite systems. If you look at those companies, and they include AOL TimeWarner, Disney, Viacom, Sony, Vivendi-Universal, Rupert Murdoch's News Corporation, Bertelsmann in Germany, four of the eight are companies that are based outside the United States—they own the film studios and the magazines and TV interests (in the case of Murdock, they own a network) that are American and we identify much of their product as American.

What we're seeing in the last 10 or 15 years is the rise of these massive companies that have huge interests across the globe. Not just making movies here and selling them around the world (they've been doing that for 80 years), but owning TV stations and networks in other countries.

MH: Not only do they make the movie, but they can advertise it on their TV show. They can put advertising in the newspapers they own. They can actually manipulate us from every area of media and all of that owned by the same factory. That was so amazing to me, and I don't think most people know that. The only way you guys can know that is to read books like yours. This book was written in 1999, so this was obviously before the election massacre here in America and the corporate media spin that happened during that election. I would love to know how you feel about the newspapers' and television's responsibility, as far as the coverage of the election.

RM: They did a terrible job. It's one of the darkest moments in American journalism history. Interestingly, the reason why the coverage was so bad was only partially due to the sort of hyper-corporate control and concentration directly, although indirectly it was definitely due to that. The primary reason the coverage was so bad, especially of that period between the election day and the Supreme Court decision when it was sort of up for grabs in Florida, really owes to the professional journalism code that developed in this country. This is a very important point that I don't think many Americans are aware of. The idea of journalism being neutral, objective, non-partisan, is a recent idea. It's only about 100 years old.

In the first 120 years of this republic's history (certainly the first 50 years), the whole media context of the First Amendment, of [Thomas] Jefferson and [James] Madison and [Alexander] Hamilton, journalism was seen as *highly* partisan. The role of journalism used to be partisan. The idea was, whoever owns the medium, the viewpoints of the newspaper would clearly and explicitly represent their political views. The idea that someone would try to write an article and not have an opinion was considered ludicrous. Why else would you write an article? Newspapers were part of our political culture. The journalism, therefore, was stridently partisan. In fact, for the first 50 years of the country's history, many of our newspapers were even subsidized by the government, through printing contracts.

In the second half of the 19th century, or during the 19th century, our press system became much more commercial. The goal of newspapers was to make money for investors or entrepreneurs, but it, even in that context, had a strong partisan and political component. Newspapers could be identified by their political views. In most American cities, as late as the 1870s and 1880s, you had a very competitive market, with lots of newspapers in every community. A major city like a Chicago or a St. Louis or a New York could have 20 or 30 daily newspapers, but even a mid-sized or small city could have five, six, seven. They'd be commercial and they'd be *highly* partisan. The journalism would not be neutral or objective.

All this really began to change in the late 19th century and it came to a head in the early 20th century, because most newspaper markets became increasingly concentrated, oftentimes with just one owner. It became impossible to start new newspapers. The reasons for this are due to economics and, significantly, the rise of advertising—because advertising tended to always go to the largest newspaper in a market, and then all the other newspapers couldn't survive. As a result, what happened was that journalism hit a major crisis in this country in the early 20th century, in what we call the Progressive Era, because stridently partisan journalism is a fine thing if you've got 10 or 15 newspapers in a city, each with a different viewpoint. If you don't like any of them, you can start your own newspaper; you can try to and have a chance to do it to introduce a different viewpoint.

Partisanship not only *isn't* a bad thing, it's probably a really good thing. It promotes debate. It's healthy for political culture. But when you've only got one or two newspapers in your community and they are owned by big, rich companies or big, rich people, then if they represent the viewpoints of their owners, it smells like month-old fish. If you can't start a competitor, it's like an authoritarian society. You're stuck reading the party line. And that was the problem our journalism faced in the Progressive Era. It really was a crisis for the big newspaper publishers because if people didn't trust the news, they wouldn't buy the paper and then the owners wouldn't make money.

It was in this context that you saw the rise of what we now call "professional journalism" or non-partisan journalism. For the first time, you could read a newspaper and the viewpoints you'd read in the news would not explicitly represent the views of the owner. There would be separation between the editorial side of the newspaper and the business side of the newspaper. The owners and advertisers would make all the money. The editors and reporters would be professionally trained, and they would use their professional judgment to determine what the news was and how it should be covered. If you understand this, you can get a sense of how that election was covered, and you can also get a very good sense of how the War on Terrorism has been covered since September 11th, because you can't have really neutral journalism. That's absurd. It's impossible to be objective or neutral. You have biases built into any professional code. And the way professional journalism developed in the United States in the first part of the 20th century, and the key values that still determine the way news is covered, had certain crucial biases built in.

First and foremost, and this is the one that really matters for this discussion, is the reliance upon official sources as the basis for news stories. This is a new thing for American journalism. By official sources, I mean people in government, governors, senators, business leaders, people in power. Prior to professional journalism becoming the rule in the 20th century, if the governor of the state said something in 1880 or 1870 or 1830, and they thought it was stupid, they wouldn't report it. They'd just ignore it. But once you get professional journalism, if someone in power says something and they're powerful enough, you'd certainly report it. That's what they're saying, and that's news. If the President says something, it's news. Before the 20th century, the President of the United States, for example, only accounted for 2% or 3% of the news in the United States. By some surveys, in the last 50 years, it's grown up to the point where the President's up to 25% of the news stories.

MH: Don't you think it was a little strange that the whole world had to hear about him [President Bush] choking on a pretzel?

RM: Because of the reliance on official sources for the way you gather news, you plant reporters on beats around official sources, and what they say becomes news. It's a very inexpensive way to cover news. It's a lot cheaper to put someone at the White House and sort of report what's going on than to have to go out and do investigative stories. It also removes the controversy (this is the crucial thing) of story selection. So, if someone calls up the editor of your Phoenix paper and bellyaches that they don't like this story about what Senator [John] McCain said, the editor can say, "Hey, don't blame us. Senator McCain said it. We have to cover it. That's our job. We report." And that was the crucial thing for professional journalism. It removes the controversy over story selection because you are just reporting what people in power, or what official sources, say.

The weakness of that for democracy is that it means it gives official sources, people in power, tremendous control over the news indirectly. If they're talking about something, it gets covered and becomes news, and if they *don't* talk about something, it's very difficult for journalists to raise that issue without being accused of being unprofessional or partisan.

MH: We live in a society where people believe everything they see in print. If Ari Fleischer says Bill Clinton ran away with the country's jewels, everyone believes it because it was in print.

RM: Even if everybody *doesn't* believe it, if he *says* it and it's covered, it will be out there. Some people will believe it and that will do sufficient damage. If you understand that bias, you see that journalists basically are stenographers to official sources, for the most part, and if they step outside that, they're accused of not being professional or of trying to raise their own opinions.

MH: How many people have been fired for writing stories that were true? We could even look at Pacifica Radio, people actually bringing out a different type of news from the rest, and they find themselves broadcasting from a parking lot.

RM: So, look at the election in Florida. You had John Nichols [*see* Chapter 9] on, who is really the premier expert on this topic, in my opinion. What we know now in Florida was that on election night, you had a race that was too close to call. You had a race where Al Gore, on election night, had won the popular vote nationally by half a million votes, roughly, but Florida was way too close to call (it was split by a hair) and there were rumors of irregularities. Now, how the press handled the coverage of that story from election night until the Supreme Court decision was a very interesting example of the weaknesses of our journalism system. What they did is, they volleyed between what the official sources were saying to them—the Republicans on one side and the Democrats on the other.

Republicans from election night on, starting from when John Ellis, Bush's cousin, got FOX News channel to declare Bush the winner, were claiming that George Bush had *clearly* won the election and that Al Gore was struggling, trying to come up with some gimmick to *steal* it away from the rightful winner. That was their party line. That was their consensus, from that moment until this day.

MH: So, they mesmerized a lot of Americans into believing it.

RM: Every Republican in the country held to that party line with even more rigor than I think the most scared Politburo flunky held to Stalin's line in the 1930s. That was simply the given: "We won the election, Gore was trying to steal it," regardless of any empirical evidence to the contrary. Whenever they were covering this story, the Republican side was uniform. It was *always* that position, so any story reflected that and always had that in it. The Democrats, the other official sources the reporters were dealing with, did not have that unanimity. They did not have the opinion that Gore won it and Bush was trying to steal it. Their line was much more mobile. It was, "Yeah, well, it's up for grabs. We just want to figure out who won. We think we've got a chance."

Journalists reporting these two sides, invariably, made it sound like one side won and the other side [was] hemming and hawing. It sounds pretty goofy. Even without any intent to report pro-Bush, just following the codes of professional journalism would put you in that spot. We know why the Republicans were that way, they wanted to take power, period. Why were the Democrats so mealy-mouthed? Why weren't they as aggressive? Why weren't they fighting as hard as the Republicans? That's the great, unanswered question. But we do know they weren't.

One indication of just how unwilling the Democrats were to fight for what we now know they clearly won came in the *New York Times*, which is a very strong pro-Gore newspaper (it's a Democratic newspaper), just two or three days after the election. Above the fold on page 1, the most important real estate in American journalism, ran a piece saying, "Leading Democrats Wonder Whether It's Time for Gore to Throw in The Towel." There were leading Democrats at that point already saying maybe we shouldn't be contesting this. There were no reports of leading Republicans wondering whether Bush should throw in the towel. That would be unthinkable. Those people would probably be sleeping at the bottom of the East River if they even *thought* that. I'm being facetious, but the point remains that since the sources of the Democrats were mixed, they weren't anywhere near as eager to go to the mattresses to defend what they had rightfully won.

The press coverage always carried the tone. They had Bush as having won the darn thing and Gore sort of middling around, trying to figure out what sort of legal gimmick he can use to steal back what he hasn't really won. And that was a real distinct limit of professional journalism. One example of how that played out came with Greg Palast [*see* Chapter 2], who has also been a guest on your show. Greg Palast broke the story, for example, about what happened to the felons on the felon lists in Florida and why wasn't this story all over the news? Was it because journalists were conspiring against Gore? Not really.

What happened was simply this. Palast breaks the story in England. And then it gets some play on the Internet. People are talking about it. For whatever reason, Al Gore decides not to run with it. He doesn't want to push it. He doesn't want to have Jesse Jackson and 300,000 African-Americans going on demonstrations demanding that fairness be done, that this was disenfranchisement. He makes the decision not to go to war over that, so he's going to downplay it.

The Republicans dismiss it as completely irrelevant. It becomes difficult for a reporter to cover the story because they're not getting support from official sources. Palast gives the example of when he broke the story, a CBS producer called him up and said they wanted to work on it. Palast said, "Yeah, go ahead, sure, it's yours." Palast said, "Look, there are a few loose ends you've got to check into," and he gave them some information. They said, "Yeah, we're going to get right on it. It's a great story." A few days later, the story still hadn't broken. The time was short; this was running into late November. Palast called up CBS and talked to the producer and said, "What happened to that story?" And the producer said, "Oh, we decided not to run it." Palast said, "How come?" And the producer said (and I'm not making this up), "Well, we called up Governor Jeb Bush's office and asked them if there's anything to it, and they said, 'No.'"

MH: And that was that.

RM: That was it. And since no Democrats were pushing it, they didn't have the guts or the willingness to get into that fight. A reporter didn't have the source cover they needed if they wanted to pursue that story. If they had pursued that story without having the Democrats backing them up, they would have gotten fired or tremendously harassed. It's terrible. The problem with our professional journalism is that it reflects the debate among the elites, but no journalists, except a Greg Palast, were representing those of us in the general population who just wanted the truth. Who won the darn election? Who had the most votes? Who should be president? And, for me, it was frustrating because it wasn't that I was an Al Gore supporter—I just wanted to know who actually had won. I think whoever gets the most votes deserves to win.

MH: But why should *that* be the case?

RM: Yeah, who am I? I guess I'm old-fashioned.

MH: You figured if the guy won, he should be in office.

RM: I guess in the *new* American system, whoever can steal it and get away with it, wins.

MH: What do you suggest we do now?

RM: Become more aware. Study so you know what you're talking about. I've got a website, www. robertmcchesney.com, where I list many of these groups that are working on various issues in media reform, and also other groups that do media literacy and have information, such as a wonderful group called Fairness & Accuracy in Reporting. There's a lot of momentum building right now, on local and national levels, to try to reform aspects of our media system, to blast it open to give more space for non-commercial, non-profit media, and to improve the system. I think people should start tuning in. It's going to happen. Also, increasingly, whenever you're dealing with politicians, press them on this. Let them know this is important. Republican, Democratic, Green, whatever politician—let them know that this is an important issue. Our goal will have to be to make this a debated issue, to get people to say that the control over the communication information channels in this country cannot just simply be turned over to Wall Street and Madison Avenue without any strings attached.

MH: I can tell you that just based on the success of my show, a lot of people are asking me, "Why aren't we hearing you on the radio?" Do you *really* think what I do on this show is something the corporate owners are going to want to put on their shows? The people who are putting out Rush Limbaugh? We can change it; just the popularity of online news has to be changing it.

RM: And also, in the case of a show like this, you're not going to get advertisers, no matter how big your audience. The advertisers aren't going to want to be sponsoring shows of this nature. They're very comfortable sponsoring Rush Limbaugh and Gordon Liddy because those are shows that extol business control over our society, and advertisers are businesses.

MH: I'm going to suggest over and over that my listeners get these books because education is power.

ELEVEN

SPIN THE MEDIA – DANGEROUS GAME!

Meria with Norman Solomon

Norman Solomon[12] is the Executive Director of the Institute for Public Accuracy (a nationwide consortium of public policy researchers), author of *Media Beat*, a nationally-syndicated columnist, and author of nine books, including his latest, *The Habits of Highly Deceptive Media: Decoding Spin and Lies in Mainstream News.* Solomon discusses how to tell the difference between "spin" and news, the press responsibility in the Election 2000 fiasco, the reinvention of John Ashcroft from bigot to "saint," the travesty of comparing George W. Bush to Franklin D. Roosevelt, why Americans think the U.S. is the center of the Universe, how to get people more informed and more responsible as citizens of the *world*, the U.S. dollars that go for foreign political campaigns, how we could have avoided becoming involved in Vietnam, the Enron meltdown and how the press is covering it, why the "dumbing down" of Americans in television and print is necessary for certain ends, and how to break out of "trance" news and realize the truth about our country, the world, and why the world views us as the "big bully" on the block. (Interview taped/broadcast on February 7, 2002.)

MH: I learned from Norman's book that a lot of our money goes to fund political parties in other countries. I had *no* idea that we have actually put $10 million from the

CIA into Italy for campaigns, and in Chile, $20 million from the U.S. Treasury. Why? Because we want *"our"* people in power even in other countries. We have the nerve to involve ourselves in places where we do *not* belong. This book by Norman actually is a compendium of a lot of articles he has written through the years on many different subjects. We need to really start holding our government accountable for where they spend *our* money. Today, we will also discuss whether or not the United States really *is* the center of the Universe or whether other countries should have the right to also live their lives the way they want and run their own countries the way they want. What's the latest stuff you're working on now?

NS: I write a weekly column that goes out to some daily papers. There are a few in the country and, as you know, the kind of media criticism I do is really not the sort that will run in mainstream papers, liberal or conservative. But I do write a weekly syndicated column that runs every Monday in *The San Francisco Examiner* and it runs in a few other dailies in the country.

MH: I've seen it everywhere, even *Online Journal*. I usually get at least 10 copies of your latest articles from my listeners. They don't want me to miss it. After reading your book and many of your articles, I said, "How do I interview someone who knows so much about everything?"

NS: The world is so vast, including the media world, I feel like I just scrape along little bits and pieces of the surface and yet all of us are just trying to make sense of what often seems to be a pretty chaotic media universe. I think there are ways to decode the media patterns. I think that without being kind of reductionist or simplistic about it, there are some basic paradigms usually in play, and some similarities to help crack the code.

It begins to make a lot more sense or to have a pattern in its *nonsense* when we can crack the code. A lot of it is that the news media, particularly we are saying the mass media here, are not about making sense. They're about making money and even though, on the surface, that may not seem to be what is going on in the programming on CNN or in *Time* magazine or whatever, that's really kind of the backdrop, the underlying dynamic. Decisions are made as to what the priorities are and those decisions are setting the limits within which journalists, reporters, producers, and editors function. When they function within those kinds of contexts, they internalize the limitations. It is coming to seem like journalistic professionalism to observe the limits that really are handed down arbitrarily.

What is considered to be appropriate journalism is often nothing more or less than what some bunch of rich guys decided should circumscribe what we do or do not get in the news media. Just to give you a quick example, whether you work in the *San Francisco Chronicle* newsroom or at the *New York Times* or any one of another thousand daily papers in the country, you do not have anybody walking into the newsroom in the morning and saying, "Gee, I picked up this morning's paper. We have our business section, but where is the labor section?" It just does not occur to people because the limitations are so internalized and so solid.

MH: I noticed that on the back of your book, Robert McChesney [*see* Chapter 10] wrote some high praise on your book.

NS: Bob McChesney wrote *Rich Media, Poor Democracy*. He cuts through a lot of the fog to talk about, as he puts it, the severe limitations that commercialized media put on us. It is not that good work *can't* be done in commercial media, but the limits are so extreme. I think that also goes, for the most part, for what is called public broadcasting, you know, NPR, PBS, and so forth.

MH: I had Bob on the show a few weeks ago. One of the things he said, which you just triggered again, is that there really is nothing that covers the labor section or the common people any more, which is really something that newspapers should put as first page stuff. That's what people want to know about.

NS: Is it about some people cashing in on big mega-corporate maneuvers and investments? Is it Main Street or Wall Street, is another way to put it. Really, it is about Wall Street one way or another for the most part.

MH: Many years ago, I realized that when I wanted to read the news, what I had to read was between the lines, what they *weren't* telling me.

NS: Between the lines is where the almost ineffable, but definitely powerful, messages come from, like the assumption of who is important and who isn't; what matters and what doesn't; who should be heard from, repeatedly and at great length, and who else should just be presented in snippets. A great example is what just came down in New York where we had the world economic forum. If you read in what we are told is the nation's newspaper of record, the *New York Times*, there were easily several dozen, perhaps as many as 100, news articles in the last week talking about the world economic forum and the nuances and chic interactions of the rich and powerful, the top corporate executives from around the planet who were there. Those were chronicled in great detail. There were several articles about protesters in the street who were challenging corporate globalization and so forth. Those stories tended to be more distant; just snippets of quotes, kind of cutsie, and I think you could say somewhat condescending. The contrast there is really great.

MH: I read your article about [U.S. Attorney General] John Ashcroft and how he has been reinvented from a bigot to a follower of Martin Luther King, Jr.

NS: In one year. It is enough to make our heads spin. If we were watching it in historical terms, we would get whiplash, just the total reinvention of this guy. He praised profusely, back in 1998, in an interview with *Southern Partisan* magazine (which, according to *The New Republic* is the leading neo-confederate journal of the country) as great patriots Stonewall Jackson, Robert E. Lee, Jefferson Davis, who were political supporters of slavery. He said they did not have a bad agenda, a perverted agenda, as he put it. He bristled at the idea that these advocates of continuing slavery had what he called a perverted agenda. Just in the last few weeks, he has in national TV appearances said he is walking in the footsteps of Martin Luther King, Jr. This only can go without comment in the national media if, and only if, there is a contempt for history. You have to destroy history if you want to promote demagogues. I am afraid the news media have very little interest in that sort of historical accuracy.

MH: Yet I saw there was more than enough coverage about Ashcroft insisting that naked statue be draped.

NS: Yes, indeed. The guy happens to be a fundamentalist. The folks who are supportive of a rigid Taliban sort of society are, in a way, mirror images of this fellow. He personally refuses to dance. He thinks that dancing is immoral. As you said, he wants to cover up what he thinks is not moral. If he lived in Greek times, he would be covering up their statues.

MH: I figured maybe he wasn't breastfed long enough.

NS: I don't know what the deal is, but he certainly has a political agenda that is very fundamentalist, very far right, and the news media have pretty much accommodated themselves to him.

MH: I can recognize the humor in your articles. It is very advanced tongue-in-cheek stuff, like the article where you were talking about people comparing George Bush, especially with his state of dis-union speech, with Franklin Delano Roosevelt.

NS: We don't know sometimes whether to laugh or scream or kick telephone poles when we see news media coverage of our purported leaders, and this notion that is put forward with a straight face of George W. Bush being akin to Franklin Delano Roosevelt would just be hysterically funny if it didn't have such a barbed and vicious political agenda behind it. As I point out in the column, the kind of things that FDR said about the rich, about corporate power, about the need to challenge corporate power in the 1930s, is exactly the sort of political position that George W. Bush and the interests he represents find abhorrent. We are left, again, with history being whitewashed. It's like Martin Luther King, Jr. is now a martyr on a postage stamp, who had a dreaming affect and, meanwhile, as I say in the article, not only does it boost George W. Bush in the media, but it's a way of cutting FDR down to Bush's size, which, in terms of historical stature and certainly depth as a thinker, is rather small.

MH: I would think that Roosevelt must be spinning in his grave.

NS: At high RPMs and, of course, that's as a result of other kinds of spinning that have been going on through news media on a daily basis.

MH: Most Americans only have what they hear/see on television and read in newspapers, so they really take that and make it their "Bible." It becomes their truth. What do we need to do to snap them out of it?

NS: You set the context in which they think very well, because few of us have first-hand experience with news events that we can form opinions on. I've never been to Afghanistan. I have my impressions of events, whether across the state or around the world, filtered through the media access and information that is available to me. I think our challenge is to find additional sources of information and analysis and perspective, and also to be willing and able to challenge, read and, as you said, read *between* the lines, to perceive differently the mainstream media.

I don't advise people to just dodge the existing mass media. I think we need to look at it in different ways. Always ask ourselves, one way or another, why are *these* voices being heard and *these* perspectives being put forward? Who can we plausibly assume would have other perspectives that don't have money behind them that are being excluded or downplayed or very limited in terms of getting through the mass media? Then, also, go to other sources. I don't think the Internet is any cure-all, because it is increasingly dominated by corporate interests, but there are some great sources. We are speaking in a venue right now that *you* have created that is a different sort of window into world events and human possibilities.

I think this is an example of how grassroots-based national and international media, through the technology of the Internet, is tremendously important and has an aggregate effect. We could rattle off the names of 50 or 100 websites that are not dominant like CNN or MSNBC, but they're significant. Whether we are talking about fair.org or commondreams.org or others. It's significant that that work's being done and we need to stay in constant touch with these other perspectives to sift it out for ourselves.

MH: My show is now heard in 60 countries. I hear from people as far away as the Czech Republic, who tell me that my show gives them solace because America right now is scaring the hell out of them.

NS: I think for people in Czechoslovakia and anywhere in the world, it is quite plausible that the United States of America would scare the hell out of them. I'm here in the San Francisco, California area and it scares the hell out of *me*. U.S. society has always had strength, but, overall, there's been a strong undertow of arrogance, of dislocation, of dominance from money, of media estrangement, of conceits being built on oppression. We have never effectively come to terms with the original sins of our own country—the massacres of Native Americans and slavery, the enormous racial and class injustices in our society. Of course, injustices such as that exist around the world.

You mentioned Czechoslovakia, where the treatment of gypsies has been pretty horrendous. [Czech Republic President Vaclav] Havel, as a leader there, has sometimes played along with that. The United States is not unique in being a place where terrible oppression has taken place, but the U.S. *is* the world's super-power. It does cast the largest shadow. It does have, *by far*, the biggest military. It is the biggest bully on the world block and for those reasons, especially now, more than ever, we need to be aware of and willing to challenge U.S. military and economic and political power around the planet, because the military is at the service of those who are very wealthy and who are determined to become even more so. Many, many people, obviously, are suffering as a result.

MH: In your book, you say that a lot of Americans really are under the impression that the United States is the center of the Universe.

NS: As I call it, jingo-narcissism. The jingoistic self-centered notion that we are where it's at gets accelerated and accentuated by this media machinery that keeps telling us that, indeed, we are *so* important. Of course, it is a barbed compliment because it also has the goal of making us feel we're the center of the Universe, but we don't quite have as much as we need or *deserve*. That's the purpose of advertising, for instance, is to tell us that we're great, but we're not *complete* if we don't buy and consume "x," "y," or "z." So, this discontent is fed even while the self-centeredness is fueled as well.

MH: What did you think of after September 11th when Bush said that to be a good American we all needed to just go out and keep consuming?

NS: It's kind of like "show your patriotism by buying things." That's the flag that is so compelling to people like Bush. It may not be the Stars and Stripes really quite so much as the dollar sign hoisted above, flapping in the breeze. I think that's really what turns these people on. It's a sickness. It's a terribly deranged political economy that pursues profit above everything else.

MH: Bev Conover [*see* Chapter 8] at *Online Journal* is really trying hard now to get a movement going against spending and against people supporting these corporations. She was trying to come up with a slogan and she asked whether I could think of one. What I thought was, "Starve a corporation, feed a democracy."

NS: I think that's well put. Resources are currently necessary. To do a small Web project that can put itself out there at all effectively, you need a modicum of financial resources. When you look at how the society appropriates its resources and how money is spent, it's kind of a map of the ideology, not the rhetoric, not the high-flying flowery phrases of how much we care about human beings, but when you get down to it, when the U.S. already is spending about $1 billion a day on the military, this is staggering. How do you spend $1 billion a day on the military?

MH: I always try to figure out, where does all this money come from? Do they just manufacture it? Is it out there like the Internet, out in cyberspace?

NS: I think it's coming from you and me and other people who pay taxes, for the most part. Of course, there is a borrowing process and a deficit because the government has good credit. I'm no economist, but it's our tax money and the promise of *more* tax money that then enables the government, while it is moving into deficit spending, to go ahead and borrow. Of course, then, the banks are going to get the interest on the borrowed money, so I think where it all comes from is often from our obedience or our belief, our willingness to tolerate what I think is really a system of skewing priorities much more for the benefit of the few than the many.

MH: At $1 billion a month, I think they said it's costing us for this war, can you imagine how much food we could buy for these people? That's where it's *really* going to change the terrorism, is to feed and clothe people all over the world so they don't have this collective anger. Two-thirds of the world is starving, so that means two-thirds of the world is angry.

NS: The figure I saw is that in an hour's period, well over 1,000 children on the planet die from preventable diseases. I've also seen, and this is a Noam Chomsky figure, if you took 1/10th of the Pentagon budget and applied it to solving some of those problems of preventable illness and disease for children, you could largely prevent their deaths. That's a real commentary on where the government priorities are.

MH: Think about how much popularity we could buy saving 1,000 children every hour.

NS: If the values were in a different place, I think we'd have a very different sort of a response. Not that the world would be rosy, but you put positive energy in, you're more likely to get positive energy back.

MH: Gandhi said, "Violence only creates more violence." One chapter in your book just jumped me right out of bed one night. I said, "This *can't* be true." It was your article on "Money Scandals: 'Mr. Smith' Goes to Washington." You talked about how we interfere around the world in political affairs of other countries and about all the money we pour into political campaigns overseas.

NS: It's just such blatant hypocrisy, it's amazing it can even be pulled off. When there was a scandal a few years ago of money from the Chinese government or interests being poured into certain campaigns in the U.S. in 1996, there was quite a big media uproar about it. Yet, *routinely*, the U.S. has taken its prerogative to do that, bragged about doing it through the conduits like the National Endowment for Democracy and other means to send money to Russia, for instance, to get [Russian President] Boris Yeltsin re-elected. We interfere with the electoral processes of *dozens* of countries. This is kind of the essence of the arrogance of a super power. Whether it's funneling money into another country's political campaign to support certain candidates or sending missiles over to another country, the notion is "do as we say, not as we do." When *they* do it, it's interference or it's terrorism, which it usually is. When *we* do it, it's benign, it's to promote democracy or simply to *stop* terrorism.

MH: In other words, it's okay for the United States not to play by the rules, but everybody else has to play by *our* rules.

NS: It is the subverted definition of the Golden Rule: "Those who *have* the gold make the rules." Also, those who have the weapons to back up *their* implementation of the rules are able to do so. I think that certainly extends to what is called free trade; that essentially the U.S. lays down the markers, sets the rules, decides when free trade exists, and when it's to be totally dispensed with because the U.S. has the muscle, economically and politically, and sometimes militarily, to get its way.

It's a matter of breaking down protective barriers in other countries, but that's portrayed in the news media as simply "reform" or "free trade" or "modernization." Privatization has now gotten a bad name because of Enron, but it's really the same notion. You allow private interests to trump the interests of the public and you let private interests that are smiled upon by the U.S. government to prevail.

MH: My feeling is that if most Americans knew the *real* truth, they would be up-in-arms.

NS: That brings us back to news media foursquare because news media create and sustain an impression we have of the world, the way the world is, what the world is, and how events have unfolded. That's our filter. Whether it's Americans or people anywhere else in the world, we respond to the information we have and *don't* have. I find, in general, that whatever their political perspectives are, people have a *moral* sense. They have a sense of ethics. They want to be part of what they perceive as the "right" thing. I don't believe that support for the U.S. military in the United States is primarily based on a bloodthirstiness, although there is that, but there is such a skewed picture of the world presented by news media that people's humanistic impulses are funneled in the service of an agenda that is anything but humanistic.

MH: Bush said the reason these terrorists strike us is because they're jealous of our lifestyle. Don't you find that to be an insult to the intelligence of the American public, to *any* human being, not even an American?

NS: We would think that people would be offended by that, but it's the kind of a dumbed-down, very simplistic line—to say they don't like us because we are successful; they don't like us because we're good. That was another part of the message. They don't like our democracy. I think that's been overplayed and it's even *more* than exaggerated, it's a way in which those who support the *status quo* can portray all resentment towards us as being basically based on evil, and they are resentful of what's positive in this country.

MH: I've traveled a lot to many different foreign countries on the planet and I haven't seen anyone in their own country, whether it's Italy or France or the backwoods in the Caribbean somewhere, who didn't like their own lifestyle. They didn't say to me, "Oh, you're an American, I'm *so* jealous of your lifestyle." These people seemed pretty happy living the way they live.

NS: The real problem is often poverty. Of course, most people don't like poverty, but they do have enormous positive feelings about their own cultures and their own societies.

MH: When I moved to Phoenix from New York [City], it was like being on another planet. So many people had already made up their minds what New Yorkers are like, in order for me to get a compliment here, it was a twisted compliment. Someone would say, "You know, you're not bad for a New Yorker." I think it's the same thing that carries over with foreigners. Once they really meet a living, breathing American, they say, "You're not all the terrible demons that we thought you were."

NS: We suffer from enormous stereotypes. Some of those are carried word-of-mouth, but I think a lot of them are media-generated. The news media do filter our impressions of each other. It reminds me of a statement that was attributed to the American humorist, Will Rogers. He was talking about someone and he said, "It's not what he *doesn't* know that bothers me, it's what he knows that just ain't so." That kind of deficit is a lot more difficult to dislodge. If I *know* I don't know something, maybe I can learn about it. But if I believe I know something and I'm pretty sure about it, then how can that bogus knowledge be dislodged if it's inaccurate? The news media has made us feel that we know other people because we've seen images of them. As you know from traveling, that is so often different from what is actually real.

MH: One thing I've learned is that all people are the same, all around the world. They all have the same concerns. They all worry about feeding their family, having a place to live, whether their kids are going to get sick. That's a total human thing. To believe this latest most ridiculous line that ever could have come out of his mouth, this "axis of evil," is really a slap in the face to millions of people.

NS: I've gotten e-mails from Iran, for instance. People are really stunned by that. It's such a weird notion and it reminds me of when [former President Ronald] Reagan thought he had been in World War II because he was in a *movie* about World War II. This is a media-driven sense of what societies are like and, of course, it's like the Jerzy Kosinski novel, *Being There*, that was made into the film with Peter Sellers. The notion if something is consistent with what we've already seen on TV, then it's really captivating and compelling. I think when stereotypes are put out through a political media apparatus, it doesn't seem so weird to people because it's consistent with what they've gotten before.

MH: Do you think we have a "Chauncy Gardner" in the White House?

NS: He's been very skillful. He's been learning. They used to say that Reagan was a quick study. I think George W. Bush is good at that. He's able to pick up the cues from his handlers and he's really improved on TV in the sense of being more phony than ever.

MH: They're good actors. Reagan was already an actor, so at least he knew how to learn his lines.

NS: Production values. Media commentators and political journalists quite often (and we've seen this with a vengeance in the last few months) will evaluate the leadership of a president or a senator based on what a drama critic would call "performances" and "production values" and so forth. That's one of the most disturbing things about the media coverage of politics in general—that the basis to evaluate a president, or whoever, is really on appearances in the most often very superficial way. You have these supposedly very perceptive and sophisticated pundits on television and in the *New York Times* and so forth, and they really are evaluating as though they were watching some stage play.

MH: A lot of people are into body language and facial gestures—and even somebody like Mark [Crispin] Miller, who wrote *The Bush Dyslexicon* [*see* Chapter 13]—have looked at Bush. All I ever saw was somebody you can't trust. Just looking at his facial features, I still feel the same way. Every time he's out there, it looks like, "Is today the day I'm going to get caught?"

NS: He's pretty frightened, but these folks are, in their own way, quite insulated. It's not so terribly hard to read a teleprompter and if you do have the basic skills, or can develop them, to talk in certain ways, to know how to navigate questions. Bush has only a limited repertoire of tape loops. He's kind of like a random-access memory or a very little hard drive.

MH: I think he's got a 486.

NS: Maybe it's one of those old floppy disks. You can see the internal disk drive spinning. You can see that he's just groping to try to remember which tape loop to activate.

MH: I've seen him lock-up quite a few times. Control-Alt-Delete, George. Anyway, did you happen to see Al Gore's speech that he gave in Tennessee? Al did it *without* a teleprompter. The whole thing is online if you want to see it. It's worth watching because it seems that the personable Al Gore that everyone complained they only saw at the end of the election is totally there. It seems to me like he really needed that downtime. It's at Gore-04.com. They have the whole speech. Here's a guy who speaks from his heart, the way Kennedy would have spoken, without notes, without prompters, without Cheney in the background lip-synching to him. Here's a man who's really of, by, and for the people, who gets *elected* by the people, and is still not president.

NS: He was elected by more popular votes. That's just an objective fact—by more than half a million more popular votes than Bush. He never, of course, would have gotten there without enormous support from corporate America. He's been a big patron of theirs and vice versa. He's a big corporate guy. I think the nature of U.S. politics in presidential races and senatorial races and so forth is that we choose between varieties of corporate candidates. I think that's what we had in 2000.

MH: What do you think was the media's responsibility in that whole election fiasco?

NS: For one thing, corporate media are evaluating corpo-
        rate candidates. We have these divisions among and
        between those candidates and Rupert Murdoch on
        Fox versus AOL TimeWarner on CNN and so forth
        (at that point, TimeWarner). They are going to have
        splits and divisions.

MH: It's like watching the Battle of the Titans.

NS: And from my vantage point, they let Bush slide a lot.
        If they'd done tough reporting, instead of winking at
        the guy and saying, "Well, he doesn't know his facts,
        but that's okay," I think Gore would be in the White
        House, even given what went on in Florida.

MH: You have another chapter [in your book], "Retractions
        of Reporting are Quite Selective."

NS: Working on that piece really blew my mind. I just got
        a question stuck in my mind. We know about the
        Gulf of Tonkin coverage in 1964. It really opened the
        floodgates to the Vietnam War in terms of leading to
        the Gulf of Tonkin Resolution a few days later, which
        passed almost unanimously in the U.S. Congress and
        was as close as the U.S. ever got to a formal
        declaration of war on Vietnam. The reporting of it
        was absolutely false. The first time in the Gulf of
        Tonkin, the North Vietnamese did *not* unprovokedly
        attack the U.S. We had been shelling the North
        Vietnamese coast prior to that. The *second* reported
        attack, it seems, never really occurred. It was kind of
        a trumped-up way to stampede the U.S. further into
        the Vietnam War.

        I got to wondering whether the major outlets, the *New
        York Times* and the *Washington Post* ever retracted
        their stories, which were basically out-and-out lies put

forward as facts. I did some investigation. As you know, from reading the piece, it turned out that, of course, they *never* had done any retractions at all, even though these were bald-faced lies reported as facts. When I found Murrey Marder, who had done that reporting for the *Washington Post*, he said, "I can assure you there was *never* any retraction" of the Gulf of Tonkin reporting. If there was going to be that sort of retraction, then the news media of the United States would have to retract most of what they *ever* reported about the *entire* war.

MH: Even scarier, what I want to read from here is that you said, "Marder commented, 'If the American press had been doing its job and the Congress had been doing *its* job, we would never have been involved in the Vietnam War.'" How many hundreds of thousands of lives on both sides ended up ruined because of that war?

NS: It's very chilling and it goes to a key point, I think, about why we should be concerned, angry, and active about news media. The news that we get and don't get is a matter of life and death. It is *absolutely* crucial to what happens on this planet. It's about media filtering out and steering us in certain directions. We have to be active on it because it's not a matter of whether news media affects us (of course, they do in so many ways), it's are we simply going to be passive and be done in by news media or are we going to be active enough to change the course of events?

MH: What do you think about what the media has or has not done about 9/11?

NS: I would divide that into two categories. Many of my columns on this subject are at www.fair.org, if people just click to "Media Beat" there. On the level of communicating just the horrific human toll, what it means in human terms when bombs go off or buildings explode and planes go down, at that level, I think the news media has done a good job, really evoked and communicated that human life is so much more profound when we can get down to what matters, than the glitz and commercialism that usually dances in front of our eyes through news media. I would give them a high rating on that basis.

When you get into the realm of policy, since September 11th, the kind of media coverage that's been put forward on matters of policy, what the U.S. foreign policy is, what terrorism is and is not around the world, I think the coverage has been largely atrocious. It's been propaganda-driven; it has been largely pegged to what the White House and the State Department and Pentagon *want* to be reported; and it's been fundamentally hypocritical in an Orwellian sense. If we are going to condemn terrorism, we have to condemn terrorism, whether it's what happened on September 11th or what happened beginning October 7th with the U.S. bombing in Afghanistan. Marc Herold, a professor at the University of New Hampshire, released a study in mid-December finding that about 3,700 civilians in Afghanistan had been killed by U.S. bombs since October 7th. That got very, *very* little media coverage in the United States and for those people under those bombs who had absolutely zilch to do with what happened on September 11th, they experienced terrorism.

MH: So, terrorism is defined by what side of the globe you're standing on?

NS: Absolutely. We've got to get real on this. The news media coverage is *so* locked in to U.S. foreign policy perspectives as shaped by Washington. It's so basic. We really have to think outside of that media box.

MH: I saw a piece from Canadian television where an interviewer had done a story, asking the questions about September 11th that no one in America has done yet. How could this have happened? Where were the CIA and FBI? Where did the intelligence fall down? Basically, it was accusing the Administration of complicity. This is really becoming a world view now because America has become so aggressive as the bad boy to so many countries as a result of September 11th. Why is *our* media not pressing that?

NS: I think those are universally to be understood as taboo questions that should not be raised, certainly should not be raised very loudly or consistently. Journalists are not generally more or less courageous than people in other professions. They don't want to bite the hand that's signing their paycheck. They understand, generally, what is going to be conducive to their careers continuing or moving upward, and they also understand what is hazardous to their careers. So, there is an enormous amount of conformity that's often understood simply by seeing what is acceptable, what is praised, and what we don't hear.

MH: But I think every American has a right to know, at least somebody's got to speak out for the 3,000 people who are buried under that rubble. "What happened?" is a damn good question and now we have Cheney and Bush both telling the Speaker of the House to ask very few questions and they want those to be in secret meetings.

NS: They love secrecy.

MH: But who's paying their bills? It's us little worker bees.

NS: Demagogues have always preferred secrecy because they want to stay behind the curtain and then come out with their carefully cooked books and their phony presentations. They want to pull it off. Secrecy is what you do *before* you pull the curtain.

MH: Let's hope it's not going to be time to pull the curtain on *all* American rights by the time this Administration is through.

NS: That gets us back to Ashcroft. The *New York Times*, in passing, pointed out a few weeks ago that Ashcroft is the lightning rod. He gets the blame, but he's happy to do that because it takes some of the heat off Bush. All of this is run from the very top. I'm not saying that Bush thinks of it all, because who knows what he is capable of thinking of, but he certainly signs off on it all.

MH: Ashcroft, Bush, they're all doing each other's dirty work. The real losers here are the people who are paying everybody's salaries. You, and me, and all the people working real hard to pay their taxes and just get through life.

NS: We are subsidizing their wealth.

MH: Bush is trying to distance himself from this whole Enron mess, which, obviously, the media is having a field day with. I wonder if the real truth will come out through this dumbed-down media that we have.

NS: I think bits and pieces will come out. Some of the deeper questions of the extent of corporate power are unlikely to get much ventilation. It is a "scandal" because there is a split between Democrats and Republicans that enables a scandal to emerge. Many of the problems in media coverage are when the Democrats and Republicans in Washington are *not* split. Since they both support basic corporate power, when there's not a split, those issues are not elevated to being ones that media will open up very extensively. I do think Enron is an opening, a possibility, as an issue.

I should mention that one of the hats I wear is that I am the Executive Director at the Institute for Public Accuracy. We've put out some recent news releases about Enron and people can go to our website, which is www.accuracy.org/media-beat, and you can see what we've been sharing. This includes some statements from analysts on what Enron involves at the deeper level. For instance, that Enron, through the privatization process, ran roughshod in India. The U.S. news media had no problem with that. Essentially, they went in and bribed an Indian state in West India, that includes Bombay, to build a 680-megawatt plant where they planned, at minimum, to realize $12 *billion* in profits. How do you go in and do that? It was the first privatized power plant in all of India. The U.S. media didn't have any *real* problem with it. That's where I think we need to go beyond the scandals to look at what is just business as usual.

MH: That's something that I try to figure out. I've been alive in this country for over half a century and I haven't seen any major changes, one way or the other, with what people do.

NS: If people like you and me, and thousands and millions of other people, hadn't been active over this last half century, then things would be a lot worse even than they are today.

MH: Do you think there's a cure for corporate corrupt media by maybe making law changes?

NS: I think there are many potential cures. Those changes will come from the bottom up as they always have.

Even if they're ultimately implemented by the powers that be, it's always under pressure from the grassroots.

MH: I really feel it is going to be a peoples' movement that has to change this. I don't trust either political party to do it. I've been around too long and I really haven't seen any changes. At the beginning of last year [2001], I thought, "Are we back in the '60s?" because it seemed like all our news was basically the same. I felt like we were thrown back in a time tunnel.

NS: There is certainly that feel and that's all the more reason we've got to raise our voices. The First Amendment is like a lot in life, you use it or you lose it. We really do have to enliven the First Amendment by using it.

MH: I'm just going to keep using my voice and voices like yours. I'm giving my listeners the best minds on the planet, but I can't do their reading for them.

TWELVE

FOLLOW THE MONEY – OOPS, THE FLAG

Meria with Stan Goff

Stan Goff[13] is the author of *Hideous Dream: A Soldier's Memoir of the US Invasion of Haiti*, which describes his experiences in Haiti. As a man with over 24 years' experience in our armed forces (a Master Sergeant in the Army Special Forces), his views and revelations *must* be heard by every Ameri-CAN. Goff took the oath "to protect the U.S. Constitution," yet now says that at no time in his 24 years did he truly uphold the Constitution. He discloses that racism is rampant in our armed forces. He states that "the flag follows the money and the troops follow the flag." He discloses information concerning the use of the CIA, for many years already, more for covert operations than intelligence, culminating in the WTC disaster. He also speaks about the Department of Defense and NSA [National Security Agency] as the groups responsible for "intelligence."

Goff discusses how the U.S. is still interfering in Haiti, the "laboratory nexus of CIA and local thugs." He exposes the National Endowment for Democracy as a front group that interferes in the outcomes of elections in other countries to serve U.S. corporate interests. He expresses his opinions about "the idiotic foreign policies of Bush," U.S. imperialism, and the growing fascism in America. He states that "war is about money and money is about domination," and expresses the view that the "war on terrorism" is being used as a pretext to restructure the global architecture.

Goff discusses how 9/11 was used as a means to accelerate the foreign and national policies of militarism, why there is such political complacency in America and what we can do individually to change things. He identifies John Ashcroft as an unrepentant racist, who is systematically destroying services to the public sector to impose militarization of domestic policies. Goff knows the game inside out. He's been involved in many U.S. military campaigns, finally realizing that what he thought the missions were, had nothing to do with the *true* goals. (Interview taped/broadcast on February 13, 2002.)

MH: The book is published by one of the bravest publishers out there, my friend Tennessee [Jones, Director of Sales and Marketing] over at Soft Skull Press. The blurb on the back says, "In a distinguished career in elite Ranger, Airborne and Special Forces counterterrorist units, Stan Goff went to Vietnam, Guatemala, El Salvador, Grenada, Panama, Venezuela, Honduras, South Korea, Colombia, Peru, Somalia, and, in 1994, Haiti. There, he refused to turn away from the implications of his own experience. He chose to defy the contradictions between what the foreign policy establishment said and what the U.S. military did, and took sides with Haitian democratic forces over the U.S.-supported death squad apparatus.

"Conflict escalated with his men who were steeped in racist, anti-Haitian propaganda, as well as with commanders who depended on him to support a massive campaign of deception aimed at both the Haitian and American people. *Hideous Dream* is a revealing look inside U.S. foreign policy, inside the elite echelon of the Special Forces, and inside the racist history of American imperial domination of Haiti. It is also a deeply personal account of a man trapped between his emerging political consciousness and the cynical mandates of his life as a professional soldier."

Maybe it's because I'm female, but war books are never usually what I sit down and read out of choice. Once I started reading your book, I couldn't put it down. The book is really written from the heart. It's in everyday terms. What prompted you to put this book together?

SG: It didn't start as a book. I think it started really as therapy almost. The lion's share I wrote in the first two or three months after I got back and then, I set the thing aside and thought about it for about 4-1/2 years. I was writing some other stuff and some of it was being published by a fellow named Nick Mamatas up in New York who went to work for Soft Skull as an editor. He said, "Hey, you still got that stuff laying around that you wrote on Haiti?" And I said, "Oh, yeah, I got it." And he said, "Well, turn it into a manuscript and send it up here." I knuckled down for a few weeks and finished off the last few pages and sent it up to him. Soft Skull took a chance on me because it doesn't really fit into any genre, which is one reason that nobody else was particularly interested in publishing it.

MH: I think anybody who comes out and talks about anything that's not part of the patriotic fever in this country right now is being compared to some kind of traitor, etc. There's so much in this book that people really need to know about U.S. foreign policy. It would help them understand why the whole world *really* hates us. Reading about your experience with the people in Haiti, and I know they're beautiful people, really touched me. Of course, I'm sure that didn't make you too popular with the rest of the boys in your group.

SG: I would say the Haitian people are *my* heroes. It's a country that's gone through some really remarkable hard times and most of those hard times have really been imposed externally even though it's always portrayed as some sort of innate perversion of African people that they're incapable of governing themselves. In fact, external influences have always had a profound influence on what happens in Haiti. The people there still have the same really revolutionary spirit of resistance that caused the revolution through which Haiti won its independence in 1804.

I really didn't know anything about Haiti when I got there, but the more I learned about it, the more I discovered how connected [and important our histories are]. I'm not sure it's really possible to completely understand the history of race or racism as an institution in this country without integrating Haiti into that interpretation.

MH: A lot of people in America want to believe, or at least want to make themselves believe, that racism doesn't exist in this country any more.

SG: Denial springs eternal. That, to me, is a feat of mental gymnastics to even make such a claim and for people to make that claim, or to repeat that claim, is pretty disingenuous.

MH: Just yesterday, I got sent a story from the *San Francisco Chronicle* about the police who went into a black neighborhood and for no reason whatsoever beat up kids from 12 to14 years old. And when the mother was pleading for her daughter's life, the cop says, "As long as you people are here, this is what we're going to keep doing." I mean, this is America in 2002. This was in California. This wasn't on another planet.

SG: No, and there's a lot of that stuff going on. That's why it's interesting to me that I had to go to a lot of other third-world nations to discover how many third-world nations exist right inside our own borders. There's a third-world nation that exists 10 miles as the crow flies from where I'm standing right now and it's probably true of most of the people who are sitting here listening to this. Racism is the ideological ornamentation on this system. It's really an economic system that, in some ways, is almost a colonial system inside our own borders. It's being exacerbated now by the introduction of Hispanics/Latinos. Since NAFTA, in North Carolina, where I live, the introduction of Hispanic/Latino workers in this state has caused the biggest demographic shift since reconstruction. The whole racial and national dynamic is complicated. It just shows you this relationship that exists between economic elites in this country and the people on the bottom of the ladder has been pretty naked colonialism in a lot of ways.

MH: You spent 24 years in the military service. You report that you got yourself in trouble quite a few times. At the end, when you were really being grilled, it was for exposing the racism within the Special Forces.

SG: I think I contributed to it. I think there's not a subtle causal explanation for how that came to pass. I just started moving in the wrong direction. I wasn't moving with the flow of everything else that was going on there and, over time, the force of those institutions will pick you up and carry you away. The fact that I had been openly confrontational over issues of race certainly didn't help matters and it elevated my visibility in the Special Forces community where it was problematic.

My personal identification with a number of Haitians, and even the fact that I'd made friends with Haitians, made me suspect in some people's eyes. They were claiming I'd "gone native," that I'd turned Haitian, which is not that uncommon. That's the kind of thing you start hearing if you even question what the mission is or, not even the mission, if you just start questioning the narrative that's superimposed *on* the mission, you become visible in a very perilous way.

MH: You make it very clear in your book that what you thought the mission was and what you ended up finding out it was once you got there, were two different things.

SG: If I had known what I know now, I wouldn't have been that naïve in the first place. But, I was very naïve going into the mission. I thought history had conjured up a set of circumstances where the United States was finally going to go in and be forced to do the "right" thing—and that was just stunning naiveté on my part.

MH: You were young. You've got to forgive yourself for all those young, wonderful ideals, you know. Then, reality set in. You have some pretty interesting characters described in your book. There were parts where I was just laughing out loud, but it was kind of a nervous laugh because I could really feel what you were going through there, being torn in your feelings for these people. And how could you not? A lot of people, including the former leader of Afghanistan, are saying the same thing you just said about Haiti. How can we have a government from, say, Germany tell *our* people how to live? And I don't think what we did in Haiti was any different.

SG: It's still not. In fact, the United States is still interfering vigorously in the internal affairs of the Haitian people. The United States is going to declare whatever process takes place in Haiti to be undemocratic until the democratic process provides them with the results our government expects. I've been back about nine times since the intervention, and I was there last year during the [Haitian President Jean-Bertrand] Aristide inauguration. This stuff is still going on. The Haitians call it "the laboratory," and what they're talking about is that nexus between the political section and the U.S. Embassy, the CIA, and the old McCoot sector, that sort of thug-ish sector that became enforcers.

Different dominant classes in Haiti are at war with one another. What they have in common and what will bring them together and solidify them in a common front, is their *intense* fear of their own people. Any time anyone has a real connection with the great mass of Haitian people, it terrifies them, and that was really their terror of Aristide. That was also the U.S. terror of Aristide.

Even though they co-opted Aristide and they put his face on the front to go back in, they needed him in order to justify going back in. They fought very hard behind the scenes through organizations like the National Endowment for Democracy. These are front foundations run by U.S. embassies to manipulate and interfere in other peoples' elections, even though we would be incensed if anybody tried to influence the outcome of our elections here. We do that all the time. Not "we"—you and I didn't do it—I should quit using that pronoun. It's the United States foreign policy establishment that interferes enthusiastically.

MH: And their front organization is the National Endowment for Democracy?

SG: The National Endowment for Democracy (NED). I would encourage anybody who doesn't know what that is to just sort of do a web search or go to the library and look up some information on that. It's an organization that's designed for the sole purpose of interfering in and influencing the outcomes of other peoples' elections. There are some problems within Aristide's organization, but those are internal problems. All organizations are imperfect and, as a friend of mine in Haiti says, the Haitian people have a *right* to be wrong. It's nobody's business what kind of problems they have. What the U.S. is doing now is withholding loans and foreign aid to Haiti and they've created an intense crisis there for the purpose of destabilizing Haiti, while they continue to put up this fake opposition, which has been cobbled together with NED funds.

The name they're using now is Converge Democritique, the Democratic Conversion. They've cobbled together 15 different political parties that together couldn't garner 8% of the vote. They *obviously* have no popular base. Their base is a lot of funds that are being funneled to them through the NED and through members of the Haitian economic elite to try to go back and seize the reins of the country down there. And that's been the ongoing process. I fully expect the Bush Administration, when they disentangle themselves from some of the not only wicked, but fairly idiotic, foreign policies they're pursuing right now, to turn a baleful eye back on Haiti and go back, through one means or another, and attempt some sort of a *coup* there again.

MH: What do you think the U.S. wants from Haiti? I mean, we obviously want oil from the Afghanistan mess, but what do we want from Haiti?

SG: They want subjection. Haiti doesn't exist as an isolate any more than anything else.

Right now, what the United States is experiencing as a hegemony, as an imperial nation in this hemisphere, in particular, are some pretty thorough-going threats to their domination of the region, so you have to see Haiti as part of the region. It cannot be allowed to exercise autonomy because it gives other people "bad" ideas. The super-exploited half of the island keeps the wage levels down and keeps popular forces out of power next door in the Dominican Republic. The Haitian workers are the most exploited sector inside the Dominican Republic, and the deeper poverty of Haiti in turn puts a downward pressure on wages. This elevates the profit margins of investors who are in the Dominican Republic next door, which is a vassal state of the United States and has been since we invaded them back in, I think, 1965.

There are other problems in this hemisphere and Haiti is part of that equation. Ecuador is about to come apart at the seams and has been for about a year and a half. Argentina has already gone into default and their economy has collapsed. Popular forces there are beginning to question the dictate of the International Monetary Fund and the U.S. foreign policy establishment.

Colombia has been engaged in a long-standing civil war and the people who would win that war without U.S. assistance going in there are not people the U.S. particularly wants to see in power.

Venezuela has gone off the reservation as far as the United States is concerned. Cuba still exists. Puerto Rico is beginning to have a nationalist current. All these things have to be taken together to understand how Haiti is going to be perceived by that establishment. Nicaragua wasn't a place where there was particularly a lot of investment, but to allow the Nicaraguan revolution to succeed would have been a "bad" example. They had to be knocked back down because that would threaten power more generally throughout the region.

MH: Up until maybe the last year or two, I was pretty much in the dark about U.S. foreign policy, too. I wanted to be like everyone else, thinking we were so great. I think most Americans have no idea how much death and destruction we've done in so many other countries just for the almighty buck. You have a quote in here in your chapter called "No Conspiracies," where you say, "As Smedley Butler, a former Marine Corps Medal of Honor winner turned critic of capitalism, once said, 'The flag follows the money, and the troops follow the flag.'"

SG: That sums it up about as tidily as I could think of.

MH: In other words, it really is, bottom-line, everything is all about money?

SG: I think it's about money, but I think money is about domination and I think that's important to understand, too. You can take a handful of dollar bills and if everybody didn't accept that you could exchange them for something real, what can you do with them? You can't change a tire with them. You can't eat them. I think the question goes deeper than just the money. The money is a means by which a very small group of people manage to continue to have this entitlement to the bodies and labor of everybody else, and to exist parasitically off those people. I know that's a real radical conclusion for someone to draw; people will red-bait me, but they're going to do that anyway.

MH: I'm not arguing with you. I had Howard Winant [*see* Chapter 5] on my show, who wrote a book called *The World Is a Ghetto*. He says that throughout history, the whole idea of domination and control was to keep the darker races down. It's still happening. It's right here in America. We don't really have to go to distant shores to have that kind of twisted thinking going on.

SG: And I think it's real important for people to understand this. This is an example of cognizant dissonance, racism as an ideology. I believe it was something that was a kind of window-dressing they had to put on there. I discovered (and wrote about where I describe some of my experiences in Vietnam) that if you're in a situation where you're obligated to do bad things to people, the only way you can continue to live with yourself is to find some way to dehumanize those people so that you can rationalize what you're doing. If you go back and trace it, historically, racism grew directly out of the expansion of capital into colonial zones. If you're going to be stealing African bodies for labor, you have to find a way to justify that. The way you justify that is to dehumanize them.

MH: Say they don't have a soul or they're not as intelligent as you or come up with a million other stupid things.

SG: For me, it was important to understand that. It was a big discovery in my own growth process, and Haiti stimulated that thinking a lot.

MH: In reading some of your experiences, there seemed to be a couple of times where you basically almost totally lost your mind. And you have to be a pretty strong man to have pulled yourself back from some of the things that were going on around you. You described how you would get a little tanked and then go and float in the river to just get yourself back in touch with reality. We take our young boys and we raise them with mother's love and then the Army or Navy, whatever, gets them and trains them to kill. They go do these unnatural things—I don't believe killing is a natural act. Then, they're supposed to just come back home and be normal. You really put all those feelings so well in your book. I thought, "I can't believe I'm reading a war book, but okay." It really isn't about war; it really is about how you became a human being through it.

SG: I don't think there's any way to talk about this stuff seriously if we don't talk about gender. I don't think boys are raised strictly with their mother's love and then, all of a sudden, turned into monsters by the military. I was socialized as a boy starting very early, just like every other boy is. The socialization of boys is a pretty creepy process when you start taking a close look at it. We teach boys to commit a form of emotional suicide and it begins very early on. The price we pay for our privilege as males is a fragmentation of our own personality, and it's a lifelong thing. It's something that disconnects us from society in a way. It leads us to believe that our lives are involved with confronting everybody else and being prepared to do things like take peoples' lives, to resort to violence and all that. We do some terrible things in the way that we raise boys.

MH: I have been thinking about my own son, if they start reinstalling the draft.

SG: They're moving toward that pretty quickly too. The militarization of this society is one of the most alarming things I've seen in a long time.

MH: What happened in the book is, you really shifted. I see the shift in you as a human being where you really started to see what all the real problems were in the world. I would say it is a fact that human beings are working towards an extinction of themselves. Can it be stopped? A lot of these wars and things we've been fighting are mostly because there are people who are poor and hungry and starving around the world and nothing is being done about it. When I read that you were in Somalia, I wanted to know what you thought of the movie *Black Hawk Down?*

SG: I won't go see it. I've already heard from enough people about it. No matter how accurately they portray some details, that was part of their task force. That's one reason I don't particularly want to see it because I just don't want to put myself through it again. I was expelled from that mission and from some of the best units in the Army. It is my understanding that the portrayal of Africans in there is as having no value.

MH: I understood there was a lot of propaganda in it. Then, I found out that the United States chipped in $2.2 million to make that movie.

SG: That's worrisome all by itself.

MH: Isn't that a scary thought? I won't see it and I've asked my listeners to boycott the movie, too. People need to realize they have the *right* to do that. What do you think about the current war on terrorism?

SG: It's just another pretext to go out and restructure the global architecture in the midst of a terrible crisis they don't know how to cope with. I've been in on a lot of mobilizations for operations, and it took us *months* to prepare for something as logistically supportable as Haiti, which is only 120 miles off our shores. You are talking about them putting this operation together and going in to invade Afghanistan with the level of inter-service coordination and sophistication that we saw going into Afghanistan, and they did that in under 30 days? That's preposterous. It's categorically not possible. Those war plans were on the table before September 11th. That's not saying this is a conspiracy that September 11th was ordered by the White House and all that stuff. There's some of that going around, too. It *is* saying that this Administration pounced on that event in a deeply cynical and opportunistic way to go out and accelerate a foreign policy and a domestic policy agenda of militarization in the face of what's shaping up to be a deep and protracted global economic crisis.

There was a crisis of empire in this hemisphere that I described earlier, a political crisis of legitimacy that this Administration had starting out because they lost the election by judicial fiat. This resolves a lot of problems. This pulls all their cookies out of the fire. And, now, it's allowed them to do pretty much anything they want because they've got these weak-kneed, spineless Democrats who are just going along with them because they're afraid they're going to lose some political capital if they speak out against this stuff.

MH: A lot of people are saying the same thing. Where the hell *are* the Democrats? Let's face it, they laid down for this stolen election and it's been downhill ever since. Maybe we need to have that election overseeing unit oversee *our* elections instead of worrying about Haiti and all these other countries.

SG: The most interesting thing when I was in Haiti for the inauguration was all this criticism coming from the U.S. Embassy over the Haitian elections where they had won with 98% of the vote. They criticized them as illegitimate when they only got 49% of the vote and took the election here. The Haitians were saying what gall we have to criticize them.

MH: Remember when you were a kid, that expression, "It takes one to know one"? My mother used to say, "The guilty party always talks first." What a travesty. I hear all the conspiracies about September 11th, as well, but there are a lot of people, including Canadian television, who are accusing the U.S. government, at the very least, of complicity.

SG: It's impossible that there wasn't some sort of complicity. I don't mean complicity in that they participated in some conspiracy, but there's certainly complicity in some sort of a cover-up. Let's face it, if the folks who they say did it, *did* do it, they are people our own foreign policy establishment armed, equipped, trained, and advised. They were *not* Afghanis; the vast majority of them were Saudis. The bin Laden family has economic connections to the Bush family. For them to suddenly come up and turn them into this cartoonish international heavy is pretext.

        I heard at one point, when Argentina was at a very turbulent time, that al-Qaida members may be in northern Argentina. It's just one pretext after another.

The way you can tell whether a Foreign Service person or anybody working for a presidential administration is lying is if their lips are moving. If they tell the truth, it's accidental. That's my experience working directly out of embassies. Everything they tell you is instrumental. It's designed to gain consent or acquiescence. It's not designed to represent reality. If it represents reality, that's purely an accident. It's how they exercise power.

MH: A lot of people now are comparing George Bush to Teddy Roosevelt because of his speech, his State of the Union address. Does that sit well with you?

SG: I don't know that much about Teddy Roosevelt. I know he was a populist demagogue. Bush is not a populist, but he's certainly a demagogue, so I guess they have some things in common. They're both racists.

MH: What did you think about his "axis of evil" bullying?

SG: It's amazing to me the level of political complacency in this society that people will sit by and listen to stuff like that. I'm still a little bit stunned from time to time at how easily our own culture seems to accept it. This is supposed to be a statesman talking like this.

MH: He made it a pissing match.

SG: People should know better than that, just from their own life experiences.

MH: Maybe people just don't want to be bothered. You call it a de-politicalization. Isn't what we try to do when we go into other countries is get those people not voting and not caring about politics? And that's the same thing that happens here. Even with all the hubbub about this past election, how many Americans *really* went out and voted?

SG: If they're strictly local elections and don't have a general election with all the hoopla behind it, we're real lucky to see a 12% to 15% turn-out where I live. It is a system that does demobilize people and I think it's by design.

MH: In your chapter, "No Apologies," you say you had only sworn to protect the Constitution of the United States, but you didn't take an oath "to conceal stupidity or ignore perfidy." It seems you were thinking you were representing the truth of the Constitution of the United States and you found out that really had nothing to do with it.

SG: Never has. That's the irony that I hope comes through. The people I'd like to see get this book are the soldiers. It's not a great work of literature or anything like that (I'm not going to make grandiose claims), but I wanted to give an accurate representation of what went on. I want soldiers to see this book because I can't believe I'm unique, that I'm the only one who has questions about the kinds of things I was involved in. That defies commonsense. One of the things that kept me in the dark for so long was that I really didn't have any alternative information to plug into my own interpretation of the events that were going on around me and the types of things I was involved in.

        One of the key things that soldiers should question is when we take our oath, that's all we take an oath to do. When a soldier takes an oath, the soldier's oath is, "I swear to protect the Constitution of the United States from all enemies, foreign and domestic." I can't remember one occasion, in a single conflict area, in 24 years of service, not one single time *ever* being called upon to protect the Constitution of the United

States. Not once. I don't care how many hairs you split, you can't explain to me how killing Vietnamese people protected the Constitution of the United States or how providing support to people who were involved with death squads in El Salvador is protecting and defending the Constitution of the United States. It doesn't fit. And it's a real simple thing. It's not complicated. We don't even have to get into critiques of political autonomy and all that.

MH: We were talking about how much courage Soft Skull Press has because Tennessee was the one who picked up *Fortunate Son* [by Jim Hatfield] when the original publisher punked out after threats from the Bush Administration to get rid of that book about George. What do you think the solution is to us bombing the hell out of the whole world? What we've done in Afghanistan is a total waste of money and has just killed a lot of innocent people to accomplish nothing.

SG: I think that's pretty succinct and probably very accurate. I don't think this Administration right now is acting out of a position of strength. I think there's a perception that they're operating from a position of strength because they have their domestic opposition cowed right now. But in terms of what their situation is economically, militarily, politically, etc., they're in a real tough spot and there is no easy way out for them. It seems to me that they're just sort of lunging around at random, saying, "What we have now is not going to work, so let's, for God's sake, do something."

I don't think Afghanistan is the target. Ultimately, what we're looking at right now is that this is an administration of energy oligarchs, which this Enron thing is going to bring out more and more. Given the fact that world oil production right now (and oil is the lifeblood of the global capitalist economy) is peaking and will soon begin to go into permanent and precipitous decline. In the year 2012 or thereabouts, the only remaining oil that will not have peaked is probably going to be under the ground in Saudi Arabia. That makes Saudi Arabia a pretty important place strategically.

This is a Saudi opposition really that's represented by al-Qaida and this opposition exists even within the officer corps in the Saudi military. The Saudi government is very unstable right now. The king has been debilitated with a stroke for a couple of years. There are palace intrigues going on. The standard of living is going down domestically and since the U.S. foreign policy establishment 25 to 30 years ago wiped out pan-Arab nationalism and wiped out Arab socialism as an alternative that would provide a voice to the popular misery in that country, the only thing left to them now is Islamic fundamentalism. So, it really *is* a threat and it's a threat against the government that the United States is supporting there right now, which is deeply corrupt and very unstable. I think what we're seeing is an attempt to put these new military bases around the world to prepare a military solution for what they perceive to be in the very near future a deep crisis of profit throughout the world, based on a lot of things, but energy being central to that equation.

We're not going to see these bases in Isbekistan or places like this disappear. Those are not temporary bases. They have no intention of ever leaving those bases. To support that kind of militarism, the expansion of that kind of militarism, in the face of ever-higher resistance throughout the world is, in the long-term, a no-win proposition.

It's going to break the bank at home and it's also going to require that as a domestic economic crisis is generated at home, the Administration is about to launch a merciless attack on the U.S. working class. It's already begun with the systematic destruction of public sector resources, schools, social security, Medicare. They're getting rid of these things to free up some more liquidity to pour into this Ponzi scheme they call the stock market. They've got some problems. It's not sustainable in the long-term and they're going to rely more and more on direct repressive measures. That's why I think we're seeing the militarization of domestic policing. You had a pretty graphic description of some of that a little while earlier. We're talking about the reinstatement of the draft.

With this militarization of society and this kind of militarist nationalism underwriting it, I think we really are in danger in this country right now for the first time in a long time of an emergent form of fascism. It won't look like the fascism of the 1930s. If people are looking for the jackboots and the "Heil Hitlers" and all that stuff, they're looking for the wrong thing. It's going to be a uniquely American form of fascism, but it's on its way. Look at the cabinet of this man. John Ashcroft is an unrepentant racist and he's right now running the Justice Department. He's the most important law enforcement officer in the country and he's a fanatic. We're already holding people without warrants. We're detaining people that haven't even officially been accused of anything yet.

MH: It makes you wonder why *they're* not upholding the Constitution.

SG: They're getting away with it because the people are foreigners. If you think back to Germany around 1935, the majority of the non-Jewish citizens of Germany weren't suffering any direct repression. They were sitting by while somebody else suffered it and allowing a certain portion of the population to be scapegoated. That's how this thing increments its way in. Fascism is something that intervenes whenever the system is in a crisis. When there's a crisis of profit in market forces that can't be resolved, they resort to non-market forces. I think that's what we're seeing right now on a global scale. We're not going to be immune here for very much longer. We're already seeing a lot of job losses and things like that right around where I live now, and there will be a lot more.

MH: Do you think we're going to end up in a depression?

SG: I think it's quite likely. I'm not a professional economist, but I can count.

MH: You've got eyes in your head. It's easy to see. What do you think, if anything, the citizens, the regular Joe in the street in America, can do?

SG: Organize, organize, organize. Get involved with people who are already involved. There are a whole lot of organizations out there and the more locally based the organization is, the more effective it's going to be. If you're working with progressive people, then work with progressive people who are not afraid to go out there and fight for a county commissioner's seat. Work with people who are not afraid to go out there and make a demand for a civilian review board against the local police. Work with folks who are out there fighting for a tenants' union. Those are the kinds of organizations that create the individual cells that will eventually coalesce into some sort of a mass movement that can actually make a direct and open challenge for political power. That's what it's going to take, because we are eventually going to have to quit thinking about this pluralist model of democracy where we give a little and take a little.

The people who are in charge right now have no intention of giving anyone anything. They've got to be directly and openly challenged for the political power and there's got to be some form of popular democracy that substitutes for this technical democracy that's controlled by a handful, by this clique of very wealthy and powerful people.

MH: It's been proven that 14 or 15 of the supposed terrorists aboard those planes that hit the World Trade Center were Saudis, not Afghanis, so why didn't we go after Saudi Arabia?

SG: Because we've got a lot of business over there.

MH: Starting with the Kennedy assassination, I began to realize that my country doesn't tell me the truth. Every day, there's a new story that comes out. It's like these people can't even die and just be left in peace because it's got to keep coming up.

SG: I don't believe these polls that are claiming 90% support of the Bush Adminstration. I work as an organizer now. I'm an organizer for a group called the Network for Popular Democracy in North Carolina. I've been doing this for about six years and it's very difficult to turn out 100 or 200 people for an event on short notice. Anybody who's ever done any organizing in their community knows that. When we set up a teach-in five days after September 11th here at UNC [University of North Carolina] in Chapel Hill, and did a real quick e-mail outreach to the community, we had 800 people show up. That told me that when they're constructing these polls, they're constructing the questions in a way that is creating more consent for a particular point of view.

What I'm seeing out on the streets doesn't square with these outlandish numbers. And even if there are 10% opposed and they're being intimidated by this sort of climate of post-McCarthyism right now, I think it's really our responsibility on the left to go ahead and speak out and show that we've got the courage of our convictions. It's not our speaking out that's going to endanger us. It's our silence that's going to endanger us because it encourages these people.

MH: I hope everybody heard that. That's a really good line to remember.

SG: That's what Audre Lord said: "Your silence will not protect you."

MH: I read that you had a few run-ins with some of the CIA. What do you think about the CIA? How many hours do we have, right?

SG: Those guys are everywhere. You can't make a blanket judgment about them any more than you can about any other institution.

MH: A lot of people are asking the question, "Where was our intelligence on September 11th?"

SG: I think they're wrong to even think about the CIA in that regard. For decades now, the CIA has *not* been primarily an intelligence agency. It's primarily been a covert operations agency. The last time I looked, I think their budget was about 80% committed to covert operations. Very few people are actually handling the human intelligence side of the house. It's an internal fight within the agency. The vast majority of the intelligence collection in the United

States is handled through the National Security Agency which uses very high-tech electronic stuff. They really don't get the human dimension of things and there's always a big failure of human intelligence. I think that's a constant. The CIA has their little cliques and supporters like everyone else, but it's important to understand they're a covert operations agency. I personally think their moon is waning right now and has been for quite some time, because their mission has been challenged by people within the Department of Defense [DOD] for a long time.

People in DOD have made little incursions into their territory and, as it turns out, many people who worked on covert operations on the defense side of the house have been much better at it. The CIA has been involved in a string of completely buffoonish operations. I think it's important to understand and look at something like Colombia. I'm not at all sure the Central Intelligence Agency has as much to do with what's going on down there as the DOD does. And DOD *contracts*. Normally, the Department of Defense, according to the Constitution, is supposed to be *subordinated* to some sort of civilian authority. That's why there's a Secretary of Defense who's a civilian, and it also means they're supposed to be subject to congressional oversight. The way they get around that now is the Pentagon contracts to some corporation like DynCorp and then they can go out and put mercenary forces on the ground.

Since they're a contract agency, they can claim they're a private agency and, therefore, their actions are not subject to congressional review. So, it disallows us, through our elected representatives, the opportunity to monitor and hold accountable what goes on with these outfits. I'm pretty sure this helicopter that was shot down here two or three weeks ago, the U.S. military helicopter with "civilians" on board, had employees of DynCorp on board. The DOD has taken over a lot of the kinds of functions that the old Central Intelligence Agency did under their covert operations department. They had a covert operations side and an intelligence side. They have stolen the intelligence piece from them and DOD has probably stolen a lot of the covert operations from them, so I think they're really a very weak component of the whole thing.

MH: September 11th made it look like we were caught with our pants down.

SG: Well, somebody was.

MH: Everybody sooner or later has got to ask, "Who was *supposed* to be watching the store?

SG: Not just watching the store, but who was supposed to be *responding* after the first thing happened? If you look at the sequence of activity on that day, the response to the whole thing just reeked of incompetence of some kind. There were no interceptor aircraft put up. The FAA [Federal Aviation Agency] tracks all these airplanes. Now, you got four airplanes hijacked simultaneously? Four airplanes that are simultaneously deviating from their flight plans that they've already filed with the FAA? And nobody alerts anyone? Then, you sit there and watch it live as they crash into the World Trade Center and it takes them another full hour to crash into the Pentagon, and that's after planes going clear out to Ohio conducted an unscheduled point turn and headed back toward Washington, D.C.?

MH: A lot of people online are saying that someone had to have ordered a stand-down on that.

SG: I'm not sure about that, because I was in the military long enough to know that the military makes a lot of claims about what their rapid-response capability is. Every time they meet those rapid-response times, they have to have some advance notice and they fudge a lot. There are people whose officer evaluation reports depend on those kinds of performances and that's what they are a lot of times, *performances*. I'm not convinced that's proof positive of complicity, even though I think it *is* suspicious. It at least points to incompetence, that the President of the United States is going to continue to read about goats in a third-grade classroom when 30 minutes earlier, they'd just blown up the two tallest buildings in New York. That strikes me as, at the very least, grotesquely incompetent.

MH: Let's face it, [former New York Mayor Rudy] Guiliani became President for a couple of days after that. We now, more than ever, need to support publishers like Soft Skull Press who are willing to put out *truly* informative books because so many publishing houses seem to be controlled by this Administration. It really is like fascism leaping ahead.

SG: And it's going to go as far as we *let* it go.

THIRTEEN

A DANGEROUS DYSLEXIC – BUSH

Meria with Mark Crispin Miller

Mark Crispin Miller[14] is the author of *The Bush Dyslexicon: Observations on a National Disorder* about George W. Bush. Miller discusses "the man behind the man," his constant misuse of the English language when Bush is not really interested in what he is talking about (or to whom he is speaking), and how he seems to able to command the language when he is talking about "war" or something that fits the "image" he has of himself. Miller postulates we currently have an extremely reckless (and dangerous) regime, beginning with the blatant stealing of the election in 2000. It has been gung-ho all the way since Bush started his first week in office as President, with radical anti-abortion moves, installing John Ashcroft as Attorney General, putting a gag order on doctors abroad, and so much more. Miller identifies this as a demented over-reaching of power. Bush's "axis of evil" speech created distrust and turmoil in North and South Korea (and the whole world), yet we receive Bush's dictatorial response, "It's not open for discussion," and "That's that."

Miller contends that fighting "evil" in the name of Jesus with sayings like "smoke them out" is no different from the al-Qaida fighting "evil" in the name of Allah. Bush's use of the term "evil ones" is distressing and makes him sound like a simple-minded, moralistic terrorist himself. Any person or nation threatening annihilation of an entire population could be recognized as a terrorist. Is our government itself terroristic? What about the media? The losses of freedom? The cover-ups and lies? Miller contends that Bush has contempt for the American people and relishes the role of self-appointed executioner. Are Bush and Cheney reconfiguring the world? Miller discusses why he thinks Bush and Cheney are allying this country with the countries/societies that hold the worst records for humanitarian rights for their people and dissidents. (Interview taped on February 19, 2002.)

MH: If you've read Mark's work, you'll know just how *dis*orderly he is. Last night, I was watching the news and it said that on President's Day, they debuted at the George Bush robot at Disneyland. How can they tell the difference? I wonder if the robot was programmed for his particular speech patterns.

MM: I have an elaborate theory about his speech. I don't actually think he's a robot. I think we might be better off if he were. I think there is a creature in there who is all too human. Bush is a very, very angry man and one who has spent his whole adult life, certainly his whole political life, trying to conceal his anger. The rap on him, the line everybody was uttering about George W. Bush after 9/11, was that he had been fundamentally transformed by the event, that he was completed changed, that he was now eloquent, self-restrained and wise. That was all wishful thinking.

MH: They were even comparing him to Roosevelt.

MM: And to Churchill and JFK. They're all spinning in their graves.

MH: The only people I've seen who make any sense are those comparing him to Hitler.

MM: He has that kind of demagogic impulse and, more importantly, he has exactly that same tendency to divide all of reality and all of humanity into two groups, the dark and the light, the good and the evil. In this way, he's uncannily similar to the al-Qaida types. He is not eloquent, and never will be eloquent. The first couple of days after 9/11, he really had trouble.

MH: He was missing in action, like his service career.

MM: After about 9/13, he spoke with what was, for him, unusual assurance and confidence, and I argue that has *everything* to do with the fact that he relishes the role he's now in. The George Bush as righteous warrior is the George Bush that George Bush *himself* admires. It's the George Bush that gives him a theme he can finally speak about without having to bullshit anybody, not having to pretend to be a compassionate conservative, not having to pretend to any higher ideals. All this guy really wants to do is kick ass in a righteous spirit. The fact that he has comported himself with relatively more assurance since 9/11 has to do *solely* with the fact that he's doing the only thing he's built to do, which is to go on the attack. That, too, is a kind of Hitlerian tendency.

I'm always leery of people who invoke Hitler for comparison because he was such an incredible monster and murdered so many people. On his worst day, Bush hasn't been able to match that record, but as far as temperament is concerned, and as far as his vision of the world is concerned, I would say Bush's vision of the world is a fascistic vision.

People around him, not just him, but the people around him, are really contemptuous of democracy. As we can see from their broad-based assault on civil liberties and due process, they are taking full advantage of this so-called war on terrorism to crack down big-time on a form of government they basically detest. I think they represent a real danger to American democracy, probably the greatest danger we've ever faced in our 200-year history.

MH: One of my listeners sent me what Republicans are sending around the Net about how great George Bush is because he's fighting this fight in the name of Jesus. I don't think people really get it. What's the difference between that and the al-Qaida? Nothing.

MM: There isn't any. Talking about the "evil ones" is distressing, not because we should sentimentalize the terrorists and not because they're *not* evil. It's distressing because it *sounds* like the terrorists. It's got that same simple-minded, heavily moralistic, metaphysical way of casting the other as a demon. I've been studying his language recently since *The Bush Dyslexicon* came out, and I've really been struck by how many of his descriptions of "them" sound exactly like him.

MH: You can interpret terrorism according to what part of the world you live in.

MM: Anyone who threatens whole populations with annihilation unless they go along with the program is engaging in terrorism. Now, this is not an original argument. It's an argument that [Noam] Chomsky has been making for years. It's an argument that Caleb Carr has just made in his new book [*The Lessons of Terror*] from a very different point of view, on the history of warfare where he says there is no difference between governments and rag-tag militias and freedom-fighters. They all engage in terrorism to the extent that they deliberately target civilian populations in order to intimidate them into taking some step or other. We have a government that is itself terroristic.

We have the only government in world history, as Chomsky points out, that was actually arraigned before the World Court in the Hague on charges of terrorism because of our policy in Nicaragua. Our government media dismissed that as an aberration, as perverse. Here's a good example of the kind of wild, self-description we engage in when we demonize "them."

You may recall that the Pentagon and White House refused to grant prisoner-of-war status to the soldiers captured in Afghanistan. It was irrational in the first place because Bush had defined the attacks of 9/11 as acts of war, explicitly and many times, and all of a sudden, in a conflict following an act of war, the prisoners taken are *not* prisoners-of-war, they are criminals, he says. The Pentagon then went on to say they could not be considered prisoners-of-war because *they* don't wear uniforms and carry their weapons openly. Now, I have looked extensively at the photographs in the newspapers and at the TV footage of our soldiers and, strange to say, they don't wear uniforms and *they* don't carry *their* weapons openly. So, does this mean that if al-Qaida captured some of our soldiers, they wouldn't have to observe the Geneva Convention in treating them? I don't think our government would see it that way. This kind of blindness is really, really frightening.

MH: One of the latest news bits on all the news services today (off *Reuters News*) is that we have U.S. planes now in southern Afghanistan dropping envelopes containing $100.00 bills and glossy pictures of George Bush.

MM: Are you kidding?

MH: No. I also read it on Truthout.com. I didn't get a chance to read the whole story, but some of my listeners sent it to me and asked, "Have we witnessed the end of the world here, or what?"

MM: I know we're now bombing rival factions inside Afghanistan, that was in the *New York Times* today.

MH: Doesn't this kind of smack of a world dictator?

MM: It smacks of a *would-be* world dictator. All the propaganda about Clinton, which cast him as this sort of raging, post-'60s, overgrown adolescent hippie, allowed the Bush people to cast *themselves* as very sober, buttoned-up-to-the-neck, well-behaved adults.

MH: Meanwhile, all of *their* kids are going beserko.

MM: That has obscured the fact that this is an extremely reckless, irresponsible regime. Not to put too fine a point on it, but they *did* steal the election, which already puts them in the doghouse as far as any serious American is concerned. If you cast your mind back, the very first week of the Bush presidency, they hit the ground running, trying to put in place a very radical anti-abortion program despite the fact that throughout the campaign, Bush was careful to try to represent himself as a moderate on that issue. The first week, they put John Ashcroft up for the Attorney General. They enforced this gag order on doctors working in clinics abroad that receive federal funds, and they tried to make illegal all stem cell research.

That's how that whole controversy started because that last step aroused controversy among activists against disease and scientists, which led to that ridiculous speech he finally gave in August [2001] where he tried to split the difference. That was one example of a tendency to over-reach, that's really pretty demented. They didn't get the popular vote, the anti-abortion platform is not a popular platform, but they came into office making no bones about their intention of imposing this on the country and, indeed, on the world. We've seen, now, a similar kind of over-reaching, only much more serious, with this "axis of evil" speech. That has created a tremendous amount of distrust and turmoil in South Korea and North Korea, which has strengthened the hands of the radicals in Iran whose basic purpose seems to be to facilitate a war with Iraq.

MH: We've been warned by Russia and China not to go there.

MM: And Europe. Again, this is over-reaching.

MH: And Bush's attitude is, "We're going to do whatever we have to do, and, bam, we're not going to talk about it any more. Next."

MM: Bush has been mistakenly cast by his critics as a moron, a puppet, that there's nothing inside, that he's an empty suit and "they" pull his strings. That's not, strictly speaking, accurate. Bush is an ignoramus and they *do* keep an eye on him, that's all true. And he's not really capable of a higher reasoning, to put it mildly, but he does have extremely sharp political instincts. And, more importantly, his impulses, his temperament, his character, are completely in sync with the larger political vision of the cabal that's running the country. This is a guy who is completely punitive in his impulses, clearly cynical. This tax refund that he keeps taking credit for, when are the media going to report the fact that it's *not* a refund, that it's an advance?

MH: It's a loan.

MM: I'm been waiting for somebody to report this.

MH: I reported it last year.

MM: You did and other people online reported it, but the establishment is continuing to let Bush get away with the outrageous lie that this was a refund, which expresses a level of contempt for the American people that is breathtaking. Bush *is* that cynical. Bush *is* that punitive. This is a guy who really relishes the role of an executioner, so it's not enough to laugh him off and say he's just a dummy, he's just a front man. He is *not*. He's someone who wants to go on the attack. If you read the news accounts of that "axis of evil" speech, there were several people in his circle who tried to get him not to do that, tried to talk him out of it, but it was at his insistence that they throw that in. I think we're dealing with a very dangerous man here.

MH: The White House seems to always be apologizing for him. That was clear in the fact that his stupidity in Japan actually dropped the yen just because he said the way to fix their money was devaluation instead of deflation. Why do White House officials have to continually explain what he means? Porky Pig even spoke more clearly than this.

MM: I keep thinking back to that pop quiz a TV journalist in Boston subjected him to in the Fall of 1999, asking him who certain world leaders were. Ironically, they were [Pakistani President Pervez] Musharref, and [Prime Minister Atal Behari] Vajayee of India, people he would end up being very closely involved with. Bush didn't know the answers. And he was smirking with contempt that anyone would even think he *should* know this. All kinds of people defended him, including Democrats.

MH: Does that mean that most Americans are *also* that stupid? And needed to identify with somebody who doesn't even know where Iran is?

MM: A sizable number of Americans have tended to like him because they identify with him. Unbelievably enough, this guy, who comes from one of the richest families in America, has been able to come across as a "regular Joe." A lot of it has to do with the Clinton contrast. Because of his limitations, stiffness, nastiness, simple-mindedness, his anti–intellectualism—a lot of resentful people think they *are* Bush. Go online to the Amazon site for *The Bush Dyslexicon* and you'll see a fair number of really vicious reviews by people who have obviously not read the book. They attack it because they think it's actually an attack on them by a snooty East Coast professor. The book is nothing of the kind, but that's what they think.

I wouldn't say that most Americans are stupid. I think most Americans demonstrated their intelligence by voting *against* him in the last election. I think we're talking about an aroused plurality of extremely resentful people whose influence is disproportionate to their numbers because they are well-trained to get on the phone or fire off an angry e-mail or flame somebody online or make a phone call to a network office. They're much better trained than people on the other side who aren't necessarily that easily organized. So, when we get depressed, we think, "Oh, the whole country is stupid."

MH: We've got to buy these crappy polls they keep giving us, like 80% of the people think Bush walks on water.

MM: That's very soft support. If you read down in the fine print of these polls, you see that on specific issues, they don't support him overwhelmingly; they have a lot of qualms about his policies. But let's not underestimate the power of national calamity to give leaders a sudden surge of popularity. This *always* happens. Your Hitler analogy fits in very well there. When they burned the Reichstag down, it was very useful to the Nazis because it happened a week before the election (the last election in that country for 12 years).

MH: That was also supposedly a set-up.

MM: The Nazis set that fire. I don't believe the Bush people were behind 9/11, but they certainly took advantage of it.

MH: I don't think they were behind it, but a lot of people have accused them, including Canadian television, of complicity in 9/11.

MM: There was some kind of passive collusion. I think there are a lot of unanswered questions like, for example, how it was that those aircraft entered Manhattan airspace so easily? How it was that an aircraft hit the Pentagon when there's an air force base 10 miles away? Those things are outrageous and there's, so far, been no investigation, in part, because Bush and Cheney don't want one.

MH: The fact that they don't want *any* investigations into *anything,* and all their secrets, certainly make them look even more guilty than they might actually be.

MM: They're obviously very guilty of many things.

MH: Mark Elsis [*see* Chapter 14] with lovearth.org, has something called AttackonAmerica.org. He figured out all the timing of the response since NORAD [joint U.S./Canadian North American Aerospace Defense Command] supposedly was notified on 9/11, and he figured right away that something was seriously wrong with what happened that day. He's in Florida. There's the recent story about Bush at the opening event at the Olympics. A 17-year-old

Hungarian girl, who was thrilled to death to be sitting next to the President of the United States, asked if he would say hello to her mother on her cell phone, so he spoke to her mother. The girl said to him, "Will you be sitting here and staying for the whole event?" and his answer to her was, "No, I have a war to fight," and he got up and left. What kind of an idiot are we dealing with here?

MM: The apple doesn't fall far from the tree. There was an interview that Diane Sawyer did with George Bush, Sr., I think before Desert Storm. It was one of these get-to-know-the-President type of interviews, and it took place in his study. He was showing her around the room, pointing to his various artifacts, curios, and what-not, and there were all these toy soldiers on his mantle. She made much of this. It was hard to tell if she was being ironic or what, because it seemed infantile to me.

If you go back to 1990 and 1991, it's really quite striking how similar that moment was to this. That wasn't as dangerous as this one because it was a more contained military "adventure." This one is completely open-ended and, apparently, eternal if Bush has his way. There was the same effort then as there is now to spin the President as agonizing in his study on his knees, praying, "Take this cup from me, oh, Lord," with the awful responsibilities that are on his shoulders. Yet, when you saw the guy, he was practically skipping, he was so excited. He couldn't hide the fact that this was the role he always wanted to play, this John Wayne or Abraham Lincoln role.

MH: "I've got a war to fight." I'm like, "Holy frijoles, Batman!" Is this guy totally whacked or what? How about his remark about taxes getting increased? "Not over my dead body."

MM: I urge people not to focus on these kinds of trivial stupid mistakes that he makes all the time. There were two books that came out at the same time, one was mine, *The Bush Dyslexicon*, and one was this book, *Bushisms* [*George W. Bushisms*, by Jacob Weisberg]. I don't mean to speak ill of the competition because there's a lot of good stuff in *Bushisms*, but all it is is a collection of funny grammatical mistakes. I argue that that kind of comedy actually strengthens Bush's hand.

MH: They make him like a player on *Saturday Night Live*.

MM: They make him a benign dumbbell. What's striking is that he has himself gotten a lot of mileage out of self-effacing humor that he uses to poke fun at his own inability to speak English. In fact, he gave one of these self-parodying talks (I think it was at the Grid Iron Club) and he actually read out of Weisberg's book to show his own mistakes. My book's different. My book puts these things in context and my book demonstrates how very often a witless remark is actually worse than you think at first. It isn't just that it's dumb and funny. And, also, the things he says are very revealing about himself. My favorite example was his line in New Hampshire, which was, interestingly enough, the same place where his father had campaigned, and said "message, I care." You may remember that he accidentally read a stage direction as if it were a line in the speech. He said, "Message, I care." It was also in New Hampshire that George W. was campaigning and he said, "I know how hard it is for you to put food on your family," and this got a lot of laughs, but as I point out in *The Bush Dyslexicon*, that's one of several lines he's delivered that demonstrate when it comes to trying to talk about the have-nots, when it comes time to express concern for the disadvantaged, he can't really do it.

MH: How could he? I don't remember which book it was, I think it was *Fortunate Son*, where they talk about when Bush, Sr. and his wife left the White House and were living in the *real* world, they were totally charmed and surprised to find out that pizza was delivered.

MM: That's in my book.

MH: These things shock me. People still don't get that these people are so rich and so above the ordinary American that they could have no comprehension of what it's like to worry about paying bills or getting health insurance or, God forbid, you get sick.

MM: The thing is, there have been rich people in our political history who have been very concerned about the poor. There was FDR [former President Franklin Delano Roosevelt], there was Eleanor Roosevelt [former First Lady]. There was Bobby Kennedy. These people are a different matter, these Bushes. These are people who just couldn't care less about the poor. If you read the gaffs that I collect in *The Bush Dyslexicon*, you can see what Bush really thinks of them. That's why he has so much trouble speaking. That attitude of his is much more worrisome than the fact that he mangles his English. When he's talking about stuff that he believes in and really likes, when he talks from the heart, he has no syntactical problems; he's perfectly clear. When he talks about the death penalty, when he talks about war, when he talks about his property, when he talks about baseball; when he talks about these things, he's perfectly articulate. Bush is someone whose gaffs are very revealing.

MH: He seems to flub when he really doesn't care about what he's talking about. When he's not really listening or paying attention. He's got that cowboy way.

That State of the Union address was the scariest thing I've heard in a long time. When this guy uses terms like, "We're gonna go in and smoke 'em out," this is really scary stuff. People in Japan have said, "This Bush is a Dracula." The rest of the world is basically shaking in their boots because he's out there like some guy with his gun cocked and anybody who pops his head up is the bad guy.

MM: And this from a guy who dodged the draft. His vice president was a chicken hawk, too, so there's bad faith. He's not even an authentic militarist, he's just a guy who likes to posture as a big daddy kind of tough guy.

MH: The old armchair warriors.

MM: This is a guy who actually has said, and I've collected these quotes, as a matter of pride, "I'm the kind of guy who, when he makes up his mind, he doesn't change it." That's *not* a sign of character, that's a sign of pathological rigidity. You can't be a great leader if you refuse to change your mind. It's one thing to be constantly looking at the polls and having no principles, which is the way they always cast Clinton, but Bush's alternative is actually worse because he's not *only* not principled, but he's got a mind like an oyster—nothing will enter it. The fact that the United States is now acting with complete indifference to what the rest of the world thinks means that the nation, under his supervision, is behaving like he does, if you see what I mean. We will not listen to anybody. "Don't bother me with the facts." If, for example, you tell me global warming is a problem, I'll tell you your science is faulty. On the other hand, I will justify the teaching of creationism in school by saying that the science of evolution is faulty. I mean, they use science in any way they want.

MH: They strike me like any religious fundamentalist. They distort things to make sense to their belief system.

MM: Or Bolsheviks, for that matter. They're very much like Lenin's generation. They're completely ruthless and they will say whatever they need to say. When you read books like *Too Close To Call* [by Jeffrey Toobin] or John Nichols [*see* Chapter 9], who wrote *Jews For Buchanan*, you know, those guys in Florida might just as well have been Bolshevik cadres. They were just as committed, just as ruthless, just as ingenious. Democrats were completely outgunned and outmanned. They didn't have the necessary fanatical resolve and total immorality that you need to win a victory like that. I can't emphasize this strongly enough, these people pose a great threat to democracy.

MH: We've been talking about some of the flubs—deliberate and non-deliberate—by George W. Bush, but we really haven't gotten much into talking about some of the real hot spots in your book, especially the way you break down the seriousness behind this person, the actual human being behind the persona he puts out there. Al Gore has suddenly re-energized his batteries and he's been out slamming basically everything Bush is doing now. What do you think about that?

MM: I was not a Gore supporter. I would never have been a Gore supporter, but I would have voted for him if I lived in a swing state. I was disappointed *after* the election by both [2000 election Green Party candidate Ralph] Nader and Gore for the same reason. Nader, out of his rage against the Democrats (which I can understand), basically shrugged off the theft of the election, and he does that in his new book too, *Crashing the Party*, which is a good book. When it comes to dealing with that shameful episode, his position is just terrible. Gore, I think, had a certain moral and patriotic responsibility to continue to speak up on behalf of the people who *did* vote for him and he simply let that go because Gore, as we know now, cares above all about what the elites think of him, what the newspaper editors and Washington opinion-makers think of him. And they were all telling him to throw in the towel. Their interests and the interests of the masses who voted for him were not the same.

During the whole thing in Florida, Gore was just gone. Jesse Jackson tried to get somewhere and they smeared him with that love-child thing, so he was sidelined. I'm glad Gore is out there being critical, but I think he ran a miserable campaign. He was insufficiently different from Bush in the first place, so he was unable to really criticize him in a way that counted. I wish he wouldn't run, because I don't want to be faced with a choice like that again.

MH: What does it matter? Even if you win, you lose. I am reading Ralph Nader's book and it is pretty good. He says if Gore really stepped up to the plate, or the Democrats become alive and do something before 2004, maybe we can change things.

MM: They'd have to reverse course and embrace their old constituencies. I tend to think there are ways of doing that that would not play into the hands of the Republican propagandists. Of course, I am not a democratic operative, so it's easy for me to say. Despite the fact that I was not a Gore supporter, the guy got screwed royally by the Republicans and especially by the media. *The Bush Dyslexicon* goes into that chapter and verse. The thing that astonishes me now is the persistence of the ancient myth that we have a media with a liberal bias. We've got this guy,

Bernard Goldberg, who wrote a crappy book called *Bias*, which purports to expose the "true liberalism of the media machine." And wouldn't you know it, Bush himself was seen a few weeks ago schlepping the book around as a kind of advertisement for the book.

MH: As if he reads.

MM: It's a terrible book. It doesn't have a shred of evidence in it. I believe, obviously, in paying attention to what the opposition says, but it's always depressing to see how little substance there is to their charge. I don't know how anyone can claim a media system is liberal when it so wholeheartedly participated in Clinton-bashing for eight years, was gung-ho about the Gulf War, and then went on to savage Gore and give Bush such an easy ride that Bush actually *praised* his treatment by the press in the last campaign.

I counted them up, between mid-January and the end of April [2001], the major media, by which I mean all the networks, the news weeklies, the *New York Times*, the *Los Angeles Times*, the *Washington Post*, *USA Today*, and *AP* [*Associated Press*], in that three and one-half month period, they did 1,876 stories on the Marc Rich pardon. This, at a time when a *really* radical regime was taking power, a regime that had stolen the election, was getting ready to impose this radical anti-abortion program, was getting ready to privatize social security, increase military spending, and put through these huge tax cuts for the very rich. All this stuff's going on and they're focusing on this Mark Rich pardon. That's a *liberal* media system?

MH: That's all misdirection.

MM: Where was all the coverage of Ralph Nader's campaign, if we've got a left-wing media system?

MH: Ralph was right about that. The guy didn't get a chance for any kind of coverage. He didn't get into the debates. It kind of reminds me of Bob Kunst, who's running for Governor in Florida. He's shut out of everything and he's a legitimate candidate.

MM: He's got the incumbent Governor "Boss Hog" down there.

MH: It's really, *really* unbelievable. How can we change the political system if other people can't get in there?

MM: It has everything to do with campaign finance reform, as well as media reform.

MH: In your book, you say, "George W. Bush was forced on us as president, and then, after his inauguration, hailed almost universally for his amazing charm, his democratic ease," but you also talked a little further down about something that I noticed right away because I'm a real student of body language. You said, "His body language bellows his un-interest, his distraction, his uneasiness, his callousness; and he tends to blurt out all or part of what he's really thinking, even as he's trying to lie about it." Before the stolen election, I asked, "How could anybody look at this guy and not read his body language?"

MM: This is anecdotal, so take it for what it's worth. The book came out in mid-June of 2001, and it had a pretty good run up until the attack on the Twin Towers. Even then, it kept selling, although I couldn't talk about it anymore. I think your show was the last time I could actually talk about it. Now, it's becoming permissible again to discuss it. I did a lot of talk radio, and I gave a lot of readings. I traveled around and discovered that a *lot* of Americans, I mean a *lot* of people, hundreds, just out of the ones

I met, would tell me readily that they could no longer watch the TV news because of him, and they could no longer read about him. I think there's been a *tremendous* amount of tuning out in disgust.

MH: But here's a guy who's going to put us in WW III and put all our lives in jeopardy. He's already made Americans look like crap to the rest of the world. We *have* to tune in to do something to change this.

MM: We do, and I think people have got to come back to life, but I think all the poll results that we hear don't factor in.

MH: CNN was forced to un-scrub one of the polls they scrubbed off their site, which was that 73% of Americans wanted a special prosecutor on this Enron mess. They took it down. Because of pressure from a lot of groups online, including Democrats.com, they put it back up. Yesterday, I was talking about how the White House called *The Courier*, which is in Littleton, New Hampshire, and had them fire their editor for speaking against Bush. The guy just got fired, along with a cartoonist, Mark Markham, I think. He's been there for 20 years. And then, Joe Jackson, who was doing a liberal talk show in Utah, also got the ax for the same thing. I'm going to have Joe on the show to tell his story. At least people know they can tell their story here, because if the audience gets to hear first-hand from these people, maybe they'll come out of that Bush trance, and say, "Hey, wait a minute, this is leaping fascism in America."

MM: I understand the dynamics of what happened on 9/11 and I know that on 9/13, Bush suddenly became assertive, and because people were so terrified, they warmed to the sight of that sudden confidence. What I don't understand is concluding, on that basis, that

Bush has done something remarkable. There is not a shred of evidence that this guy has done *anything* more than cheerlead. We don't know that he had anything to do with devising military strategy and I'm sure he didn't.

MH: Why would he have picked his father's war cabinet otherwise?

MM: As I point out in the book, I have a lot of his quotes—he can't even articulate the simplest notions of deterrence. He gets it's all screwed up.

MH: When you talk about "King George" and the dark side, he says, "I'll never apologize to the United States of America. I don't care what the facts are."

MM: That was his dad, actually, but same mentality.

MH: Like you said, the apple doesn't fall far from the tree.

MM: The point is that a lot of Americans are still gripped in this illusion that *this* Bush has come through in some way. There is *no* evidence that that's the case. All we know is that he has spoken forcefully when he's spoken off the cuff since 9/11. He says the same things over and over, "We're gonna get 'em running," "We're gonna smoke 'em out," "They can run, but they can't hide," "We're gonna catch 'em."

MH: They said they were going to catch Osama bin Laden in three days. It's been a little longer than three days.

MM: That doesn't phase him. To use their parlance, he stays on message. That's all you can say for this guy. He has done nothing else, and yet people are—maybe *fewer* people—but a lot of people are terribly impressed by this performance. It's been based on nothing. I think that has a lot to do with what you're describing as the media's complicity in shoring him up, which, of course, they've done from the moment he threw his hat into the ring. Now, it's become much more serious because he's attacking civil liberties right and left.

MH: There's the quote from Bush that everybody uses all the time, "I'm all for dictatorship, as long as I'm the dictator."

MM: That's in my book, as well. He made that joke twice actually. When he went to China in October [2001], there was a press conference, and [China's President] Jiang Zemin stood up at the end and said the press conference is over. Of course, all the reporters scurried away. Bush said, "I like the way they handle press conferences in China." That's so typical of him.

MH: And how come he left China out of his "axis of evil"?

MM: China, Syria, Lebanon, Saudi Arabia. But *you're* trying to be consistent, trying to be rational. Bush doesn't operate in that universe. He operates in the universe of the irrational, and, as such, I would argue that he does an intelligent job. He's not a moron.

MH: If he's a puppet, he's a damn good one. He's like Jerry Mahoney's puppet.

MM: Within that universe of the irrational, he's very adept at pushing certain people's buttons. If he were a retard, he couldn't do this. He has a certain shrewdness. He has certainly played the Democrats for suckers. When people got these rebates for $300.00 and $600.00, that was specifically a democratic initiative that Bush opposed for months. He only went along with it at the last minute to get the Democrats to back his plan for long-term rate cuts for the rich. Having done that, he took credit for it. He went all around the country telling people how lucky they were to get all this money back. People are going to discover at tax time this year that they didn't really get that money back.

MH: They're going to have to pay it back.

MM: But Bush has been masterful and shameless at not only stealing credit for this thing, but representing it as a gift when it was no such thing. That takes something more than stupidity.

MH: You are familiar with the way Bush conducted his business in Texas, which is similar to what he does now. What do you think of the way they're handling this whole Enron mess?

MM: They're trying to weasel out of it. They're handling it as a propaganda drive. First, what did we hear? It's not a political scandal, it's a *business* scandal. That was a Republican talking point. Then, we would hear that it's a bi-partisan problem, and not just from Republicans that we heard that. We still tend to hear that. Remember when Clinton said, "I did not have sex with that woman?" How many times did that run?

MH: A million, at least.

MM: I counted them. I'm that kind of person. The month after he admitted he had the affair, the four networks showed that tape 42 times. Bush basically said the same thing about Ken Lay, "I did not have political relations with that man," and he said he was an Ann Richards supporter. That was a bald-faced lie that was also disproved completely. They ran that 12 times.

MH: If you give people a lie often enough, they'll say, "Okay, that must be true."

MM: I don't think it's going to fly. It's a major, *major* scandal.

MH: He's got a lot of Republicans turning against him now. One person wants to actually to hold him in contempt of congress.

MM: That's Dan Burton, right?

MH: Right. And Cheney is right behind him. I try to tell people that people who don't have secrets, people with nothing to hide, don't hide anything. This administration is hiding *everything* and meanwhile, slashing our rights at the speed of light.

MM: Slashing our rights and slashing all the budgets for social improvement. It's a really be-knighted, crazy, irrational thing. How many times did we hear Bush say that this is a different kind of war that was going to be fought in a different kind of way?

MH: I don't remember that we have ever before rained money down on any country we just bombed. Or the $1,000.00 a head he gave to the families of the people to whom he said, "Oops, we made a mistake and bombed the wrong village in Afghanistan."

MM: His military budget includes enormous subsidies for *extremely* conventional weapon systems that have nothing to do with fighting terrorism. This is another one of these bald-faced contradictions that nobody's bothering to point out in the media. If the "different" kind of war is going to be fought in the dark and if we're not going to know what's going on and all this stuff, and if he's going to use the CIA in a military capacity, why are they spending tons of money on all kinds of systems, including one, a huge Howitzer called "The Crusader," which is manufactured by the Carlyle Group?

MH: Because his father's part of the Carlyle Group. Keep the money in the family.

MM: How is this enormous Howitzer going to help fight the war on terrorism when this is supposed to be a different kind of war? The contradictions are breathtaking. The media just swallows it.

MH: I don't really know what the answer is except to continue to educate people about what kind of madness is going on. Every day, the news is so unreal that I say, "Now, this can't *really* be true." And yet it's always true.

MM: We *couldn't* make it up.

MH: We have a President who said, "More and more of our imports come from overseas."

MM: He also said, "Commerce and trade go hand in hand."

MH: I don't want to sound like I'm a whacko conspirator, because I'm not, but I see the whole thing as one giant leap for the whole globalization, world trade, let's-control-everybody-in-every-population thing. The scary part is that other countries are copying America now, and they're slamming people's rights. Their regular citizens' rights are just going the way of the wind in the name of what happened on September 11th.

MM: What we have to understand is that Bush/Cheney are arranging an incredibly important realignment of power in the world. Whereas, for a long time, it was obviously the U.S. against the Soviet Union and, to some extent, the North against the South, what we have now is an entirely different configuration, where we are allied with the most tyrannical systems in the world. We are allied with the Russians, we are allied with the Chinese, and each of our allies now has a free hand to persecute its own minorities. [Russia's President] Vladimir Putin, whom George Bush seems genuinely to like very much, is now going to have a completely free hand with the Chechnyians.

China is going to have a completely free hand with its Islamic population and with the Falun Gong. The Turks will have a free hand with their Kurdish population. The Mexicans will have a free hand with the Zapatistas. We'll have a free hand with our own dissidents. What's happened is that the states of the world seem to be empowered by 9/11 in a way that really spells trouble for minorities the world over.

That's basically the vision that Bush wants to realize, along with missile defense, which can allow us, if it works, to prevent any kind of small-scale military counter-response, so in these spheres of influence, basically, we and Israel and Russia and China have something like missile defense. If we can kind of lord it over everybody around us that way, it would make the whole world into kind of a garrison state. That doesn't sound to me like democracy.

MH: A missile defense system isn't going to stop the suitcase bomber or the suicide bombers.

MH: And, yet, 9/11 was used as the reason why we had to push ahead with it.

MH: He took advantage of the people's fear at that time, what you called that collective event that happened here.

MM: The trauma.

MH: While everybody was in that trauma, raising and waving their "Made in China" flags, he was going berserko with, "Let's make this system worse than the people who live in China."

MM: That's right. The *only* supporter he has in Europe is [former British Prime Minister] Lady [Margaret] Thatcher.

MH: As Confucius would say, "May you live in interesting times." He's another one who must be spinning in his grave.

MM: It's a little *too* interesting, I think.

MH: I have the feeling that you're going to be doing Book 2 because you must get more information on him on a daily basis than even I do.

MM: There *is* a lot of stuff. People must understand that it's not just him, it's the media.

MH: The media really should be pistol-whipped.

MM: *The Bush Dyslexicon* is an analysis of a disorder that doesn't just afflict one man. I use dyslexia as a metaphor for the inability of the press to lead the evidence before our senses. The TV medium, television, shows us truth about this guy, in his body language, you can see it in his face, but the TV employees, the corporate employees, will *not* acknowledge the obvious.

MH: They're all afraid for their jobs.

MM: Since 9/11, they've gone further. They've called him Churchillian, they've praised his splendid eloquence, they talked about his nimble articulation of policy. This is fantasy. This is illusion. If you read what he says, if you listen to the words that come out of his mouth, he's the same guy he always was. The book is really as much an indictment of the corporate media as it is of the Bush/Cheney regime.

MH: When the White House is going out of its way to worry about firing editors in New Hampshire or people who have a little talk show in the middle of Utah, you've got to think they're very scared. They don't want the truth to come out. And they have reason to be scared. As more Americans wake up,

I think we're going to see a revolution in this country that I've been feeling since the election was stolen. It has to happen. It's the only thing that can stop the madness. Otherwise, we can all just figure out that we're going to be corporate slaves for the rest of our lives, literally.

FOURTEEN

9/11 – QUESTIONS ANYONE?
Meria with Mark Elsis

Complaints that the "media" have not been asking the right questions about 9/11 (except in foreign countries) will not wash any more. Mark Elsis[15] (who figured out the events of 9/11 before that day was over) discusses whether a stand-down order was given and (if so) by whom. Other topics he discusses are, why did Paine Stewart's small plane get *immediate* interception when off-course, while the planes of 9/11 had major time delays when they were flying at less than their maximum speed; and whether Flight 93 was shot down and (if so) why our government does not admit to it. Elsis discusses the lack of reporting of the recovery of black boxes and recordings of air traffic controllers to the pilots on 9/11.

Elsis discusses Attorney General John Ashcroft's announcement concerning the abolishment of the Freedom of Information Act; why representatives of FEMA [Federal Emergency Management Agency] were in NYC the night *before* the WTC event; and why 21 critical minutes were lost before any plane was scrambled to protect Washington, D.C. Other topics discussed are the 2003 U.S. military budget being at $396.1 *billion*—more than the military budgets of the next 25 countries on earth combined; why the passenger lists of all four flights on 9/11 do not list the names of the hijackers (and how the FBI identified them so quickly); why the number of dead does not match up with the passenger lists; the U.S.A. Patriot Act, which disregards the Bill of Rights and the U.S.

Constitution; how the terrorists may have obtained top-secret White House and Air Force One codes and signals; and how Ali Mohammed was a U.S. Army Sergeant, maybe working for the FBI (which is a question that has also been posed by Barry Zwicker, Vision TV, Canada). (Interview taped/broadcast on February 21, 2002.)

MH: How is it that questioning the event of 9/11 is getting coverage everywhere else in every other country except here in America where everybody's happy to go into their corporate media trance and wave their "Made in China" flags? Nobody really has gotten any answers out of September 11th. Carolyn Kay at MakeThemAccountable.com keeps us aware about Canadian Vision TV where Barry Zwicker is doing weekly reports on why aren't people in America asking these questions.

Mark Elsis, who's with Lovearth.org and also AttackonAmerica.net, figured out *within hours* of the event everything that people in other countries are finally asking. At the time, I'm sure there were many who said people like Mark were crazy. Everybody else is now starting to wake up and ask what really did happen on that day. Just in case you think no one here in American media is covering September 11th, today's show is a gift to you and to your brain. This is going to be your brain on speed today. Mark, I went to your site last night and was re-reading your article "Attack on America."

ME: There's a lot of information that is quite alarming about what happened prior to and on September 11th, and since September 11th.

MH: Many people I've talked to have said they don't want to get into conspiracy theories to say the U.S. was behind what happened, but a lot of people are saying there was a tremendous level of complicity on the part of the government.

ME: That's sort of taking the easy way out. It's hard for one to blame their own government. But if you say they were complicit in some respect, then they had to know. A lot of intelligent people know some of the facts I'm going to bring up this hour and they are acquiescing, is what I call it.

MH: It's kind of like saying you're a little pregnant; either you are or you are not.

ME: I don't even like to say the word "conspiracy" because it turns people off. It's one of the magic shut-off words, "Oh, it's just a conspiracy," and you don't have to really listen to it, or understand all the facts of it, or the facts aren't the facts. There is just so much disinformation and misinformation that I try to deal with. I wrote a 25-page paper and it's growing. It's called "My Country Right or Wrong," questioning September 11th. It started with me, on waking up on September 11th, seeing the second plane go into the World Trade Center around 9:03 a.m. I'm originally from New York City and I now live in Sarasota, Florida, Siesta Key, where President Bush was that morning.

When I saw his Air Force One take off at 10:00 that morning from Sarasota-Bradenton International Airport, I couldn't believe it because there were still (and this was the first thing that tipped me off) unknown terrorists, so-called terrorists, in the sky at this time. Yet, they were putting him in a plane. The United States military and NORAD [North American Aerospace Defense Command] have stated there were seven air stations on guard that morning to protect the continental United States. I've learned since we last talked that two of these were in Florida.

To backtrack, let's say Bush took off at 10:00 a.m. The FAA [Federal Aviation Agency] and NORAD must have known the first plane was hijacked at around 8:14 in the morning. They'd lost contact with the second plane at around 8:41 or 8:42, and they knew that one was hijacked. Of course, at 8:45, the first plane [American Airlines 11] hits the first tower, and at 9:03, the second plane hits the second tower. So, you're telling me now, 57 minutes later, that Air Force One took off from Sarasota-Bradenton International Airport, with no extra military presence? Nonetheless, two of the seven stations protecting the United States were in Florida and they could have both been here in less than 28 minutes.

I always go by the precautionary principle. I know Air Force One has extraordinary protection, yet the same day, when he came home on September 11th, they showed you two F-15s or 16s off his wings when he's coming home from Omaha to Washington. They made it seem like those planes were on his wing all day, when going to Shreveport and on to Omaha that morning and that afternoon. This was not the case. I don't know where they picked him up, but what I'm stating here is that they had at least 57 minutes to get everybody they could to protect him, if they wanted him to take off.

The first few pages of "My Country Right or Wrong" deals with NORAD's own press release that they put out late on September 18th, and it was in September 19th's papers that fighter jets were eight minutes away from the World Trade Center. The amount of inconsistencies in this document that they put out is just staggering and it's fifth grade math, reverse engineering math, to figure out what they're doing. The FAA knew at 8:14 a.m. that the first plane was hijacked, and knew about the second plane around 8:41, 8:42, yet NORAD and the FAA tells us NORAD doesn't know about this. The FAA says they don't tell NORAD until 8:40 a.m. about the first one, and at 8:43 a.m. about the second one. And then NORAD holds onto this. It's one of the things that is totally impossible. NORAD now states they got the information from FAA and, of course, they don't *have* to get the information from FAA because NORAD is looking at everything, not only military aircraft and missiles that are supposed to be coming in, but *also* all commercial and private aviation. They have to track *everything*.

MH: Barry Zwicker on Vision TV in Canada said the same thing. He said the United States has fail-safe procedures in place for this type of thing and all of a sudden none of it was working and they're trying to say we never tested it before? Everybody can see the B.S. in this.

ME: It's a real huge lie.

MH: The excuse for Bush jumping all around the country on the 11th was that the terrorists somehow had obtained top secret White House Air Force One codes and signals. Of course, it is never explained how they got their hands on those. People have to look at that. This is common knowledge now, though it wasn't at the time, that 15 of the 19 hijackers were from Saudi Arabia.

ME: Supposedly, the four pilots were from Egypt, so *nobody* was from Afghanistan. This thing goes back a long way. There are so many different areas to it.

George W. Bush's first company was Arbusto Energy Corporation down in Texas, I believe in '76, '77. The bin Laden family helped finance this. George Bush's father [former President Bush] is a major spokesman in the Carlyle Group, which is the 11th largest defense contractor in the United States. It's all hand-in-hand, it's military, and it's oil, and it's drugs.

MH: And Cheney was a big shot over at Haliburton Oil before he became Vice President.

ME: He was the CEO of Haliburton. I believe it was in *Fortune* that they asked all of these Fortune 500 CEOs who they would like to see as president and they all said Cheney.

MH: And [National Security Advisor Dr.] Condoleezza Rice also was on the board of a large oil company [Chevron].

ME: We have the greatest air force by far. I just learned from the Center for Defense Information that for the next fiscal year, we have a military budget of $396.1 billion dollars. This is now more than the next 25 countries all combined. I don't know what to say about that except that this is the definition of fascism.

MH: Anybody can see the fascism happening here. I tried to see if Barry Zwicker had anything in his report that you didn't have. I had to really stretch it and read very carefully. In talking about the media, he asked whether there were stand-down orders. This is one of the questions people are coming up with now. He said, "bin Laden was a long time close ally of the CIA, according to the CIA itself. Why did he suddenly turn against them, or did he?" And then he goes on to report that there was a November 22nd [2001] front-page story in *The Globe* [*and Mail*], I guess that's in Canada.

He says, "I almost missed the startling information in this myself because the headline indulges the stereotypical Canadian self put-down. We let a terrorist, Ali Mohammed, get away." He said, "The real story was buried because Mr. Mohammed was a U.S. army sergeant, but trained bin Laden's bodyguards." The article said, "Ali Mohammed was in America's good books." And he wasn't so shadowy in those days. He said, "He was one of *their* guys, a terrorist, one of the FBI's guys." He said, "The psychological trick at the heart of September 11th is, people confuse their compassion for the victims with their certainty about who the perpetrators are."

ME: By 9:13 that morning, they had Osama bin Laden's picture up. They were already suggesting that he perhaps was behind this. This was 10 minutes after the second plane hit. This was almost a half-hour before they hit the Pentagon. The amount of coordination on this is phenomenal. At the end of "My Country Right or Wrong," I more or less ask anyone in the country to take me on concerning this. I will debate *anyone* or *any* group. Of course, no one wants to take it. One of my best friends was one of the rising stars in the *Washington Post* and he just can't touch it. They don't want to know. Everybody is just burying their heads. There was a golfer named Paine Stewart. He took off from Florida in a Lear jet and, evidently, a seal broke. They decompressured at around 39,000 feet. You only have around eight to ten seconds before you lose consciousness. They all went unconscious, froze to death, and died [in October 1999]. What happened was, within 21 minutes of losing contact with air traffic controllers, there were two fighter jets on the wing of his Lear jet. They had groups all over the country going to help this jet out, groups from at least three different air force spaces in the country. They brought the plane all the way in until it crashed in South Dakota.

The thing is that here is a private jet, and within 20–21 minutes, they were all over it. Excluding what Cheney and everybody is leading you to believe, that they didn't have orders to shoot down, that is a misdirection play. The real thing is that once they don't have air traffic control contact and the planes were going off course, there are procedures put in place that you go after them. You go up and look in the window.

MH: Didn't they do the same thing with that kid in Florida who slammed that plane into that Bank of America building?

ME: Supposedly that kid's best friend said the exact opposite of what the news said. He said this kid was gung-ho and wanted to *join* the army. This whole letter they found about supporting bin Laden, I don't know how to make heads or tails of that.

MH: What I'm talking about is the response. The kid had a plane on him immediately. The pilot could see him through the window.

ME: What he had on it was a helicopter. He actually flew over MacDill Air Force Base, which is the command center for the whole Afghanistan war.

MH: He could have dropped a bomb for all they knew.

ME: He flew right over them, and I believe it was a Coast Guard helicopter that was chasing him for the last few minutes. Then, he just slammed his plane into the Bank of America building and they found this note that said, who knows. What it comes down to is that they were on him *very* quickly. And this is standard procedure. This is *not* because of 9/11. This has been procedure throughout all time, and they can't get away from this Paine Stewart story. It's like science. Any time they can't understand it, they just sweep it under the rug. This is one of the major things, that they somehow could get to Paine Stewart's plane in 21 minutes, but they couldn't seem to get to any of these planes, *any* four of these planes? The last plane, the one that crashed in Pennsylvania, was probably shot out of the sky because they found the turbine engine six or seven miles away. This is why it wasn't on the news that day for seven hours because of the FBI. I have spoken to reporters in Pittsburgh and they don't want to talk.

MH: You know that other plane that blew up supposedly in Rockaway [New York] and all those people who were eyewitnesses are up in arms that they are not being believed by the FBI. They said, "We all *saw* it happen."

ME: That was like the other one off Long Island, Flight 800. This happened years ago. They had I don't know how many hundreds of people witnessing that one and, yes, they can sweep anything under the rug. The problem here is acquiescers, as I stated before. Let's go back to the timetable because there was such improbability with what happened, just with timing.

MH: You expressed it very clearly in your article. Most people are not going to follow the math. You said that NORAD had almost an hour and a half to scramble F-16 jets from Andrews [Air Force Base in Virginia] to protect Washington, D.C. and the Pentagon. How could they, incredibly, fail to do so? It was an hour and half from when New York was hit to when the Pentagon was hit.

ME: It was an hour and a half actually from around 8:14 a.m., when the first plane was hijacked. To preface the whole thing, it's really easy. Everybody knows that before September 11th, the first two places that terrorists are going to hit are New York and Washington, D.C.

MH: That's just common sense.

ME: The top targets are the World Trade Center, the Empire State Building, the Statue of Liberty, and the UN in New York. In Washington, it's the Capitol Building, the White House, the Pentagon, and the Supreme Court. This is where they're going to hit, so once one plane is hijacked and it's heading toward New York, you would think the precautionary principle would go into place, that these guys would scramble everything they had—not only in New York, but in Washington.

MH: You said that after 90 minutes, there *still* wasn't any air protection for Washington D.C.

ME: And then when the planes got up, an amazing thing happened. These planes that cost tens of millions of dollars, these unbelievable planes, the best planes in the world, planes that can go 1,500 miles an hour (one group left Andrews to protect Washington) and in the case of protecting New York, they can go 1,875 miles an hour or almost 2,000 miles an hour, if you really want to push it, and yet they were only going less than one-third that speed. People have no answer to this; of course, because there *is* no answer. It was all done as window-dressing. These planes were sent up for window-dressing. You cannot talk to any of these pilots. Everything has been clamped down wonderfully, and the press goes along with everything. Nobody wants to say anything and very few people have the courage you do, Meria. Bless you from everybody who has a conscience and a heart and a brain, and is a *true* patriot of this country.

What happened on September 11th is criminal. Talk about criminality, Bush went to [U.S. Senator Tom] Daschle about two weeks ago, and told him, first of all, we don't want any investigation, but if there *has* to be one, you are going to put it *only* in a secret subcommittee and it's going to get buried and that's it.

MH: As if none of us has a right to know.

ME: No one has the right to know. That brings up another point. This one went under my radar for 80-something days. On October 12th, John Ashcroft put out a memo to all the other agencies about the Freedom of Information Act. What he said was, there is only one reason right now that you can't get information under the Freedom of Information Act and it is about national security. He more or less said in this memo that you don't have to abide by this any more, this law. And no one knows this. Really very few know it because it just was not reported.

MH: I call him Herr Ashcroft. As somebody who was a New Yorker, like myself, I'm sure you've been in and out of the World Trade Center, at least a couple of times in your life. You ask a good question, and a lot of people in other countries are asking good questions. If these terrorists were *really* targeting the World Trade Center, why wouldn't they have waited until about 11:00 in the morning when these buildings would have had at least 50,000 people in each one of them?

ME: Not only that, but if this was a well-planned terrorist attack, what you would try to do is, of course, *wait* until 10:30 or 11:00, when these buildings are pretty much packed with 50,000 people and you don't hit them on the 68th floor and the 90th floor, you hit them on the 25th floor. This could have been done. They could have plowed both planes in between the

25th and 30th floors. Therefore, everybody above those floors, which would have been three-quarters of the people, 37,000 people, wouldn't have made it out.

MH: What do you think about the body count going from 6,000 to 3,000? Were those people resurrected or what?

ME: I asked that, too. When the Red Cross said there were 2,562 people asking for money, a month and a half after, I asked, "That's the count, maybe within 2%." People are going to go after the money. The first count was 50,000. Then, it went down to 20,000 and 10,000 and then 8,000, 7,000, 6,000. Now, it's 2,800. I don't mean to say that's nothing, but there was all the propaganda that came out in the beginning.

MH: I think they used the big numbers to shock us more and get us emotionally tied to it. Psychologically, they couldn't have done it in a better place and touched the human heartstrings more to allow them to basically create fascism in America over one incident of a kind that happens in places like Israel every day.

ME: It happens every day, but not quite to the magnitude of these two icons of capitalism coming tumbling down.

MH: Not even the best Hollywood producer could have done that one.

ME: And how they tumbled down. I'm out on it about how these planes took those two buildings down.

MH: My feeling is that there had to be explosives in the building.

ME: There was something going on. The fireman's magazine came out and they were saying, "You're throwing away evidence that we should be examining." And let me tell you that [former New York Mayor Rudy] Giuliani got

Bechtel Corporation to control *all* of the demolition. It's all under the control of an ultra right-wing group that has its fingers everywhere, this Bechtel Corporation, and now they have total control of taking everything away from the World Trade Center.

MH: And he got a Knighthood from Queen Elizabeth or whoever.

ME: He got the Knighthood from *Time* magazine and all of the oligarchy of this country for doing that, for playing the ultimate ball. You talk about the Freedom of Information Act, so you can't find out anything. Also, just within the last month, John Ashcroft spent $8,000.00 to cover up two statues in the Department of Justice. I put this on the side of fascistic behavior.

MH: Anybody who has a problem with a female breast, which is about nurturance, probably didn't get his mother's tit enough for his needs. He's a real sicko, there are no two ways about that. The curtain actually cost more than the statute. I wondered if there was a guy's penis in his face, that would have been okay. I want to send him a calico cat for Christmas. Maybe we can get him that one they cloned. He said they're demons and "that's the way it is."

ME: I just wrote a little piece that's on a site called September112001.net, called "The Three Top Things of the Universe." What happened on September 11th is that at least 35,615 of our brothers and sisters died the worst possible death—starvation—and 85% of these people are children of five years old and younger. Approximately 30,000 children died on September 11th of starvation. I don't hear anybody talking about this. Matter of fact, on *September 10th*, 30,000 children died and on *September 12th*, 30,000 children also died of starvation death, that day and every day since. We talk about these innocent beautiful children who are dying at the rate of 10 times more every day than [the number of people who] died on September 11th in that crash. And people call themselves Christians?

MH: The key to world peace is to feed the world.

ME: In this piece, I point out to the Christians and the Jewish people that they don't understand the Fourth Commandment, "Thou Shalt Not Kill." Is there something hard that you don't understand about that? Like Gandhi said, "An eye for an eye and we all go blind."

MH: You talk about something called "Global Hawk." I've read a lot of articles about that online and there are lot of people who are asking whether these planes were remotely controlled.

ME: There *is* something called "Global Hawk." This technology has been around for a long time. The top people doing this are, of course, the United States military. In early last year, March or April [2001], a plane flew from Edwards Air Force Base [Lancaster, California] to Australia and back remotely. This plane was around the size of a 737, not a little kit plane. An F-18 Hornet landed on an aircraft carrier four times in May of last year, remotely. These were two moving objects, no power in them, remotely controlled. They first thought about this technology in the early '70s, when the hijackers would say, "Take me to Cairo or Havana or Beirut," when they used to come in with a gun or whatever and hold up the pilots. The pioneers thought there could be a button for the pilots to push that could allow others to override him, so the pilot could tell the hijacker, "Sorry, I have no control over the plane." This technology came out of trying to help at first, but it was put in all the new Boeing planes. Matter of fact, Lufthansa, that has got Boeing planes, has taken it out of their planes.

MH: Who's to say that the terrorists didn't use it?

ME: This is a possibility. I never thought of that one.

MH: If they were able to get the private codes of the President's plane and all that garbage, who's to say they didn't get their hands on Global Hawk? Let's face it, we have a government that'll sell anybody anything if the price is right.

ME: This is almost true, too.

MH: Look at anthrax. How clear does it have to be that it came from one of our own, and yet they're still not doing anything about it.

ME: I mention in "My Country, Right or Wrong," that anthrax is like how to kill six birds with one stone. It goes on and on. Reporting of the first anthrax letter was put out in Florida in *The National Enquirer* and everybody sort of laughed and then, all of a sudden, it hit all the other mainstream news. Then, Condoleezza Rice had a meeting with all the top TV executives, chairmen, and told them about the Osama bin Laden tapes that said he may be giving secret messages, so we don't want you to play these tapes, and they all acquiesced. The next day, Ari Fleischer said the same thing to the print media. Within a week, both the TV and the print media have anthrax. Let's scare them. Who got it in the Senate? Daschle and [U.S. Senator Russ] Feingold. Feingold's office, by the way, is right across from Daschle's in the Senate Building. Nobody talks about Feingold because of something that happened on October 26th of last year, which we hadn't even stumbled upon yet, the U.S.A. Patriot Act.

You were talking about why these things are done, like September 11th. It's to get things jammed through. Representative Ron Paul, a very conservative Republican from Texas (one of the three Republicans in the House), came out against it. Senator Feingold was against the U.S.A. Patriot Act and, somehow, his office gets the anthrax real soon afterwards. It was our strain and, also, the pharmaceutical companies are making oodles off of it. The sixth one is that we're going to blame this on Iraq. Watch, we are going to say it wasn't *our* strain; it was *their* strain. I just know it.

MH: There are plenty of stories in print that we sold Saddam Hussein several vials of anthrax years ago. We're a whore country. Somebody's got bucks, we're going to sell them whatever the hell they want. It's insanity. You did all the math on the lackadaisical reaction of our Air *Farce* on September 11th.

ME: Let me make one little correction. I remember thinking I gave them very liberal times of around 10 minutes response times for these two planes, from Otis [Air Force Base] to protect New York and Andrews [Air Force Base] to protect Washington. Upon further calculations and more numbers, the flight time would have been just less than seven minutes if they went at full speed. Seven minutes for both of them because the speed of one is slower, but it's closer, so they could have both gotten there within seven minutes. And they didn't. They flew at 25–30% of their top speed. Now, there's a general who came out afterwards and said the reason the flight speed was so slow to go protect Washington was because the three planes that took off from Andrews were going to New York at first. This is when a plane is going at dead-on since 8:56. It turns around in Southern Ohio or Northeastern Kentucky and came back to hit the Pentagon. They're going to protect New York and then they said they vectored off to try to get it, but it was too late. This is a cover for that story. It is just beyond belief that they were flying at 25–30% of their top speed. It is preposterous. When *are* they going to fly at top speed? I mean, this is our nation's capital about to be attacked.

MH: I saw that old movie, *Mars Attack* recently. A lot of that reminded me of what happened on September 11th, believe it or not. Remember that bizarro movie with Jack Nicholson? Doesn't it seem unusual that there were only somewhere between 229 and 264 passengers and crew members *in total* on all four of these planes?

ME: They said there were 264 people on the planes, but when you add up the manifest list, only 229 people are on the death list. I've checked this out. I've looked up the numbers myself and it's only 229. Also, all 19 of the so-called terrorists weren't on the manifest lists.

MH: How did they get on the plane if they weren't on the lists?

ME: First of all, how did they get past security? Here's another thing we didn't talk about. There are two black boxes per plane.

MH: Where are the black boxes?

ME: What about the air traffic controllers to the pilots of those planes? Where are all those people? By the way, where are the videotapes of them coming into the terminals? Where are all the tapes of all the *cell phone* calls that were supposedly made? All of these pieces of information are missing.

MH: Yet how did they manage to find all this evidence about the terrorists intact?

ME: Like the passport that was found at the World Trade Center, four blocks away, in pristine condition, and all this other stuff. The plane that went down in Pennsylvania was the one where they supposedly took over the plane. I don't know about that, but what I *do* know is that the grieving wives of these so-called heroes got together and asked the FBI to please let them listen to the black box recordings of the last minute and a half of this plane so they can hear their husbands and get closure. The FBI told them to go take a walk. What they said is, you don't really want to listen to this. It's going to disturb you. Interestingly enough, my webmaster said to me, "Well, it's sort of like the morgue. Why not take the toughest guy in the family and he can go listen to the tape?" The tough guy; he'll be able to take it, but they won't do it. It's ludicrous.

MH: When all those people were making their cell phone calls and they were talking about the hijackers, don't you think *one* of them would have said the guy is an Arab?

ME: Also, Bob Olson supposedly made *two* phone calls. Andrews Air Force Base is about 11 miles away from the Pentagon. Andrews Air Force Base has two fighter wings. They are there to protect Washington, not Langley, which is 125 miles away, to the south. So this is another thing that no one talks about. Andrews Air Force Base is literally *right there*. And they were up *after* the fact. This is documented in *The San Diego Tribune* and in an English paper that they were up *after* the fact, but they couldn't get up for almost an hour and a half before. There were 229 people on the death list, yet 264 people are on the complete lists. The amazing thing about that is, the figures would make these four planes only about 25% full.

MH: Which is very odd.

ME: Impossible.

MH: And, then, you also said there are no Arabic names on the passenger list, but the FBI identified the hijackers really quickly. How did they do that?

ME: It's beyond amazing. There's also a little tape of Dan Rather talking to one of the top guys at FEMA. It's an audiotape that we have on AttackonAmerica.net. We have compiled hundreds and hundreds of the greatest stories on that site, videos of every plane crash, the person from Canada you were just talking about; the greatest pieces of information; you can see them all. I've been following this with care.

MH: How could you not follow this as an American living in this country where they keep giving us all these bull-crap scares? Today's a day of high terror alert and all this garbage, and they never even give us any answers to where our intelligence forces were on September 11th.

ME: We spend approximately $35 *billion* on intelligence. This event was either provoked by us or else we did it.

MH: I talked to you a day or two afterward and said, "I hate to say it, and I don't even *want* to say what I'm feeling, but I really think this is all about money."

ME: It *is* about money. I believe the top reason this was done is for a clamp-down on the whole world for the New World Order globalization. We should not forget what happened last July [2001] in Genoa [Italy] where 300,000 people gathered to protest. There was supposed to be a major rally in Washington where they were going to put up for the first time fences 20 feet high and 5 miles long to protect all sorts of IMF [International Monetary Fund] and World Bank people in Washington and it was going to be a big thing. All of a sudden, it didn't happen. The powers that be understood that this anti-globalization movement is becoming huge. Carlo Giuliani, who got shot in the head and run over, was a martyr for this whole thing.

MH: I think September 11th got out of control for the globalization people because what ended up happening, it seems to have united the protesters and angered them even more. I don't think they ever really considered how devastating on the world economy that would turn out to be coupled with Enron—and that's just the tip of the iceberg.

ME: You couldn't get any closer ties than Enron and George Bush.

MH: This is an Enron government, no two ways about it.

ME: And let's not forget the complicity of Arthur Andersen. This all goes back to a law passed in 1995, where they can do both things. They can both do the accounting for you and also do other things. They shouldn't be allowed. It's a fiasco. A part of it seems like it might be a cover. There is nothing going on in investigating 9/11.

MH: They're not investigating the stolen election either. The war on terror has taken over everybody's sensibility, it seems.

ME: We're going to be spending $38 *billion* on homeland defense.

MH: Which is insane. Where was the FBI and where was the CIA on 9/11? When I talked to Stan Goff [*see* Chapter 12], who was 24 years in the [U.S. Army] Special Forces, he says the CIA hasn't been doing stuff like that for years. He says they have been doing basically covert operations [and] who *really* was in charge or responsible was the NSA [National Security Agency] and the Department of Defense. That was a big surprise to me. What do you think of that?

ME: I believe there has to be complicity on many different levels in the higher ranks of a lot of different organizations. The Joint Chiefs of Staff are running the whole show. What happened with the Joint Chiefs of Staff was that the man was just about to leave and the new man, [General Richard B.] Myers, was just about to come in. People don't realize that Myers went in front of the Senate subcommittee and said he really didn't know anything. This was two days afterward, on September 13th. It's amazing that this guy becomes who he is. Now, he's the Chairman of the Joint Chiefs of Staff. Knowing your history, knowing about the *U.S.S. Maine* in 1898, the *Lusitania* in 1915, Pearl Harbor in 1941, the Gulf of Tonkin in 1964, the 300 babies slaughtered in the incubators in 1991, and this one. They are all akin to each other. Besides that, there's something in 1962 called Operation Northwoods.

MH: Let's talk about Operation Northwoods.

ME: This is very important because people say we would never do anything like that. Oh, really? Well, take a look in *The Body of Secrets*, written by James Bamford, that came out last year [2001] about the NSA. He uncovered that in 1962, they wanted to get back at Cuba. They had invasion plans. They had people killing people in Miami. They had all of this going on to destabilize things. They had John Glenn, who was the first person to orbit the earth for the United States, and said that if something went wrong with him, they were going to blame it on Cuba.

MH: They were going to blame it on Cuban terrorists.

ME: And this wasn't signed off by just anybody. This plan, with all these different parts in it, was all phony. It was signed off by all five members of the Joint Chiefs of Staff and brought to President [John F.] Kennedy for his signature.

MH: Of course, Kennedy wouldn't go for it.

ME: Kennedy *didn't* go for it.

MH: And we all know what happened to Kennedy.

ME: That's something I was just talking to someone else briefly about, this conspiracy thing. As soon as you say "conspiracy," people get turned off. I say, if you don't believe the staggering amount of evidence here, then I guess you don't believe the staggering amount of evidence in what happened to Robert F. Kennedy's assassination or the staggering amount of evidence that happened in Martin Luther King's assassination or the staggering amount of evidence that happened in John F. Kennedy's assassination. These are all just *coincidences*?

MH: You have a great quote by Martin Luther King, Jr. at the beginning of your article on your site.

ME: Exactly one year before he was assassinated, Dr. Martin Luther King summed up what many feel provoked the September 11th attacks: "The greatest purveyor of violence on this planet is my own government." And he goes further: "A time comes when silence is betrayal. Even when pressed by the demands of inner truth, man does not easily assume the task of opposing their government's policy especially in a time of war. Nor does the human spirit move without great difficulty against all the apathy of conformance thought within one's own bosom and in the surrounding world." This was April 4, 1967, a major speech that he came out with on the Vietnam War and everything else, and everybody went crazy on him.

I find it to be oddly coincidental, exactly one year from the date of that speech, he was assassinated. I stumbled upon this a little while ago. On September 11th of 1993, 1994, or 1995, a guy from Maryland crashed his plane into the White House. No one has stumbled upon this. It was thought that this was Global Hawk also, that this guy was already dead and they just put him in the plane and flew it into the White House. There are a lot of things out there, but the major thing that nobody can get around is this. I'm going to write a paper on it called "21 Minutes." At 8:45 a.m., the first plane hits the World Trade Center. The second plane hits at 9:03 a.m. We still have not scrambled anyone to protect Washington at this point. NORAD actually waits until 9:24 a.m. before they tell Langley to scramble. This is 21 minutes between 9:03 and 9:24. They waited 21 minutes for what? This is the bottom of the whole thing about this NORAD press release that I've dug into. No one can say anything about this. They sat on it.

MH: Don't you think Cheney was the one who was really running this whole thing and he was the one doing the cover-up when he was reporting on TV, "Oh, we didn't know what to do," all that crap? Don't you think if anybody ordered a stand-down, it was probably him? I don't think Bush is brilliant enough to do it.

ME: I don't even know if he'd let Bush in on it. Everybody says he's dumb, but he's dumb like a fox in a way.

MH: He's dangerously dumb.

ME: This guy is just a lackey. His whole family only made it because of the Harrimans. His grandfather [Prescott Bush] married into the right family, and then he became managing partner for Brown Brothers Harriman, which was the largest stock brokerage in the world, and he got caught trading with the enemy in October of 1942. He later became Senator from Connecticut, his son becomes President, and his grandson becomes President. This is what I was saying about President 41, Herbert Walker Bush. He's doing with the Carlyle Group what his father did. By the way, when President 41 dies, he's going to leave a lot of money to his son, George. And where did he get this money from? From George's actions against Afghanistan. So, in a way, our President is making a lot of money off what's going on, through his father. No one's talking about this. It's unbelievable amounts of money.

MH: There's a lot out there about whether we knew in advance about the September 11th attack. Why were Russians selling their U.S. dollars weeks before September 11th?

ME: [Russian President Vladimir] Putin and the KGB told the CIA to "look out for your buildings with jetliners." Mossad, the Israeli intelligence agency, supposedly said that to them also. There's speculation all over and it was reported in a lot of European media that there was a meeting in June [2001] where they told the Taliban (that *we* put into power, by the way) what to do. I said the first major reason why this all happened was New World Order globalization, with a clampdown on everybody throughout the world, and global terrorism, so we can control the whole world. The second major reason is something called net energy. We're running out of oil and gas. A lot of people laugh, but most experts are saying this is a fact, that within 10 years, it's going to take more energy to get this stuff out of the ground than there *is* stuff in the ground. When that happens, it's all collapsing. So, they have to get to the natural gas and oil in the Caspian Sea region as fast as possible. They told them if you want to get paid off, we'll put you in power and we'll give you a little piece of the action, or else we'll rearrange your rubble.

MH: That's documented all over the place. I've read that story everywhere. John Walker, the American who fought with the Taliban, became a member of the Taliban two months before our administration gave the Taliban $43 million.

ME: For, supposedly, eradicating the poppy plants. It's about military expenditures. It's about oil. It's about drugs. There's a vast amount of opium that comes out of Afghanistan and the Taliban, supposedly, were quite fundamentalist and didn't really care for these drugs. I'm not supporting them in any way for what they did with women, but the new people who we just put in are pretty much the same thing. It's just that now we can get our pipeline through and you will see just how fast the pipeline comes through. That's the litmus test.

And now, we're going to go through Iraq and Indonesia. Calling them the axis of evil and all that; it just comes down to this: we spent $396.1 billion on defense. This is more than the next 25 countries put together. What do you think we're doing? It's for profit. We have invaded since the early '50s, Guatemala and dozens of other countries in between. The ramifications of these military operations have cost the lives of at least 8 million people being murdered through everything we have done. We supply more arms throughout the whole world than anybody else. We are the greatest purveyor of violence. Like Martin Luther King said, "We have to look at ourselves." What are *we* doing? I just looked at it, $396 billion for defense, $52 billion for education. People are crying for education all over the place, but we're going to be adding on another $50 billion to it, that's the *whole* education budget.

MH: And there's lack of healthcare and starving here at home.

ME: We're the richest country in the world and we're the *only* western country that doesn't have national healthcare.

MH: It's a government that doesn't really care about the people. They all have their own private agendas. Do you think they care about guys like you and me who are trying to eke by and survive? And you and I are probably doing great, compared to the laid-off homeless people in this country.

ME: The average living wage since the 1970s has gone down and down and down.

MH: And we have a millionaire cabinet. They don't care. They can't fathom what it's like to live our lives. They can't imagine what it's like to worry about where their next meal is coming from. Governments don't care about the people. We are nothing to them. We are expendables. September 11th showed how expendable we are.

ME: But they did it very nicely. They only had to kill 2,800 people to prove their point. They didn't hit the buildings low. They didn't wait until 11:00 a.m. and hit them low. Of course, I didn't even bring up the major point, which was that the first plane, American Airlines 11, found the Hudson River, flew down the Hudson River, and 24 miles north of New York City *is* the number one terrorist point in the United States. It's called Indian Point and there are three nuclear reactors there. The plane literally flew over that. The other plane, Flight 175, the second one that hit, flew within a couple of minutes of there and, of course, the plane that left out of Newark could have been the third plane to hit there within a few minutes.

MH: We've *got* to start asking the questions. Get the rest of us worker bees educated so we can actually say, "Wait a minute. We don't want this. This is *not our* government."

ME: To everyone out there, please don't acquiesce. Open your eyes and ears and your hearts to the truth.

FIFTEEN

IT'S *ALL* ABOUT MONEY
Meria with William Rivers Pitt

William Rivers Pitt,[16] author/writer, of Truthout.org believes that without the stolen 2000 election, 9/11 would *not* have happened. He believes it was all about George Bush paying back his campaign supporters. He questions what exactly *did* FBI Agent John O'Neill know. Pitt postulates that 9/11 was more about a failed business deal than our lifestyle being envied; discusses how the Bush Administration is heavily invested in sponsoring big business around the world; how our "news" media system does not allow any open debate in America; how Rupert Murdoch owns 60% of all the media in New York City alone (and much of the media in foreign countries also); and about how only *10* corporations own *all* the media worldwide. Was Enron setting our energy policies? Was the pipeline to the Caspian Sea Dick Cheney's idea? What did Bush know about this, and wasn't 9/11 the best thing that could have happened to Bush?

MH: William Rivers Pitt is a writer and a teacher in Boston, Massachusetts. For the last two years, he's been writing essays about the build-up to, catastrophe of and fall-out from the stolen 2000 presidential election.

WP: I'm less trying to figure out what happened with the election and more trying to figure out what happened on September 11th.

MH: I see them as going hand-in-hand.

WP: One would not have happened without the other. In 1998, a California energy company called UNOCAL was in negotiations with the leaders of Pakistan, Afghanistan, and Turkmenistan (that whole region that we've become so familiar with) to get a natural gas pipeline running from the vast natural gas reserves that are in the ground up around the Caspian Sea, through Turkmenistan, through Afghanistan, through Pakistan to a seaport where it could be exported to the markets in Asia and the West. In the same year, 1998, Osama bin Laden, whose home at the time was Afghanistan, blew up two of our embassies in Africa using American-made symtex, which he had been given by our government during the war with the Soviet Union (but that's a whole 'nother story).

Those buildings came down. The clinton administration put a block on any company having anything to do with the Taliban government in Afghanistan and UNOCAL's project ground to a halt. After that, there was nothing happening for UNOCAL. The pipeline deal was pretty much dead in the water until January 20, 2001 and the rise of the Bush Administration, who has energy contacts with companies like Enron and UNOCAL. Basically, top-to-bottom, virtually everyone in his administration either was part of the energy industry or had stock in it and they, more than anybody else, considered American business interests to be a matter of national security to the point that the National Security Agency was giving Dick Cheney talking points in his negotiations on behalf of Enron with the Indian government about a power plant they wanted to put there.

The Bush Administration was *very* invested in pushing business contacts around the world. One of the things they *really* wanted to see was this pipeline deal get done. And they began some very heavy negotiations on behalf of UNOCAL, on behalf of all the companies that wanted to get this pipeline in. Some evidence of how deeply wound up these energy companies are in that region is the fact that the new interim leader of Afghanistan, [Harmid] Karzai, is himself a former UNOCAL consultant, as is America's consulate, our advisor to Afghanistan, a man named [Zalmay] Kalilzad, also a UNOCAL advisor. We were in some pretty heavy negotiations. A lot of this information came out in a book that was first published in France and is called *Forbidden Truth* [by Jean-Charles Brisard and Guillaume Dasquie]. It suggests that we did more than simply try to deal with them. We were putting a lot of pressure on them.

MH: So, the old "either a carpet of gold or a carpet of bombs" is very true.

WP: The very phrase. And they chose to accept the carpet of bombs or, if they didn't choose, Osama bin Laden chose it for them. In a lot of ways, the September 11th attack has more to do with a failed business deal than about anybody hating our freedom.

MH: Do you think people are a little stupid to believe in this one-man theory that Osama bin Laden was behind it all?

WP: How many people pay such a vast amount of attention to international politics? How many people had really ever even heard of Osama bin Laden? How many people had heard of al-Qaida? It's a whole new thing for Americans, but the threat has been out there for years. The Clinton administration worked pretty hard to try to address the terrorist threats that were floating around out there. The 1996 Terrorism Bill that Clinton tried to pass basically would have set up all of the things we have now and we take as a matter of course—the whole Homeland Security, the heightened airline security. Everything we have now, he tried to do back in 1996 and was shot down by the Republicans because they didn't like him, they didn't trust him, and they wanted a political victory.

[Senator] Orin Hatch [R, Utah] was at the center of that, as was [Senate Majority Leader] Trent Lott [R, Mississippi]. I outline that whole thing in an essay called "The Real American Traitors," which you can find on my website. The really creepy, maddening, thoroughly disgusting wrinkle about this whole pipeline deal is, there was the FBI's chief investigator of Osama bin Laden, a man named John O'Neill. He was a deputy head of the FBI and he was the chief bin Laden hunter in the entire United States government. He was at the World Trade Center bombings in '93. He was there at the Cobar Towers in 1996. He was in Africa in 1998. He was at the Cole in 2000. He knew *everything*.

Three weeks before 9/11, he quit the FBI in protest, saying he couldn't get his job done because his government is flummoxing his efforts to look into Afghanistan and Saudi Arabia [where 15 of the 19 terrorists came from] because they'd rather see the oil and energy interests close their business deals; and his work in exposing the terrorist links within those nations was not strategically viable.

MH: Or it wasn't economically viable.

WP: Economics is strategy and vice versa. He quit three weeks before the bombing, took the job as Chief of Security for the World Trade Center and rode those towers down on September 11th. The one man who knew *everything*, the one man who had been pursuing this bin Laden character since 1993, was kept from doing his job when the Bush Administration took office because they wanted not to anger, embarrass or discomfort the Taliban or the regime in Saudi Arabia.

MH: Do you think that John being there was just a bad coincidence?

WP: A wretched coincidence. And I am not going to look askance at anyone if they draw conclusions. Already, to three-quarters of the country, I sound like a raving lunatic.

MH: People really don't want to know the truth and I don't know why. Why is everybody so complacent about 9/11 and not asking more questions?

WP: There is a great degree of fear in the country, and that's understandable.

MH: But don't they feel like they have a right to know what happened?

WP: They have a right and an *obligation* to know what happened, but this is not a country that is trained to put a lot of pressure on their government. I teach journalism, among other things. One of the trends I've been demonstrating to my students is that within the last 10 or 15 years, the level of watch-doggedness that is supposed to be inherent in a free and open press has become more and more watered down. There's a book out there called *The Elements of Journalism*, by Tom Rosentiel. Rosentiel notes that one of the reasons why Germany's militant fascism went completely unnoticed in much of Europe was because the media at the time in Europe, the newspaper people who were supposed to be paying attention to that stuff, worked for media outlets that were owned by chemical and steel interests who were profiting heavily from Germany's increased militarism.

You ask any computer programmer and they'll tell you the axiom is "garbage in, garbage out."

MH: What do you think is going on with *our* media?

WP: In 1996, the Fairness Doctrine [died and we had the] signing of the Telecommunications Act, something that Clinton signed, which, ironically enough, was basically the one thing that cut his own throat. The Fairness Doctrine was something that said if you own a radio station in the city, you cannot own a newspaper. If you own a newspaper, you can't own a TV station. If you own a TV station, you can't own either a radio station or a newspaper. It, basically, kept the rule alive that a broad variety of voices is necessary to an open debate in America and open debate is the lifeblood of an informed democratic populace.

When the Fairness Doctrine went down, Rupert Murdoch could then buy and own two TV stations, a newspaper, and a radio station. He owns something like 60% of the entire market in New York City alone. You have Viacom Corporation, you have GE, which has interests far afield from anything having to do with the media. I think *The Nation* broke it down that virtually every media news and media outlet source in the country is owned now by 10 corporations. It's a narrowing of scope.

MH: That's pretty scary. I understand Murdoch owns quite a bit of media in Europe as well.

WP: He does. He owns half the planet and he's reaching for more. They just recently pushed through even more deregulation. There was something in the *New York Times* about that just last week.

MH: A lot of people believe America was complicit in what happened on 9/11. Some people are even saying that somebody must have ordered a stand-down, as slow as our reaction was to those four planes. What do you think?

WP: I've heard the point being raised that when Payne Stewart died in his airplane, there were two F-14s on his wing within 20 minutes. I am not informed as to the standard operating procedure of the air wings in and around New York to say with any degree of certainty if people were asleep at the switch or if there was an order to stand-down or what. I think if I ever find out there was an ordered stand-down of the jets, I will just light myself on fire and be done with it.

MH: It is a really terrible thing to even have to think that our government may have had a part in that or just sat back and let it happen, so they could push out all our rights here under the Constitution in the name of national security.

WP: I've had to go a million miles in my own head to believe what I believe now. I'd have to go a million more to come to that conclusion. I think the final analysis of this entire thing really is that September 11th was so catastrophic, so awful, and such an egregious failure of virtually every level of security, intelligence, and preparedness in this country that I have half a mind to send bulldozers to the FBI, the CIA, and the NSA [National Security Agency], bulldoze them to the ground, salt the earth with lime, and start all over again.

MH: I grew up in America, my whole life, and I always felt so safe. I thought you didn't even have to doubt that we had the best intelligence and the best protection and the best military, etc. That day really did rock us all to our knees. What an awakening.

WP: Where have the tax dollars gone since the unprecedented Reagan build-up? I remember the $900.00

toilet seat and I remember everything else in this massive gear-up for a threat like the Soviet Union and 3,000 nuclear missiles in the air. Osama bin Laden was talking about it on the telephone. There's another really excellent book by James Bamford called *Body of Secrets*. It is a deep, deep look into the workings of the National Security Agency. The National Security Agency is the largest, yet most little known agency in the entire government and they have ears everywhere.

MH: Pretty dangerous.

WP: That this was missed, stands as reason number one why a complete top-to-bottom church committee-esque reinvestigation of how our national security work needs to happen.

MH: Don't you think we should have a major investigation of this and that this should be top news *every* night on TV?

WP: It is, frankly, beyond my wildest imaginings why they're not talking like that, why it's pooh-poohed to talk about it.

MH: I'm sure you discuss this with your students. What kind of reaction do you get from the kids?

WP: I try to keep my politics out of my students' ears, my journalism students, especially. Frankly, if I get started, I won't stop. I don't want them for one-half a second to believe they have to believe what I believe in order to get a decent grade out of me. It's a far better thing for them to come to their own conclusions. I'll give them one, two, three, four, five sides of an issue and let them figure it out for themselves.

MH: How did you get through the first few days of the stolen election in front of your class? You had to be freaking out.

WP: As far as that, I was just more of the news source. I'm an Internet junkie. The students were on fire to find out about what was happening. It's a fairly liberal school community to begin with. This is Boston, Massachusetts, so I did not have to worry too much about offending anybody. We had lots of discussions in school about who was going to vote for whom and why, and I had made it fairly clear that I was going to pull the lever for Gore. During the whole 36 days, I was just basically a font of information and that was actually kind of a neat phase of school because you have all of these kids who usually sit around talking.

MH: Who are actually interested.

WP: I walked over to a table one day and they were talking about the punch cards. Without anyone prompting them, they were just on the subject all by themselves. The marvel of that whole thing is that it woke everybody up to the beauty and sort of fragility of our democratic institutions, but the really wretched part about it is that it came down in such a dirty way. For 36 days, the entire generation was plugged in and then on the 37th day, they plugged right back out again. And it was just as clear as day. Hopefully, what they will get from the Supreme Court decision is that *every* vote counts.

MH: How do you connect 9/11 and December 12th?

WP: I don't think Al Gore would have charged right out and begun dealing with the Taliban to get an oil company, to satisfy the desires of an oil corporation to get a pipeline through there, nor do I think he would have called off terrorist investigations to do that. Al Gore was the gentleman who drafted in 2000 a marvelous report about the needs for heightened airline security that went virtually ignored by Congress.

MH: They just laughed it off.

WP: It doesn't stand to reason that he would have behaved, immediately upon arriving in office, the way the Bush Administration did. The people he would have brought in would not have the same sort of divided loyalties. Half of Bush's top people are Enron people.

MH: If Bush weren't promoting his oil agenda, chances are we wouldn't have had September 11th happen?

WP: If Bush had not been paying back his campaign contributors in the manner in which he was, to the detriment of national security, dealing with a terrorist regime like the Taliban, which we have since been told is the worst thing to come along since polio, it would not have happened. The terrorists have been around a long time and nobody paid much attention to them, except for a little while when they blew up a couple of Buddhas. I don't think a Gore administration would have been so involved with the energy industry that they would bend American foreign policy, American energy policy, American diplomatic policy, American security, and American intelligence policy around the needs and desires of energy interests. It would not have happened.

MH: Now, Cheney has actually had a lawsuit filed against him on his energy policy by the GAO [General Accounting Office]. What do you think about that?

WP: Frankly, this is one of those things where I start sounding like Cassandra or a complete barking lunatic. First of all, the reason why he doesn't want to tell anybody about what happened in those energy meetings is because I think Enron executives were sitting at the head of the table setting policy. Since they're the worst thing we've ever seen in this country in terms of business practices, he doesn't want to admit how cozy he was with them. I also think there is a good chance that the real reason he does not want to get into too much detail about that is because one of the discussions at the table at those energy policy meetings was likely, how are we going to make ourselves less dependent upon foreign oil? That's a national security policy conversation I agree with. I think there's a strong powerful legitimate argument to be made that Bush is but dust in the wind when you consider 50 years of foreign policy aimed towards getting all the oil out of the ground out there.

Virtually every problem we have in that region stems from that, and the solution for these guys is to go out and find more oil. The solution I would advocate is putting at least as much money into developing renewable alternative sources of energy as we have into developing petroleum. I think one of the reasons Cheney doesn't want to talk about it is because of that discussion about getting out of the Middle East and getting out of the oil embargo over there. His solution for the situation could well have been to go dig up this oil in the Caspian Sea and get the pipeline deal going. It's likely that Enron had at least something to do with the development of that policy, because one of Enron's strongest subsidiaries to this day is their gas and oil pipeline division.

According to the *Forbidden Truth* book I referenced earlier, the last meeting between agents of the Bush Administration, the oil people, and the Taliban folks happened on August 27th [2001]—the same day that Kenneth Lay sent out an e-mail to all of his employee stockholders telling them the future of the company has never looked brighter, their stock was about to go through the roof, they should all invest in a new employee stock options thing that they had going.

The timing of that is a little suspect. I also have it in the back of my head that one of the reasons why Arthur Andersen went on such a shred-fest is because when you are planning to do something as massive as a program to run a gas pipeline from the Caspian Sea through Afghanistan to Pakistan, there's some documentation involved dealing with how you're going to do it. And there's documentation involved in dealing with how you're going to finance it and Arthur Andersen would have had all that.

It's not too far of a stretch to imagine if they're willing to fight this GAO subpoena, if they're willing to fight any other questions having to do with this, that Arthur Andersen would turn around and burn those documents. The damage of those revelations would far outweigh whatever damage will be done by them shredding those documents.

MH: Where do you think Bush fits into all that?

WP: Part of me really wants to say that he is too much of a bucket-head to mastermind all of this stuff. I think it probably has a lot more to do with Dick Cheney than with George Bush. Then, again, I remind myself that people have been underestimating George Bush for 20 years. I think he probably knew all of this stuff was going on or, at least I'm sure he knew we were dealing with the Taliban to get the pipeline through. I'm sure he knew that security and our intelligence in that region and in Saudi Arabia were being de-emphasized. I'm sure he knew what was going on in those energy meetings.

MH: Last week, I heard that Cheney's old company, Halliburton, which was getting ready to declare bankruptcy, all of a sudden got a huge nine-year contract from the military to handle all their new military bases. All of a sudden, they went from total in-the-red to they're-in-the-money-now.

WP: That's at about the same time they came out and gave back a bunch of money to the federal government that they had over-billed them for years.

MH: They gave back $1 million. Big deal.

WP: Al Gore was talking about that during the campaign and virtually nobody in the media paid any attention to it.

MH: What do you think Al Gore's next move will be?

WP: If he runs again and wins the nomination, I'll vote for him, but there's a little bird whispering in my ear that hopes he doesn't run. It doesn't have anything to do with my idea of his qualifications, but it has everything to do with the media. It has everything to do with the erroneous perceptions that have been hammered into the populace over the last two or three or four years.

MH: What if he wins again? Obviously, it doesn't look like it makes a difference.

WP: The problem is that the opposition (the opposition being the Republicans and the media) have had their files and catch-phrases all set up on Al Gore for the last eight years. The American people, when they start hearing that same stuff again, will tune it out. It's a shortcut to thinking.

MH: So, he'd have to come out as a whole new person?

WP: I would love the Democrats to run a totally new candidate to make these people at least make up a whole new set of lies. Not get the opportunity to fall back on the old ones, because they'll have to work to make the new lies stick. The old lies, frankly, have already stuck; they're already there. People think he said he invented the Internet. People think he's stiff and wooden, that he's a policy-wonk, etc.

MH: Why do you think Gore was so quiet for so many months?

WP: I think he probably did it out of a sense of statesmanship. I think he was probably waiting for this nitwit to put his own foot in his mouth, which he was doing admirably up until September 11th. September 11th is the best thing that's ever happened to George Bush in his life.

MH: Didn't he say that he felt like he hit the trifecta?

WP: Cast your mind back. It's an effort because so much has happened and it just seems like a whole different planet, but cast your mind back to September 10th. The Senate was coming back. They were about to pull out the whuppin' stick on his budget, on his faith-based programs, on his energy plans.

MH: His nominations.

WP: This was *before* Enron. They'd spent their entire summer practicing their verbal karate in the mirror and they were on their way back on September 10th. Al Gore was about to get back into the game on September 10th. That *Newsweek* issue came out with that really damning look into the way in which the Supreme Court came around and made their decision. It was on the stand for exactly one day. September 11th was *the* best thing that ever happened to George Bush's political career since meeting Ken Lay in the first place.

MH: For him, that was a major gift from God. I see that one of your least favorite persons is probably also *my* least favorite person on the planet, [U.S. Attorney General] John Ashcroft.

WP: He's an interesting character, is Big John. Nothing like a hardcore religious fundamentalist in charge of the man-made secular laws of this country. That's not a very good fit. A guy who got beat by a dead man.

MH: *AND* who is deathly afraid of calico cats and naked statutes of women.

WP: I was speaking to a friend of mine who lives right next door to some place where Bush is going to be appearing in the next day or so. She said, "I'm going to move. I'm going to burn my house down." I told her to go down to the Animal Rescue League and get a bunch of calico cats and build a catapult in her front yard, launching them at Ashcroft and Bush.

MH: They just cloned a calico cat.

WP: *Definitely* a sign of the Apocalypse.

MH: The scary thing to me, though, is that the rest of the world is looking at America in the worst way they have looked at our country ever since I can remember.

WP: In anybody's memory. The last time we looked this belligerent and disorganized and just veering off in the wrong direction could very well be the Civil War. You think about how the French and the English were sitting here with smiles on their faces watching the Union fly apart after having been around for only a hundred years, butchering each other in great numbers out on their own countryside and everything, making really bad foreign policy decisions. I cannot think of another time when we have been such a malicious, unilateral, belligerent, dangerous presence on the world stage.

MH: What about the fact that our President looks like such an idiot to the rest of the world? I mean they've called him everything from "Dracula" to the "evil incarnate of Satan."

WP: It *is* pretty embarrassing. Let me revise that a little bit. I think we probably made some pretty good horses' asses out of ourselves during Vietnam and the Nixon Administration, so let me pull it back a little bit from the Civil War comment. I'd forgotten about Dick.

MH: But the stolen election; the rest of the world is asking, "What's wrong with Americans to lie down and take that?"

WP: The rest of the world's media was the only place where you could really get the skinny on it. I don't know how aware anyone would have been without Greg Palast [*see* Chapter 2] and the BBC.

MH: His show is always the one that gets hacked whenever I have him as a guest. Now, I don't announce ahead of time when he's coming on.

WP: You might have that problem with me. It has nothing to do with my popularity. I have a small cadre of incredible fools who follow me from website to website.

MH: The truth does tend to attract that. Look what happened to Jesus, Martin Luther King, Jr., John Lennon, and we could go on and on. I don't like to throw them all in the same group, but anybody who comes from an actual thought process, can see how stupid all of this is. At least, what the media gives us is so stupid. Last night, out of boredom, I put CNN on and Larry King was interviewing Gary Condit. With all the important questions he should have been asking Gary Condit, all he did was circle around the Chandra Levy case. I'm not putting that case down in importance, but why wasn't he asking him about

September 11th? Why wasn't he asking him about this U.S.A. Patriot Act?

WP: It's a distraction. And I *am* putting down Gary Condit. The very last thing I had published before September 11th was on September 7th. It was something called "Late to the Party" and it was about the massive, horrible, ridiculous distraction that was the Gary Condit story. The last lines in the essay I wrote were, "If we don't start paying attention to things very soon, there will be a tombstone over the place that used to be America." You know, "Here lies America. They didn't pay attention."

MH: We pay more attention to everybody's penis in this country than to what's going on.

WP: If you weren't a shark attack victim killed by a crazy Russian or supposedly murdered by Gary Condit, you don't deserve a lick of notice. That's something that's been a trend for years. The de-emphasis on foreign news in this country is 10 years old. All of the other major networks de-emphasized it. The majority of CBS' revenue used to come from the news, particularly their foreign news. Last year or the year before, I think the revenues from the news realm was 4% for the overall business that came from the news. So, of course, it's de-emphasized. It started with the Gulf War, when the media rolled over and allowed the Pentagon to dictate what was and was not news.

MH: That's insanity.

WP: It was raised to a high art during the O.J. [Simpson] trial and it was consummated for all time during the impeachment. Everything else since then has just been noise.

MH: You've got a little piece on your website called "Whoring the American Flag."

WP: Now, *more than ever*, it's important for you to buy a cell phone. Now, *more than ever*, it's important for you to get new tires on your car. Now, *more than ever*, it's important for you to have term life insurance. Give me a break.

MH: What really annoys me is that since September 11th, now we have military ads in front of movies.

WP: And on MTV.

MH: And they are all the heroes, today's heroes. People really don't get how much money the Pentagon now is spending with Hollywood. I understand they're going to put on a 13-week series with Disney about war.

WP: Disney is one of those companies that owns half the media.

MH: And Rumsfeld's going to be sitting in on that. We're going to see American war by the Pentagon. More propaganda like *Blackhawk Down*.

WP: They hired some Madison Avenue company a couple of months ago to set this up.

MH: Doesn't anybody think this is ludicrous, or is it just me and you?

WP: I think part of the problem that we're living in right now is the self-same media that is sort of pumping all of this stuff is also the one telling us that Bush has an 80% approval rating or something like that. A ham sandwich would get an 80% approval rating after September 11th, as long as it looked good in a suit. I think that is less a statement about the effective leadership of George Bush and more a statement on the profound loyalty the American people have to their leaders especially in a time of crisis.

MH:	It's almost like a dependency, like a "Daddy, take care of it."

WP:	And that *is* the deal. We're a republic. That's the way it's supposed to be to a certain extent. It's not a democracy so much as it is a republic. We put people in government to take care of *our* business. And the fact that nothing has been blown up yet . . .

MH:	Is a miracle.

WP:	People take some comfort in the idea that Bush is actually doing something.

MH:	I will admit that he does look good in a suit. He wears some pretty good suits.

WP:	He looks good in a suit, but that's about it.

MH:	I am worried about him as a human being because he looks like hell. You look at him in a photograph from six months ago until now, I swear he looks like he's rotting from some dreaded disease. I can't believe it's the same person.

WP:	It happens to every president.

MH:	But it usually takes the full four years. With Bush, it's taken only 4 months.

WP:	Clinton, after his first year, looked like he'd been beaten with sticks.

MH:	His eyelids were all swollen.

WP:	The 80% approval rating has kind of cowed a lot of the loyal opposition. They're political weathervanes, with a couple of exceptions. Fox News, of all places, put out a poll about a month ago that didn't really get a lot of play anywhere because it was too freaky to be explained. The question was, "Would you vote for George Bush again for President of the United States?" 49% of the people said "Yes." That's the same 49% that he got in 2000. Nothing has changed. A lot of people may think he is doing a decent job holding things together in the aftermath of September 11th, but a majority of Americans, as in the year 2000, think he is an idiot on healthcare, education, Social Security, Medicare, the energy policy, environmental issues—an idiot on everything they thought he was an idiot about on December 6th. Nothing has changed.

MH: He's got his big war on terrorism and he thinks he's going to be able to ride that. You wrote a piece recently, "Bush's War on Terror is a Total Failure."

WP: To date, total failure. *To date.* Osama bin Laden is alive and free. Mohammad Omar is alive and free. By the Pentagon's own estimate, we've killed exactly six al-Qaida leaders and let hundreds and hundreds and *hundreds* of them go because our little proxy warriors down there on the ground have divided loyalties, to say the very least. Civil war is beginning to return to Afghanistan, as it always does in the aftermath of any war. Karzai, in my opinion, will be dead in a year. What else? Before we've even finished our business there, we're spreading off over into other countries after that incredibly stupid comment about the "axis of evil."

MH: The guy who wrote that into Bush's speech resigned.

WP: Resigned? I heard he got fired.

MH: He's saying he resigned on peaceful terms and, interestingly enough, Jimmy Carter said it'll probably take the United States many years to live that one down.

WP: They're talking about us in North Korea and Iran the way they were talking about us in the '70s. It's the dumbest thing I've ever heard of in my life. And we're going to go and fight a war in Iraq? Without anybody really supporting us? Britain, it sounds like, is getting on board even though a majority of people in Britain don't want to have anything to do with it.

MH: Russia and China warned us pretty strongly not to go there.

WP: As did Saudi Arabia. Don't make any mistake, Saudi Arabia is the most important country in the world right now.

MH: Because they've got the oil.

WP: They've got the oil. And they've got the terrorists. And they've got the ear and interests of the Carlyle Group, which, by the way, is Papa Bush's main gig right now.

MH: What do you think is going to happen? Do you think Bush is still going to go "my way or the highway" and go after Iraq?

WP: Every time I think I've figured out what this clown is going to do, he goes off in a totally different direction. He does exactly the worst possible thing and manages to get away with it.

MH: Do you remember a few months ago when he said he realized he had a mission, that he was basically on a mission from God?

WP: He and Ashcroft are both anointed with Crisco by God to take care of all the metaphorical calico cats in the world.

MH: Whatever happened to separation of state and church?

WP: The separation of church and state has been under siege since the beginnings of the Reagan Administration.

MH: For him to say that we're a Christian nation is an insult. *He's* an insult and so is Ashcroft to even use the term Christian.

WP: It's an insult to the vast number of people in the country who are not Christian.

MH: And the ones who *are* Christian.

WP: Who believe in the sacred institutions set up by the founding fathers.

MH: Do you talk to your students about national security and the U.S. Patriot Act?

WP: I have mentioned some of the grimmer aspects of it in my journalism classes. Without really raising my voice or saying this is terrible, I've said, "Well, this is what this thing can do. Now this is what's happening with this thing." One of my students actually wound up writing an article for the paper about it. This is, Section 213, the sneak-and-peek provision, which says they can come into a suspect's house, search it, put a device in their computer that basically tracks every stroke of the keyboard, do all this stuff, and leave without ever serving a warrant or notice that they were there in the first place. They could be in my house right now, for all I know.

MH: How is *this* America? People say they're out there fighting for freedom, but we're losing our freedom, so what are we fighting for?

WP: Their argument is it only applies to non-Americans or terrorist suspects, right?

MH: But you know that's not true. I get stories every day of regular Americans who are being razzed in their own houses. People who are getting killed by these gung-ho agents who blow in and don't even check to see if it's the right people.

WP: It's just the very idea of how elastic the definition of terrorists could conceivably become.

MH: I got in my hand a few months ago a copy of the brochure that was put out by the FBI to the local police here in Phoenix, Arizona, defining a terrorist. One of the definitions was anyone who talks about the Constitution too much. It was actually posted online. They tried to scrub it, but too many people had already seen it. Of course, there was no description of anybody who would fit the terrorist description of the people who were supposedly on those planes. Anybody who was considered a loner. Anybody who talked too much about the environment.

WP: Anybody, according to the definition of John Ashcroft, who tries to frighten people about losing their freedoms. Do you remember that fabulous line?

MH: That was as juicy a line as the "axis of evil."

WP: That's what I mean about the definition becoming elastic and, therefore, dangerous.

MH: I believe he said anybody who spoke out against the government or incited fear was also to be considered a terrorist.

WP: "Those who scare peace-loving people with phantoms of lost liberty, my message is this: your tactics only aid terrorists, for they erode national unity and diminish our resolve."

MH: That's madness. Part of being an American is the freedom of speech.

WP: Dissent was the first thing to go when this whole thing started, and that is a common fallout from war. That's happened in virtually every large-scale conflict that we've had.

MH: But you know what's even scarier is that since this is happening here in America, other countries are emulating what we're doing as far as human rights in their own countries.

WP: The bastards are getting away with murder, not to put too fine a point on it.

MH: When I read the news now, I can't even believe that what I'm reading is not from *The National Enquirer.*

WP: Or from *The Onion.*

MH: One of the stories is that in Britain, because they have too much traffic, they're going to force people to put some gizmo in their car so that every time they go out, they can be tracked by satellite. They're going to be charged by the mile for every time they use their car. They said they're going to "try to respect people's privacy."

WP: I guarantee that will not fly here in America.

MH: My point is that Australia, Europe, Italy, all these other countries, since September 11th, have clamped down even though they were not the people attacked. Wait a minute, didn't that happen in New York City? Why is the whole world suffering because of it? You have to give credibility to the connection with globalization and that One World Order.

WP: Greg Palast's book [*The Best Democracy Money Can Buy*] is worth paying very much attention to because the acceleration of that has been manifest in the days since this happened. The Americans who are driving the whole globalization thing in the government think, and it has been proven time and again, that they can get away with whatever they want.

MH: They bought an election. They can do whatever else
        they want. I understood Bush wanted to support a
        Republican candidate for governor in California.

WP: He can support anyone he wants to in California.

MH: If California ever voted Republican, I would know it
        was time to leave the planet.

WP: It would break off and fall into the sea. The people
        I know in California were telling me that well before
        the rest of the country ever heard of Enron, they were
        protesting in massive demonstrations in the street,
        carrying pictures of Ken Lay, because Enron had a lot
        to do with the lights going on and off in California
        37 times.

MH: That whole thing was nothing more than a scam
        on California.

WP: The Enron debacle has been nothing more than an
        absolute validation and reinvestment of political
        power in Gray Davis. I don't think he is in any
        trouble and if he is in trouble, another Democrat will
        take his spot.

MH: Last night, on CNN, they said it would take two years
        to get all the legal papers and everything filed to begin
        going against Enron.

WP: It will take awhile, but in the meantime, we beat
        the drum.

MH: In the meantime, what happened to all that money?

WP: It's an important drum to beat. All that money is in
        offshore accounts right now. All the money they took
        out of California is in the Grand Caymans.

MH: Don't you think the principals of Enron are terrorists
        and they should have their assets frozen?

WP: Did you watch [former Enron officer Jeffrey] Skilling today on the television? It was one of the most extraordinarily shameful things I have ever seen in my life. "The framers of the Constitution are watching," he said. You're damn right they are and they're wondering how many of the Senators across the aisle from you were paid by you before you got your butt in a sling. In an essay I'm working on right now is a breakdown of all of the ways Enron has helped and will eventually heal American democracy if we pay attention to what we're supposed to pay attention to.

MH: Sometimes you need something dastardly to wake up. There's a site online, witcity.com, where they supposedly have the current answering machine at Enron. It's something like, "For all you people who still have your Enron stock and want to find out 42 ways to turn it into Origami, press 3; if this is Dick Cheney, press 6; if you want to file a lawsuit, press 7." The Enron collapse has awakened a lot of Americans to take a closer look at their 401(k)s.

WP: The reason I've decided the principle fear, the principle horror, of Enron and the principle reason why your description of them being terrorists is so fitting is that Enron and their actions, aided and abetted by the Bush Administration (half of whom are either Enron former employees or holders of Enron stock)—what they have done is undermine the fundamental principles and the underpinnings of Wall Street, of the accounting industry, of the banking industry, and of the safety and security people feel in putting any kind of money in stocks whatsoever for their retirement portfolios. There's no such thing as a safe 401(k) any more. There was a report in the *LA Times* the other day that some investigators fear there could be dozens of Enrons out there.

MH: There are a lot of other companies already going belly-up because of it.

WP: Williams, Tyco, the list just goes on.

MH: Even some big steel firm I reported on got screwed by Enron, too. Global Crossing and so many others, I think it's just the tip of the iceberg.

WP: And *that* is the real crime.

MH: Do you think Enron can bring this administration down?

WP: Everything depends on whether or not the shredders are working in the White House basement right now concerning those energy meetings with Dick Cheney. I think all roads lead to Cheney. I think Cheney is the big operator in this administration and I think the stuff they were talking about is absolutely vital to an understanding of how deeply in the pocket of Enron this administration was. Never mind all this pipeline stuff that I've been talking about.

MH: Never mind that they bought an election. He has nominated terrible people since he got into office. Pickering; Poindexter, who was convicted of terrible frauds and conspiracies during Iran/Contra.

WP: He's not the only Iran/Contra who's in there. Don't forget that John Negroponte represents us at the United Nations.

MH: He's a real killer of human rights.

WP: He's also as pure and vivid a definition of a terrorist as we have in the American government. He was the one down there in Central America when all the butchery was happening and claimed not to know that anything was going on—all of which was going on at the behest of American foreign policy in the Reagan Administration. At the very least, he must have heard a couple of screams in the night.

MH: There's also scuttlebutt that gets around that Colin Powell is kind of trying to distance himself.

WP: He tried to get himself fired the other day. His next job is going to be spokesmodel for the Trojan company.

MH: Let's really take a look at the Bush family. Their kids are all totally wired and out of control and he wants to support abstinence. It's 2002, you know what I mean?

WP: The whole "family values" thing.

MH: It's all bupkis. George Jr. was one who used to like to party-hearty, dancing naked on tables in nightclubs. Now that he's too old or he's too tired to do his drugs and his sex tricks and stuff, the rest of the world shouldn't?

WP: Clinton said he didn't inhale and we spent eight years talking about that. George Bush says, "Well, I had a revelation. I was 40 years old," and, okay, we'll stop talking about it now. That's really all we need to know, George: that you're a better man for having done all that coke and drunk all that scotch. Evil Dewars, indeed.

MH: And never go through any kind of rehab program. A lot of people ask me, who do you think beat Bush up that day with the pretzel story? I don't know. It could have been anybody. Maybe it was his father, who always seems to be behind the scenes at the White House.

WP: I think it was either Laura [Bush] or Dick Cheney or maybe even [White House Senior Advisor] Karl Rove.

MH: *Saturday Night Live* showed Dick Cheney beating the hell out of him.

WP: He had just said something stupid. I can't remember what it was, but he had just said something stupid the day before and made life difficult for a lot of people in the White House, so there's a theory in the back of my head.

MH: What could he say that's even more stupid than what he's *already* said? How about what he said to Japan about us being such good friends for the past 100 years?

WP: Or mixing up the words "devalued" and "devaluation" to annihilate the Japanese stock market for a day?

MH: He's not only embarrassing, but he makes the rest of the countries, at least the few countries that used to be our friends, hate us now. And if they don't hate us, they're laughing at us.

WP: They're laughing at us with a sort of a nervous tremble in their voices. They don't know where all hell is going to break loose next. The next couple of years of my life are going to be really interesting because I do firmly believe that the Bush Administration represents a clear and present danger to the best interests of this nation. I, for one, do not intend to rest or become demoralized. I'm going to do whatever it takes to just absolutely dam up whatever political power he and his people have to keep them from pushing the agenda they have been pushing. It is deadly.

MH: They say Bush believes in God—Gold, Oil, and Drugs.

WP: And power. The fundamental difference between a liberal and a conservative, I believe, is that a liberal may be wrong, but will act from a core of believing they're doing what they're doing in the best interest of the country, the planet, and the people. Republicans can be wrong, but that doesn't even matter because they will do what they do for the sake of power and nothing more.

MH: It goes back to domination.

WP: It is simply a matter of doing what needs to be done to gain and hold power. And that is our Achilles heel because, in a way, the things we have to do in order to seize back the agenda, seize back the power, seize back the message, is to do the kind of things they do. Learn from the victors. Let's not fool ourselves. We do not hold the high ground here.

MH: Do you think Gore should have maybe been a little nastier than he was?

WP: I think if Gore runs again in 2004, we are going to see a whole new person. I think the days of wine and roses are over. I think if there's going to be a success-ful Democratic presidential campaign in 2004, the idea that we're too smart, too good, too decent to play rough needs to go right out the window. We need to be an army of James Carvilles. I saw [political consultant] James Carville on television the other day on *Meet the Press* and he was marvelous. He erased everyone who was trying to make the ridiculous claim that Enron is as much a Democratic scandal as it is a Republican scandal. He said, "Excuse me, the percentages were 73% to Republicans and 27% to Democrats, as far as the campaign donations go." He said if you play a game and the score is 73 to 27, it's *not* a tie, but it *is* a marvelous lie to be repeated over and over again.

SIXTEEN

WHAT'S THE SOLUTION?
Meria with Dr. Arun Gandhi

Dr. Arun Gandhi[17] is the grandson of Mohandas K. (Mahatma) Gandhi and is the co-founder (with his wife, Sunanda) of the Gandhi Institute. He discusses some of the lessons he learned during the time he spent with his grandfather, the obligation he has accepted to carry on the work of his grandfather; his endorsement of the Hollywood movie *Gandhi*; and his work for world peace. After having experienced prejudice firsthand growing up in South Africa, Dr. Gandhi truly understands how anger, hatred, and violence only create more of the same.

In a time on Earth where there is so much violence, hatred and war, Dr. Gandhi's refreshing voice of reason, compassion, and non-violence is very welcome. Mahatma Gandhi said "an eye-for-an-eye justice only means the whole world will be blind." Dr. Gandhi explains his statement, "We can stop being enemies when we stop being pawns in the hands of unscrupulous politicians." Dr. Gandhi also explains how participating in a democracy is more than just voting once every four years and how a civilization can be judged by its treatment of its animals and prisoners. Mahatma Gandhi said, "We must be the change we wish to see." Meria says, "We CAN be the peace we seek."

MH: Dr. Gandhi travels around the world teaching theories and practices of non-violence. I understand you got to spend quite a bit of time with your grandfather.

AG: I spent 18 months with him between the ages of 12 and14. This was back in 1945-1946. This was a very crucial period in my life because I learned a lot of important things from him. It was also a crucial period in *his* life because India was about to get independence, but he was disappointed that the independence didn't come the way he wanted it to.

The country was divided by the British between the Hindu India and the Muslim Pakistan. That generated a lot of violence and killings. It sort of negated all of Grandfather's work in one sense.

MH: Given what's going on in India and Pakistan today, what are your feelings about that?

AG: It's a very sad situation, but this was foreseen. This is why Grandfather didn't want the country to be divided. He said no country should be divided on the basis of religion. He was even willing to wait for 10 more years to get independence, but some of the Indian politicians were in a hurry to get into power. They went behind his back and accepted partition of the country and now we are paying the price for it. Grandfather cited the example of Ireland, which Britain had divided into Catholic Ireland and Protestant Ireland and they are *still* fighting over it. He said the same thing is going to happen in India, and we are still fighting in India 50 years after independence. The same thing is happening in Israel and Palestine.

MH: Your grandfather was known for saying that he was a Hindu, he was a Jew, he was a Christian, and he totally understood that concept.

AG: He said that a friendly study of all the scriptures is the sacred duty of every individual. He found that all the religions of the world basically preach the same thing. They come from the root of love, compassion, understanding, and peace. Over the years, all kinds of dross have been added to it. Now, the fundamentals of all the religions have been forgotten. He wanted us to go back into the roots of all religions and see how equal we are, that it doesn't matter which religion you want to believe in. He used to also tell us, "Religion is like climbing a mountain. We are all going up to the same peak, so why should it matter to anybody which side of the mountain we choose to climb up from?"

MH: I want you to talk more about your institute and how we can actually teach people non-violence. I have grandchildren. I try to teach my granddaughters the peaceful way of life, and things that are important to me. I watched the video on your site and I did re-watch the movie *Gandhi* a few times. What is it like being the grandson of probably one of the greatest men who ever lived on the planet?

AG: It's awesome. It's an awesome responsibility.

MH: Is it a lot of pressure?

AG: Yes, if you look at it that way. My mother taught me a very good lesson. She said, "It can be a burden if you want to make it a burden, but it can also be a light that is shining and making your path clearer for you. It all depends on how you want to take it." Many people have taken it as a burden. Many of my cousins feel this is a very big burden for us to carry.

MH: Do they feel they have to try to be perfect because they're his relative?

AG: People *do* expect you to be perfect and all that. Of course, we are *not* perfect. I make it very clear to people that if you are expecting me to be another Mahatma, I can't be, because everybody cannot be a Mahatma. I am trying my best in whatever way I can, to pass on his legacy.

MH: You've seen the movie *Gandhi*, the American version of your grandfather's life.

AG: I have seen it many times and, in fact, I use it often in my workshops.

MH: Do you find the movie to be an accurate depiction of your grandfather's life and struggle?

AG: I think, basically, it is very accurate, provided you look at it as a movie based on his philosophy and his personality. Those are depicted very truthfully.

MH: As his grandson, when you watch that movie, how does it make you feel?

AG: It makes me cry every time I see it because it brings back the memories of the time I spent with him.

MH: But can you really understand that this whole big nine academy award-winning movie is about *your* grandfather, I mean on a personal level?

AG: Yes.

MH: I don't know how I could handle something like that, and I wondered how his family must feel when they watch this movie.

AG: You do feel a part of it; you *do* feel overwhelmed sometimes, but I, personally, feel very proud to be associated with him.

MH: The word "Mahatma," I understand, means a great soul.

AG: It's a title. It's the Indian equivalent of a saint. He didn't like it. He used to say he is not a saint, he is just an ordinary person. He pleaded with the people not to call him Mahatma, but the people wouldn't listen. The title stuck with him and, so, he came to be known popularly as Mahatma Gandhi.

MH: Why do you think as human beings, we need to have somebody we can create or look at as a saint on the planet?

AG: I think, in some sense, this is a wrong attitude. We don't always need to have a great personality to guide and enlighten us. We have to learn to shoulder our own responsibilities. I think we can always look at somebody close for guidance and as a mentor, but, unfortunately, today, because of the lifestyle and because of the materialism we have gotten involved in, our relationships are not what they used to be. In the past, our relationships, when we were not so materialistic, were more positive and were built on positive principles. Now, increasingly, they are built on very negative principles.

It's all selfishness and self-centeredness. Each one is trying to grab as much of the pie as possible and by any means possible. We teach this to our children also. We tell them they have to succeed in life and they have to get to the top and it doesn't matter how they get there. They just have to get there. These kinds of subliminal messages that we give to children have created a very selfish, self-centered society. In that kind of society, you don't have respect for your parents or your uncles or your friends or anybody, and that's why we always want somebody up there to latch onto.

Often, you don't find somebody up there, and then you feel neglected. If we went back to the old principles of building relationships based on positive principles, of love, compassion, understanding, respect for each other, then we would be willing to respect our parents, our uncles, anybody who is within our reach, and have them as mentors for us. Then we wouldn't be so lost.

MH: I know your grandfather totally believed the whole human family was *his* family. He wasn't prejudiced against anybody. He didn't seem to have any rules about somebody being good enough for him to associate with or care about.

AG: He was really concerned about all these prejudices that exist in human society, and he tried to eliminate that. Unfortunately, what has happened is that we, as human beings, have focused a lot on eliminating racism, for instance, in this country and eliminating hatred. But we have to realize that the tree of hatred comes out of the seed of prejudice. Racism and gender prejudice and all of these other prejudices are just a small branch on the tree of hatred. If we attack only one small branch on that tree, we are not going to harm the tree in any way. It will go on surviving. What we need to do is to focus our attention to get rid of that *whole* tree from the roots. We need to get rid of the prejudices within ourselves, because those are the prejudices that give rise to these kinds of hatreds and all the other ailments.

MH: I know you were born in Durban, South Africa and lived there pretty much for the early years of your life. You faced a lot of prejudice there which was part of the reason, I guess, you went to live with your grandfather.

AG: That's true. In fact, if you look at his history, his whole philosophy of non-violence took birth in South Africa because he suffered prejudices there. He went to South Africa as a young lawyer to make money and pay back the loans the family had taken for his education, but after reaching there, he became a victim of racial prejudice. He was beaten up by white people and there was a lot of hatred and anger and apartheid towards non-white people.

When he saw and experienced that, he realized something needed to be done. Instead of taking the negative attitude of fighting violently against oppressors like this, he decided to take the positive action of developing the philosophy of non-violence and seeking justice through non-violent action. That's how it all developed in South Africa. In a sense, that's the experience I went through but, in my case, I didn't have the sense he had to work out a theory of my own, so my parents decided to take me to India and give me the opportunity to live with Grandfather.

MH: What an opportunity that was. My listening audience should also know that your website is www.gandhiinstitute.org and that you have a video of a yourself giving a full lecture in San Diego [California]. You [tell] a funny story that shows that even though Gandhi was your grandfather, he didn't give you any special treatment. It's a story about you trying to get his autograph.

AG: It *is* funny, but it has a tremendous moral and a tremendous lesson for all of us to learn.

MH: The best thing was that your grandfather never pushed you away when you were doing what most children do, which is trying to wear us down.

AG: Exactly.

MH: He always seemed to respond to you from love. It was such a wonderful lesson.

AG: We tend to get angry at little things. We shoo our children away and tell them to get out, we'll talk about it later. We show our anger and that creates a wall between us and the children or between us and other people. Actually, it is that anger that really generates so much violence in our lives, both passive as well as physical violence. If we look at all the violence we experience in our lives or in the life of the nation, we'll find that 90% of the violence comes from anger. Whether it is individual or collective, we get angry and we say things or do things to people that leads to violence, and that violence then perpetuates itself and grows and multiplies. The first thing we need to do in understanding non-violence is try to learn to understand our anger and use that anger positively, rather than abusing it. As you learned in that story, I was beaten up at the age of 10 by some white youths because they thought I was too black and I was beaten up by some black youths because they thought I was too white.

MH: Unbelievable.

AG: I wanted eye-for-an-eye justice. That's what we are all brought up to believe. You have to get eye-for-an-eye justice. And that's when my grandfather reminded me that an eye-for-an-eye justice will only make the whole world blind. He looked at this whole problem and said you *can* use violence, but that's not going to help anybody. You go and beat them up, and they come and beat you up, the violence is just going to escalate and hatred will grow. Eventually, you will both perish with that hatred. The point of this whole problem is that we want to try to change the people who are doing wrong and who are believing in wrong things. That change can only come about by educating them or by bringing them to the awareness that they are wrong and that something needs to be done.

MH: But don't you also think change really begins with each of us?

AG: Gandhi always said that we have to be the change we wish to see in the world.

MH: Instead of leaving it to the next guy.

AG: When we wait for the next guy to change, nobody changes because the next guy is waiting for somebody else to change. If we change, gradually everybody changes along with us.

MH: I didn't realize just how much passive anger most people have and how it shows up in prejudice, it shows up in discrimination, and just the way we treat each other. So many of us have that kind of anger or violence inside of us even, as you say, if it's just whisking your kids away because you're busy. I never thought of that as an act of anger before, but it really is something to consider.

AG: Every time we do something that hurts somebody, we are acting in anger. We are acting in violence.

MH: Right now, we see that the whole world seems to be reacting out of violence. Do you think it's some kind of mass hallucination?

AG: That is because at no stage have we been taught about anger and how to deal with it, so we just snap when something happens and we resort to violence. After September 11th, everybody was so angry and they wanted revenge, to go and wipe out Afghanistan. All kinds of crazy notions were put forth there and we've *been* doing that. We've bombed Afghanistan and so many innocent people who have died there. We have sort of justified this by saying they gave shelter to the al-Qaida and so they deserved to die. *Nobody* deserves to die there. Somebody might say that we give shelter to the Ku Klux Klan, so the United States needs to be bombed and the Klan eliminated. How do you justify this kind of thing at all?

MH: They justify it with "might equals right." That's the American way, it seems.

AG: That's the way we have been brought up and so everybody is trying to use the same technique now.

MH: How can we change it?

AG: We have to change by changing ourselves and bringing about greater awareness. One good thing that has come out of September 11th is that there is a tremendous interest in this philosophy of non-violence. We, at the Institute, are just overwhelmed by the response, people wanting to know more and learn more and invitations to go and speak and do workshops, especially from young people. One thing that I find rather disturbing, from the letters I have received and the number of letters I have read in magazines and newspapers on this September 11th issue—is that women seem to be wanting revenge and wanting to wipe out al-Qaida. They have been sometimes even more aggressive than men. I have been really surprised by that.

MH: At the time of September 11th, some people online were sending letters around that we should just bomb Afghanistan with food and clothing and the things that created the original problems for these people in the first place.

AG: Exactly. That's what we need to look at. This is the time for us to do some introspection and to [ask] where did we go wrong?

MH: Obviously, the world can't survive if everybody's going to start threatening nuclear war with each other, so there has to be a better way.

AG: We are in a happy position where we have everything we need in the world here, and we need to be able to share that with other people and help them improve their lives. Instead, we've become so selfish and self-centered, we just want everything for ourselves. Nobody should dare to come and destroy our way of life. That kind of arrogance is going to destroy us eventually.

MH: I really would like to pray for the fact that maybe everybody will get it, maybe everybody will learn and stop the world from exploding.

AG: We have to be hopeful in this matter, and we have to just go on doing this work. People are not *all* crazy or mad. There are good people. All who believe in this need to come out and do something about it. There's no point in our sitting quietly and saying, "What can I do?" and do nothing at all.

MH: You and I are out there speaking about it and there are a lot of other people out there speaking about it. I'm assuming my listeners are going to go tell everybody they know about what they hear today on the show.

AG: More and more of this has to happen, and only then will we be able to impact the world.

MH: I'm not sure whether this is your quote or your grandfather's: "We can stop being enemies when we stop being pawns in the hands of unscrupulous politicians."

AG: That's my quote.

MH: Do you want to talk a little bit about what you mean by that?

AG: I think politicians everywhere have only one objective in mind and that is to get into the seat of power and to hold onto that seat as long as possible. To be able to achieve that goal, they will do anything at all. They are totally unscrupulous. In India, if you go and see the ordinary people in the streets, the Hindus and the Muslims, they are not even interested in religious differences. They are just interested in living together peacefully and surviving. They are doing this wonderfully, but it's only in pockets like the big cities where the wealthy politicians have their bases, that the politicians create that enmity and the anger towards each other. Then, the whole world sort of feels this is happening everywhere in the country.

The same thing happens in every country, one way or the other. Politicians are always there to exploit situations for their own personal gain and to remain in seats of power. I feel that politicians are at the root of all the evil we see in the world. If we can only make the people wake up and realize that democracy does not mean only casting your vote once in four years. Democracy means that we have to be alert and watchful of what is being done by our representatives in our name, to and by our country. Be more assertive. If we just go and cast our votes once in four years and go to sleep after that, then we have to pay the price for what's happening.

MH: I think a lot of Americans are paying the price for disinterest in their own policies and politics. [They] are now becoming aware of the mistakes we've made in the past with our foreign policy; 9/11 really woke everybody up in this country.

AG: I hope they will realize that and do something about it.

MH: We have the other side of it, of course, when we have our politicians saying that anybody speaking out against the current administration is considered a terrorist, so they try to keep that fear going.

AG: The whole problem in this kind of violent society is that the only way you can control the people is through fear. Violence is based on fear. The whole thing is about controlling through fear. As long as that fear cycle is kept on in the country, people are just going to quietly submit to whatever happens.

MH: Obviously, you don't come from a line of fearful people.

AG: Non-violence is about learning to control people through love and understanding, and that's why it's more positive.

MH: I understand, of course, that everybody is probably always talking to you about your grandfather, but a lot of people probably don't know that even your father and your mother spent many years being persecuted and in prison for what they believed in.

AG: That's true. My father was the second son of four sons. He was the only one who devoted his life to practicing his philosophy as his life's work. He was involved in South Africa where he continued with the institutions that Grandfather had started in non-violence. He also opposed apartheid in that country and went to prison. I think, cumulatively, he spent about 14 years of his life in prison. He suffered in the prisons because they gave him hard labor and tortured him in there. He died at a comparatively young age of 64 because of his life in prison.

MH: He lived and died for what he believed in, which is more than most people can say. A lot of people in America don't even know what they believe in.

AG: A lot of people *anywhere* in the world don't know what they believe in.

MH: That's true. Why limit it? I also understand your mom spent 54 years at your grandfather's ashram? Is she depicted in the movie? Is she one of those two young girls who are always helping him?

AG: She is not depicted there. One was Grandfather's grandniece, and the other is a granddaughter-in-law.

MH: Fifty-four years is a long time for your mom to have spent there. I'm assuming you weren't there all that time, so did you visit with your mom often?

AG: I visited her often and it was unfortunate that I couldn't be with her. That was because the South African government wouldn't allow me to bring my Indian wife back with me from India to South Africa. I had to choose to live in India. My Mom and my two sisters continued to live in South Africa and continued the work there.

MH: I guess people don't realize how serious and terrible the conditions under apartheid were. It just amazed me to know the population [statistics] of India at that time and being under the rule of so few white people. I happen to have been born white, although supposedly what they used to consider "black" in America, as an Italian-American, but I can't even imagine what it would be like to be under somebody else's rule just because of the color of my skin.

AG: It's something you can't really imagine, and you can't understand it until you have experienced it.

MH: When there's such a huge population of non-whites in Africa, why did they just sit back and let themselves be ruled by obviously a very small number of white people?

AG: That's exactly the point. First of all, they feared violence, they feared the rulers would become violent and suppress them. Then, people just got into their shells and they wanted to just live their own lives and not get involved in other things. It is because we have created this kind of selfish, self-centered society. We are so concerned about our jobs, our income, our family, and we don't want to upset anything, so we quietly submit to this kind of thing. A classic example is, a lot of my friends in South Africa used to say if the whites don't want us there, why do we want to go there. "Let's not go there. Let's forget about it." But that's not the point.

MH: Every human being should be free to move about the planet wherever they want.

AG: Exactly. That's how this attitude comes up and, before we know it, we are submitting to a lot of injustice everywhere.

MH: I should think it was probably a very lucky thing that your grandfather was an attorney. I bet he never anticipated where his life would take him when he was just a boy in school.

AG: He went to South Africa as a young attorney. His only ambition in life was to be able to earn money and pay back the loans his family had taken for his education.

MH: Obviously, God had different plans for him.

AG: And it was those experiences in South Africa that changed his life completely.

MH: I used to have a cute little refrigerator magnet that says, "We plan and God laughs." I guess that was a very fortuitous thing for mankind, what happened to your grandfather.

AG: I started this Gandhi Institute, but it really wasn't planned or anything. We came here, my wife and I, [to the U.S.] in 1987 to do a comparative study of races in this country with color prejudices in South Africa and the caste prejudice in India. It was during that study that we found a lot of people coming up to us and asking us about non-violence and how it is practiced; and we found there's a lot of interest in this country in that field. My wife and I decided to start an institute and teach people. We didn't have the money to do this, so we decided to sell Grandfather's original letters that my parents had preserved for sentimental reasons, which I received after my Mom died in 1988. I found that many of those letters were getting old and brittle and they would perish, and then everybody would be a loser, so we made the painful decision to sell the letters and raise the money. We got $56,000.00 and that was invested in this Institute. That's how we got it started.

MH: In a way, you did eventually end up getting that autograph you wanted from your grandfather, in the letters. Here, in America, a lot of people think that when you talk about non-violence, that means being a coward.

AG: That's a tremendous misunderstanding on the part of people. It's not cowardice at all. It needs more courage and bravery to be non-violent than to be violent. People here have a very limited understanding of the philosophy. They think non-violence is just not taking any action or just keeping quiet and suffering it, or pacifism. That's not non-violence at all. Grandfather said he would rather people be violent than people be cowards.

MH: At least you know they're alive and have a pulse in them. I think it certainly takes a lot of bravery to stand up for what you believe in, especially when it goes against what's common. Violence in America is out of control. It's everywhere. It's on TV, it's on the radio, it's in the advertisements we see, it's happening in our school system. Then, when you see parents killing other parents at children's games, violence is really out of control in America.

AG: It's totally out of control. It's also interesting to see how fearful American people are. The need to carry guns and weapons is an indication of how much fear there is in the people.

MH: How do you think we can overcome some of that fear?

AG: We have to *be* the change. We have to take courage in our hands and decide on ethical and moral values and change society by changing ourselves. Coming to realizations, for instance, that we are not going to carry guns any more. We are not going to be a violent nation. We are going to learn more about this, and we are going to be more considerate and compassionate. Non-violence is based on the principles of love and compassion and respect. When people ask me if non-violence is relevant today, I ask them, are love and compassion and respect relevant today? And if we can say they are not relevant today, then God help us.

MH: I think you also said, "We must learn to respect people not for *what* they are, or how much they are worth, but for *who* they are: human beings." In this country, I have to speak more from an American point of view because this is where I live and grew up—but here, when you meet somebody new, it seems the first question you ask is, "What do you do?" And we immediately judge them by their career, judging by what we think their earning potential is.

AG: We first want to know how much they earn, where they stand economically. The second thing we want to know is, what is their religious belief, and so on. All of these things are labels we have put on people, and whether we respect them or not depends on their answers to these questions.

MH: Is it really a matter of letting go of judgment and just accepting people as people?

AG: Right.

MH: I didn't know Mahatma Gandhi didn't believe in the melting pot like we have here in America.

AG: No, he said there's no such thing as a melting pot. You can't melt everybody down to one identity. What he believed was that humanity was a bowl of tossed salad, that you have all these different ingredients that look different, taste different, everything is very different about them, but when you put them all together in a bowl of tossed salad, they taste so wonderful.

MH: Variety is the spice of life. How boring would it be if we were all the same?

AG: Exactly. Another thing that we misunderstand and misconstrue is building communities. We think if we just join a neighborhood or build neighborhoods, those are communities. Neighborhoods are neighborhoods; they are not communities. A community, to be a community, has to be inter-related and interdependent. They have to have a relationship with each other living in that community. In our society today, half the time, we don't know who's living down the road from us and we don't care. It's not our business. We just get home; we lock our doors, and sit inside. We think that's the end of our world.

MH: And that certainly can't be healthy for our soul, to be so isolated.

AG: Not for our soul or for other people or for building a community.

MH: You also said any kind of injustice *anywhere* is a form of violence.

AG: In the American context, we live a very lavish lifestyle here. We waste a lot of things because we have so much of it here. Yet, we know that people in other countries and people in other neighborhoods in our own country don't have enough, but we don't care about them. There is a very interesting episode that occurred last year when I took a group of Americans on a visit to India. Many of these were students from a university, Wellesley College in Massachusetts. We try to live modestly whenever we go on these tours but, at one place, our travel agent was able to get us a good deal from a fairly good hotel, almost a five-star hotel. When we were checking in there, all these young women were so excited because, finally, they saw something they could relate to, which they had experienced back home. A five-star hotel was like something they saw every day in America. They were planning how they were going to have a hot bath and wash their hair, and this and that.

When they went to their rooms, they looked out the windows and saw the slums next door, where people were living in hovels and they didn't have enough food to eat; and they felt pangs of guilt. They came back to me and said, "Mr. Gandhi, we should move from this hotel to another hotel," and I asked, "Why?" They said, "Because we feel guilty that we are living in all this luxury here and these people outside, they don't have anything."

I said, "That's not the point here. There's a lesson here for you to learn. You enjoy the same luxury and the same benefits back home, but you don't feel guilty because you don't have a window to the other half of the world there. Here, you have a window to the other half of the world and you can see them and, therefore, you feel guilty about it. You have to learn to feel that guilt *all* the time, even when you are back home and you don't see the poverty. You have to feel that guilt and you have to be willing enough to share some of your good fortune with other people." This is what I've been trying to explain to the people here in the United States and in other affluent countries. They need to share and they need to share constructively with other people.

MH: If we can actually share all the resources on this planet with everybody, we'd have no problems on this planet. Obviously, there's enough for everybody. It's just all going in one direction though.

AG: Right. So, if we learn to share and learn to help other people attain a better standard of living, there wouldn't be all this strife and hate and prejudice in the world. And people would not be so envious of America and so hateful towards America.

MH: I don't think people are *just* envious of America. I don't think that was the reason for 9/11. I think a lot of people are upset with the way our foreign policy has oppressed so many people in many other lands.

AG: They look at America as a big bully.

MH: And what business do we have, going and telling another country how to run their lives?

AG: It doesn't mean America lives a secluded life, though. There are people who feel that America should just mind its own business and not do anything, that we should live our own life and let the rest of the world go to hell.

MH: They have a right to think that.

AG: They have a right to think anything they want to. That's not the point. The point is, we can't live in that kind of isolation.

MH: Imagine if all the money we've just spent on bombing Afghanistan was spent on food and clothing and shelter, how much more good it would have done for America, and for the whole world. Is it because we don't have women in office? Women, I think, would naturally think, "Gee, why don't we just feed these people and give them a place to live?"

AG: I suppose that's one of the ideas. The men in office in the United States have always had this macho image and created this image of America being the super power, so now we have to live up to that image.

MH: I think we can always change our image. A lot of people go in for make-overs every so often. Maybe we need a make-over.

AG: That's what I keep telling people, that we have proved to the world we are the super power in terms of military might. Now, we need to prove to the world that we can also be a super power in terms of moral might.

MH: Just come from love. You've said violence occurs in many different forms, and you talk about violence against nature. I know we're a throw-away society, but I never connected it to being violent until I heard that. You have said that you even see bulk-buying as violence against humanity.

AG: When we over-consume things, we are depriving people elsewhere of those resources. That is violence against people who have to live in poverty because we are so greedy.

MH: A lot of people now are of the mind that we need to learn to start starving corporations in order to feed democracy. I see that in so many other countries where our businesses have gone in and basically taken over the politics of that land. Then, it's always the people who suffer. It's the people who lose their rights and their democracy. I think if more people, not just here in America, but worldwide, realized where their dollars go, or were a little more conscious about where they spend their money, it could make a huge difference in the world.

AG: That's why I said we need to help *constructively*, not *destructively*. For instance, the government gives aid to foreign countries and it's all politically motivated. It has lots of strings tied to it when they give that aid. That kind of aid doesn't help anybody. Most of the time, it ends up in the pockets of corrupt politicians and officials at the other end. What I feel is that aid and help to other countries has to be motivated by compassion. Governments and politicians are incapable of acting out of compassion, so it has to be a community-to-community interaction.

When the people here begin to take it into their hands and build relationships with another community in a third-world country and help them develop, that is when we'll see effective and constructive development at the other end. The people themselves will benefit, and not some politicians and bureaucrats.

MH: In America, a lot of people talk about tolerance. They actually even teach tolerance in school, which I think is kind of interesting.

AG: I am against tolerance.

MH: Tolerance, instead of love and compassion and understanding?

AG: Exactly. You can tolerate somebody and not like and not respect that person, but because you can't do anything about it, you just tolerate them.

MH: What's that about? I wouldn't want anybody being in my life because they *tolerate* me.

AG: Exactly. So, we don't want tolerance and we don't want to teach people tolerance. We want to teach people *positive* things.

MH: I understand you do a lot of lecturing and have quite a few strong opinions on our prison system in this country.

AG: Justice has come to mean revenge in our vocabulary. I think justice should mean reformation. Prisons should not be places of punishment. They should be places where we reform people who have done something wrong and make them worthy citizens again, so they come out and be better human beings. Grandfather said you can judge a civilization by the way they treat their animals and prisoners.

MH: The way we treat our animals is another horror. To go along with the story you told us about those girls in that hotel, animal rights activists say that if slaughterhouses had glass windows and glass walls, no one would eat animal meat. What do you think our chances are of creating a non-violent world, or a *mostly* non-violent world?

AG: I think the chances are really good. I'm always optimistic about this, provided we decide to do something about it and, then, *do* it. We must look at the larger picture. We say, "Well, I don't have the capacity to change the whole world, so why should I bother at all?" Then, we don't do anything at all. That kind of negative thinking is why nothing really happens.

If we take positive action and say, "I'm going to make *my* life worth something and I'm going to help bring about that change," then each one of us can affect our family and our neighborhood. From that, it can grow and, eventually, the whole world will change.

MH: That's good to know. Another quote by your grandfather is, "Keep your thoughts positive, because your thoughts become your words. Keep your words positive, because your words become your behavior. Keep your behavior positive, because your behaviors become your habits. Keep your habits positive, because your habits become your values. Keep your values positive, because your values become your destiny." Peace *really* does start with each of us. Be the change you want to see in the world. Peace can happen. John Lennon said all you need to do is decide that you want it. Peace is yours if you want it.

AFTERWORD

The Meria Heller Show is webcast Sunday-Thursday, from 10:00-11:00 a.m. (MST) at www.Meria.net. The show, which opens with the familiar words, "Good morning, everybody. Meria Heller here, alive and kicking in Phoenix, Arizona," can now be heard in over 60 countries. All shows are archived onsite for listening 24/7, worldwide.

Join Meria's Yahoo group ("Meria" – http://groups.yahoo.com/group/Meria/join) to be notified of upcoming interviews and other breaking news.

From Meria: Stop supporting media that lies to you. Get educated. Strive for peace in your life, home, community, country, and the world. What happens to one of us happens to us all.

Peace. We can have it if we want it. And please stay tuned for more from Meria, the Mouth that Roars.

ABOUT MERIA

Meria Heller is an Internet celebrity. On her Sunday-Thursday live webcast heard in over 60 countries at www.Meria.net or www.MeriaHeller.com, she interviews top authors, environmentalists, political activists, humanitarians, doctors who champion alternative medicine, and other exceptional people. Meria's investigative journalism is "way ahead of the curve" because she does not limit her sources to mainstream media. Since Meria's show is not funded by corporate advertisers, she is free to cover stories obtained from the full range of media sources. Meria is credited by many for having helped them discover their passion to actively improve local, national or international situations. In 2001, The *Meria Heller Show* was nominated for the prestigious Peabody Award for Excellence in Broadcasting.

Previously, Meria hosted a talk radio call-in show, "The Meria Heller Commentator on the Human Species Show," heard throughout Arizona and the Greater New England area over a 50,000 watt station (KFNX 1100 AM in Phoenix, Arizona and WALE 990 AM in Greater New England). It was rated among the top four of all talk shows on the station. Throughout her broadcasting career, Meria has also been a frequent guest on local and national television programs.

Meria's video, *The Thirteen Stones of the Universal Wheel*, delivers her vision for world peace through understanding our fellow world citizens. She is also an accomplished writer who publishes a quarterly newsletter and contributes monthly articles to various publications. She is the author of the books, *Global Unity through the Universal Wheel*; *The Awakening of an American: How My Country Broke My Heart (Book 1)*; *and The Awakening of an American: My Country's Rights and Wrongs (Book 2)*; and has a *Book 3* in the works.

Meria is the founder of "THE UNIVERSAL WHEEL," a lifestyle and philosophy based on our interconnectedness to all living things. She is also an accomplished watercolorist and, in 1988, had a one-woman show in Soho, New York before moving to Phoenix, Arizona. She is listed in the *Encyclopedia of Living Artists in America* and her work is included in private and corporate collections in the United States and abroad.

A teacher of metaphysics and motivational techniques, Reiki Master, and ordained minister with a doctorate in religion through ULC in Modesto, California, Meria also has her own unique "spiritual therapy" consultation business. She has lectured and taught successful living concepts in the U.S. and abroad, at universities, public schools, prisons, expos, and elsewhere. Meria was the first person ever accepted to teach the Medicine Wheel and Native Americana, as she coined it, in Arizona. She is a charismatic teacher of the healing power of love and laughter who believes the secret of life is that "we're here to have a good time."

Articles by and about Meria Heller are archived at the *Associated Press*, the *Arizona Republic*, the *Scottsdale Tribune*, *The New Times-Seattle*, *Connecting Link Magazine*, *The Democracy Chronicle*, *Onlinejournal.com*, and Media Monitors.net

INDEX

(Guest Websites/Book Attributions/Recommended Websites)

[1]**BUGLIOSI** Vincent. *The Betrayal of America: How The Supreme Court Undermined the Constitution and Chose Our President*, New York: Thunder's Mouth Press/Nation Books, 2001. Vincent can be contacted through his publisher.

[2]**PALAST** Gregory. *The Best Democracy Money Can Buy: An Investigative Reporter Exposes the Truth about Globalization, Corporate Cons, and High Finance Fraudsters*, London/Sterling, Virginia: Pluto Press, 2002. Greg's website is www.GregPalast.com.

[3]**RECHTENWALD** Michael. Michael's website is www.legitgov.org.

[4]**ODEN** Nancy. Nancy can be contacted at www.greenparty.com.

[5]**FERTIK** Bob. Bob can be contacted at www.Democrats.com.

[6]**WINANT** Howard. *The World Is A Ghetto: Race and Democracy Since World War II*, New

[7]**STARR**

York: Basic Books, 2001. Howard's website is http://blue.temple.edu/~winant. Howard can be contacted at winant@blue.temple.edu.

[7]**STARR** Linda. Linda can be contacted at www.onlinejournal.com. Jim Hatfield's book, *Fortunate Son,* can be obtained through its new publisher at www.softskull.com.

[8]**CHANDLER** Dave. Dave's website is www.Earthside.com.

[9]**CONOVER** Bev. Bev can be contacted at www.onlinejournal.com.

[10]**NICHOLS** John. *Jews for Buchanan: Did You Hear the One about the Theft of the American Presidency?* New York: The New Press, 2001 John can be contacted at www.thenation.com.

[11]**McCHESNEY** Robert. *Rich Media, Poor Democracy: Communication Politics in Dubious Times,* New York: The New Press, 1999. Robert can be contacted at www.thenation.com or at his website at www.robertmcchesney.com

[12]**SOLOMON** Norman. *The Habits of Highly Deceptive Media: Decoding Spin and Lies in Mainstream News,* Monroe, Maine: Common Courage Press, 1999. Norman can be contacted at www.accuracy.org or www.fair.org or www.commondreams.org.

[13]**GOFF** Stan. *Hideous Dream: A Soldier's Memoir of the US Invasion of Haiti,* Winnipeg,

[14]**MILLER**

    Manitoba: Soft Skull Press, Inc., 2000. Norman can be contacted through his publisher at www.softskull.com.

[14]**MILLER** — Mark Crispin. *The Bush Dyslexicon: Observations on a National Disorder*, New York: W.W. Norton & Company, Inc., 2001. Mark can be contacted at mcm7@homemail.nyu.edu.

[15]**ELSIS** — Mark. Mark can be contacted at www.lovearth.net or at mark@lovearth.net.

[16]**PITT** — William Rivers. William can be contacted at www.truthout.com or www.truthout.org or www.willpitt.com.

[17]**GANDHI** — Dr. Arun. Arun can be contacted at his website at www.gandhiinstitute.org.

IF YOU LIKED THIS BOOK, YOU WON'T WANT TO MISS OTHER TITLES BY DANDELION BOOKS

Available Now And Always Through www.GoOff.com And Affiliated Websites!!

Non-Fiction:

America, Awake! We Must Take Back Our Country, by Norman D. Livergood … This book is intended as a wake-up call for Americans, as Paul Revere awakened the Lexington patriots to the British attack on April 18, 1775, and as Thomas Paine's *Common Sense* roused apathetic American colonists to recognize and struggle against British oppression. Our current situation is similar to that which American patriots faced in the 1770s: a country ruled by 'foreign' and 'domestic' plutocratic powers and a divided citizenry uncertain of their vital interests. (ISBN 189330227X)

America's Nightmare: The Presidency of George Bush II, by John Stanton & Wayne Madsen… Media & Language, War & Weapons, Internal Affairs and a variety of other issues pointing out the US "crisis without prcedent" that was wrought by the US Presidential election of 2000 followed by 9/11. "Stanton & Madsen will challenge many of the things you've been told by CNN and Fox news. This book is dangerous." (ISBN 1893302296)

America's Autopsy Report, by John Kaminski… The false fabric of history is unraveling beneath an avalanche of pathological lies to justify endless war and Orewellian new laws that revoke the rights of Americans. While TV and newspapers glorify the dangerous ideas of perverted billionaires, the Internet has pulsated with outrage and provided a new and real forum for freedom among concerned people all over the world who are opposed to the mass murder and criminal exploitation of the defenseless victims of multinational corporate totalitarianism. John Kaminski's passionate essays give voice to those hopes and fears of humane people that are ignored by the big business shysters who rule the major media. (ISBN 1893302423)

Seeds Of Fire: China And The Story Behind The Attack On America, by Gordon Thomas. . . The inside story about China that no one can afford to ignore. Using his unsurpassed contacts in Israel, Washington, London and Europe, Gordon Thomas, internationally acclaimed best-selling author and investigative reporter for over a quarter-century, reveals information about China's intentions to use the current crisis to launch itself as a super-power and become America's new major enemy ..." *This has been kept out of the news agenda because it does not suit certain business interests to have that truth emerge ... Every patriotic American should buy and read this book ... it is simply revelatory* (Ray Flynn, Former U.S. Ambassador to the Vatican). (ISBN 1893302547)

Shaking The Foundations: Coming of Age In The Postmodern Era, by John H. Brand, D.Min., J.D. . . . Scientific discoveries in the Twentieth Century require the restructuring of our understanding the nature of Nature and of human beings. In simple language the author explains how significant implications of quantum mechanics, astronomy, biology and brain physiology form the foundation for new perspectives to comprehend the meaning of our lives. (ISBN 1893302253)

Rebuilding The Foundations: Forging A New And Just America, by John H. Brand, D.Min., J.D. ... Should we expect a learned scholar to warn us about our dangerous reptilian brains that are the real cause of today's evils? Although Brand is not without hope for rescuing America, he warns us to act fast–and now. Evil men intent on imposing their political, economic, and religious self-serving goals on America are not far from achieving their goal of mastery."

Democracy Under Siege: The Jesuits' Attempt To Destroy the Popular Government Of The United States; The True Story of Abraham Lincoln's Death: Banned For Over 100 Years, This Information Now Revealed For The First Time! by C.T. Wilcox ... U.S. President Lincoln was the triumphant embodiment of the New Concept of Popular Government. Was John Wilkes Booth a Jesuit patsy, hired to do the dirty work for the Roman Catholic church – whose plan, a well-kept secret until now – was to overthrow the American Government? (ISBN 189302318)

The Last Atlantis Book You'll Ever Have To Read! by Gene D. Matlock ... More than 25,000 books, plus countless other articles have been written about a fabled confederation of city-states known as Atlantis. If it really did exist, where was it located? Does anyone have valid evidence of its existence – artifacts and other remnants? According to historian, archaezologist, educator and linguist Gene D. Matlock, both questions can easily be answered. (ISBN 1893302202)

The Last Days Of Israel, by Barry Chamish ... With the Middle East crisis ongoing, *The Last Days of Israel* takes on even greater significance as an important book of our age. Barry Chamish, investigative reporter who has the true story about Yitzak Rabin's assassination, tells it like it is. (ISBN 1893302164)

The Courage To Be Who I Am, by Mary-Margareht Rose ... This book is rich with teachings and anecdotes delivered with humor and humanness, by a woman who followed her heart and learned to listen to her inner voice; in the process, transforming every obstacle into an opportunity to test her courage to manifest her true identity. (1SBN 189330213X)

How To Have A Husband And Live With Your Lover (At The Same Time), by Pamela Peled ... "We've come a long way, baby," she writes. Who would have thought that in the 21st century you could actually live with your husband who could turn out to be your lover even after the honeymoon is long over? Here is another version of "things could be worse" for anyone who is considering a Trade-in or Extra to have around when life with the current model starts to go flat. (ISBN 1-893302-34-2)

The Making Of A Master: Tracking Your Self-Worth, by Jeanette O'Donnal ... A simple tracking method for self-improvement that takes the mystery out of defining your goals, making a road map and tracking your progress. A book rich with nuggets of wisdom couched in anecdotes and instructive dialogues. (ISBN 1-893302-36-9).

Fiction:

Freedom: Letting Go of Anxiety And Fear Of The Unknown, by Jim Britt . . . Jeremy Carter, a fireman from Missouri who is in New York City for the day, decides to take a tour of the Trade Center, only to watch in shock, the attack on its twin towers from a block away. Afterward as he gazes at the pit of rubble and talks with many of the survivors, Jeremy starts to explore the inner depths of his soul, to ask questions he'd never asked before. This dialogue helps him learn who he is and what it takes to overcome the fear, anger, grief and anxiety this kind of tragedy brings. (ISBN 1893302741)

The Prince Must Die, by Gower Leconfield . . . breaks all taboos for mystery thrillers. After the "powers that be" suppressed the manuscripts of three major British writers, Dandelion Books breaks through with a thriller involving a plot to assassinate Prince Charles. *The Prince Must Die* brings to life a Britain of today that is on the edge with race riots, neo-Nazis, hard right backlash and neo-punk nihilists. Riveting entertainment . . . you won't be able to put it down. (ISBN 1893302725)

Daniela, by Stephen Weeks . . . A gripping epic novel of sexual obsession and betrayal as Nazi Prague falls. The harboring of deadly secrets and triumph of an enduring love against the hardest of times. Nikolei is a Polish/Ukrainian Jew who finds himself fighting among the Germans then turning against them to save Prague in 1945. Nikolei manages to hide himself among the Germans with a woman working as a prostitute.

Unfinished Business, by Elizabeth Lucas Taylor ... Lindsay Mayer knows something is amiss when her husband, Griffin, a college professor, starts spending too much time at his office and out-of-town. Shortly after the ugly truth surfaces, Griffin disappears altogether. Lindsay is shattered. Life without Griffin is life without life ... One of the sexiest books you'll ever read! (ISBN 1893302687)

The Woman With Qualities, by Sarah Daniels ... South Florida isn't exactly the Promised Land that forty-nine-year-old newly widowed Keri Anders had in mind when she transplanted herself here from the northeast ... A tough action-packed novel that is far more than a love story. (ISBN 1893302113)

Weapon In Heaven, by David Bulley . . . Eddy Licklighter is in a fight with God for his very own soul. You can't mess around half-assed when fighting with God. You've got to go at it whole-hearted. Eddy loses his wife and baby girl in a fire. Bulley's protagonist is a contemporary version of the Old Testament character of Job. Licklighter wants nothing from God except His presence so he can kill him off. The humor, warmth, pathos and ultimate redemption of Licklighter will make you hold your sides with laughter at the same time you shed common tears for his "God-awful" dilemma. (ISBN 1893302288)

Adventure Capital, by John Rushing . . . South Florida adventure, crime and violence in a fiction story based on a true life experience. A book you will not want to put down until you reach the last page. (ISBN 1893302083)

A Mother's Journey: To Release Sorrow And Reap Joy, by Sharon Kay . . . A poignant account of Norah Ann Mason's life journey as a wife, mother and single parent. This book will have a powerful impact on anyone, female or male, who has experienced parental abuse, family separations, financial struggles and a desperate need to find the magic in life that others talk about that just doesn't seem to be there for them. (ISBN 1893302520)

Diving Through Clouds, by Nicola Lindsay . . . Kate is dying . . . dying . . . dead; but not quite. Total demise would have deprived her guardian angel, Thomas, from taking her on a nose-dive through the clouds of self-denial to see herself in the eyes of the friends and family she left behind. A spiritual journey from a gifted fiction writer. (ISBN 1893302199)

Return To Masada, by Robert G. Makin . . . In a gripping account of the famous Battle of Masada, Robert G. Makin skillfully recaptures the blood and gore as well as the spiritual essence of this historic struggle for freedom and independence. (ISBN 1893302105)

Time Out Of Mind, by Solar Vayanian . . . Atlantis had become a snake pit of intrigue teeming with factious groups vying for power and control. An unforgettable drama that tells of the breakdown of the priesthood, the hidden scientific experiments in genetic engineering which produced "things" —part human and part animal—and other atrocities; the infiltration by the dark lords of Orion; and the implantation of the human body with a device to fuel the Orion wars. (ISBN 1893302210)

ALL DANDELION BOOKS ARE AVAILABLE THROUGH WWW.GOOFF.COM AND AFFILIATED WEBSITES . . . ALWAYS.